THE HEALTH CARE SUPERVISOR'S HANDBOOK

Third Edition

Norman Metzger
Edmond A. Guggenheim Professor
Department of Health Care Management
Mount Sinai School of Medicine
New York, New York

AN ASPEN PUBLICATION®
Aspen Publishers, Inc.
1988
Rockville, Maryland
Royal Tunbridge Wells

Library of Congress Cataloging-in-Publication Data

Metzger, Norman, 1924-

The health care supervisor's handbook.

"An Aspen publication."
Includes bibliographies and index.
1. Health facilities—Personnel management.
I. Title [DNLM: 1. Health Facility Administrators.
2. Personnel Management. WX 159 M596h]
RA971.35.M46 1988 362.1'1'0683 87-37363
ISBN: 0-87189-757-1

Editorial Services: Mary Beth Roesser

Library of Congress Catalog Card Number: 87-37363
ISBN: 0-87189-757-1

Printed in the United States of America

1 2 3 4 5

TO BART METZGER
Another preacher in the wilderness

Our advanced society, for all its strengths, has long harbored a fundamental weakness: it has prodigiously generated goods and services, but has been seriously deficient in creating some of the basic conditions of human community.

Daniel Yankelovich New Rules
(New York: Bantam Books/Published by arrangement with Random House, Inc. 1982) p. 6.

Many men who have more than enough abstract intelligence to learn the methods and techniques of management fail because their affinity with other people is almost entirely intellectual or cognitive. They may have the "intellectual empathy" but may not be able to sense or identify the universalized emotional feelings which strongly influence human behavior.

Norman L. Paul
The Use of Empathy in the Resolution of Grief,
Perspectives in Biology and Medicine *(The University of Chicago Press, August 1967, p. 155)*

Top management is becoming more and more isolated from the balance of the workforce. It is perceived as communicating less, delegating fewer decisions, and being less responsive to employee concerns.

Managing Human Resources/1983 and Beyond
(Opinion Research Corp. Report)

Employees still like their jobs, and most still find their employers credible, but there is evidence of a growing malaise, a gradual but persistent loss of optimism.

Achieving Competitive Advantage Through the Effective Management of People, 1986-87 — A Strategic Report *(Philadelphia, PA : The Hay Group)*

Society...is a vehicle for earthly heroism...man transcends death by finding meaning for his life...it is the burning desire for the creature to count....what man really fears is not so much extinction, but extinction with insignificance.

Ernest Becker Escape From Evil *(New York, NY: The Free Press, 1975, pp 3-6 and 51)*
See also: The Denial of Death *(New York, NY: The Free Press, pp. 3 and 4)*

Table of Contents

Preface

In my last book *Achieving Excellence: A Prescription for Health Care Managers*, which I co-authored with Lawrence C. Bassett, we asked the questions "How does one survive in a paranoid world of health care management? How does a manager or an aspiring manager survive in the rapidly changing environment of the American workplace?" In suggesting the need to survive I am not talking about surviving by the skin of one's teeth, or hanging on by one's fingernails, but surviving with dignity and pride in a job well done. Such survival within the context of a constantly changing society, and a constantly changing health care industry, is made possible by continually upgrading one's knowledge and experience. To practice yesterday's management style today is to court failure. To fail to understand the changing breed of employees we deal with is to ask for alienated workers.

The challenge for today's health care supervisors and managers is to provide work experiences that give employees the sense that they "make a difference." A 1986 American Society of Personnel Administration/Commerce Clearing House (ASPA/CCH) survey reported the results of a research project, designed and executed by Professor John L. Pierce of the University of Minnesota in Duluth, on the question "Do employees today feel they make a difference where they work?";[1] these results are extremely important to all of you in health care management. It is clear that the employee who feels "I count around here" is more likely to internalize and act out the organization's values and traditions; the employee who feels that he or she does not make a difference is more likely to ignore—or even resist—the organization's values and traditions. These research results point the way to this third edition of the *Health Care Supervisor's Handbook.* The major survey finding is that a manager or supervisor who has a relaxed style and who invites employee participation in decision-making is more likely to have employees with a high level of organizational self-esteem than a "traditional" manager.

This book is directed toward a management style that steps away from the beaten path of the traditional manager and emphasizes an employee-centered approach. Managers adopting this style can gain the respect and admiration of their subordinates and look beyond the day-to-day details of their job to develop an understanding of the motivations of their subordinates.

Today's health care managers are exposed to conflicting pressures—pressures from above to perpetuate conformity and pressures from below to permit individuality. Those managers who succeed are individuals with exceptional emotional maturity. Rogers outlined certain patterns of behavior that he found consistently in people of exceptional emotional maturity. He said they almost always manifest:

1. willingness to accept experiences for what they are
2. confidence in their own ability and judgment
3. greater reliance on self than on society or friends
4. willingness to continue to grow as persons[2]

I address your willingness to grow as persons. I have, once again, conducted a thorough search of the literature and added to this third edition an illustrious list of researchers and authors, as well as those upon whom I drew in the first and second editions. I have included parts of my research that were contained in an earlier book *The Arbitration and Grievance Process*, which I wrote with Joseph Ferentino, together with material contained in *Achieving Excellence.*

In 1981, Daniel Yankelovich in his book *New Rules* told us that a new social ethic is gradually starting to take shape. He called it an ethic of commitment to distinguish it from the traditional ethic of self-denial that underlies the old giving-getting compact. He said that it will take several years before this new ethic emerges clearly from the confusion of the present.[3] I believe that this new ethic of commitment has found its moment. Many of you are committed to the responsibility of leadership. Many of you are searching for new patterns, new styles, and more fulfilling and meaningful work experiences. This book is dedicated to such supervisors and managers.

I once again wish to acknowledge the enormous contribution of Irene

Wehr to the revision of this book. She is a hard taskmaster who keeps me on track. Her advice and direction were invaluable.

Norman Metzger

NOTES

1. American Society of Personnel Administration/Commerce Clearing House, *Human Resource Management: 1986 ASPA/CCH Survey* (Chicago: Commerce Clearing House, Inc., 13 June 1986).
2. Carl R. Rogers, *Client-Centered Therapy* (Boston: Houghton-Mifflin, 1951), 12.
3. Daniel Yankelovich, *New Rules* (New York: Bantam, 1981), 10.

Part I

The New Organization: Supervisors and Managers as Motivators and Facilitators

Chapter 1

Managers and Supervisors in Health Care

> *Approaches to organizing and managing are not inherently effective or ineffective. They are effective to the degree that they fit existing conditions. To be effective a management approach needs to fit the existing societal values, the nature of the work-force, the type of product being produced and the business environment. Because all of these factors determine the effectiveness of a management approach,* its effectiveness may change over time. . . . The crucial thing is to develop and practice a style that fits the conditions at a given point in time. *(emphasis added)*
>
> *Edward E. Lawler III*
> *High-Involvement Management*
> *(San Francisco, CA: Jossey-Bass Publishers, 1986) p. 2.*

A TIME FOR CHANGE

The health care industry is undergoing incredible and rapid change. As bewildering as it is, it is also full of excitement. Those professionals who have the responsibility for the administration of sections, departments, or divisions and who are willing and able to change have an unparalleled opportunity for challenge and, in the final analysis, for fulfilling and meaningful work.

If there is a critical challenge to making health care employees more productive with a concomitant degree of self-fulfillment for them, it is in the area of management roles. Managers need not be told that the job of supervision is a frustrating one. Most managers must represent top management to their employees and balance this with representation of employees to top management. There are no more influential individuals in health care in the drive toward productivity, toward lessening worker alienation, toward building morale, and toward reducing costs than the supervisor and the middle-manager. It is a sad commentary, but nonetheless a truism, that most top management does not recognize, indeed fails to appreciate, the manager's key position as an agent of change. Several keen observers have labeled that position "the forgotten person," "the master and victim of double talk," and "the marginal person."

Sasser and Leonard state that the first-line supervisor is caught directly in the crossfire of values and priorities.

1. The supervisor often does not know the objectives and policies of top management but heavily influences what management can accomplish.
2. The supervisor is not part of the work force but depends heavily on its acceptance.
3. The supervisor is in the first line of management but has little authority.
4. The supervisor is a member of management but is far removed from the locus of decision-making.
5. The supervisor is limited by precedence and company culture but serves as the agent of change without whose action little occurs in the company.
6. The supervisor establishes standards and precedence but has little information or knowledge on which to base decisions.
7. The supervisor is supposed to spend much time on interpersonal relationships but finds that much of his or her time is needed for record-keeping.
8. The supervisor is supposed to have a position of leadership but feels that leadership traits are suppressed because of the low self-image associated with the position.
9. The supervisor is asked to identify with the values and aspirations of management but is at a dead end in career progress and development.
10. The supervisor is usually young and deals with a young, diverse staff but is evaluated, trained, and rewarded by older, more conservative, and more authoritarian supervisors.[1]

As the health care industry has moved into highly sophisticated approaches to delivery systems, advanced technology, and computer science, the job of the first-line supervisor has not been simplified but has become more complex. As the supervisor, you must be a respected leader of the rank-and-file employees: you often find a need for technical competence in the specific area you supervise, you must be able to plan the work, and you must, of course, deal with interpersonal relationships. You are the person in the middle, often the oppressed middle. Very often you are forced to curry the good will of the boss. Shorris tells us "Competition for the good will of the leader or primal father follows the patterns described by Freud, except that envy generates esprit de corps, which, in turn, generates greater envy. The horde becomes the mass, men not only permit themselves to become a means, they seek their own debasement in the hope of winning secret favors."[2]

Let us start off by looking into the mirror. The following are difficult reality-based questions. Answer them if you dare.

1. To what extent do you make decisions based on how happy you will make others?
2. To what extent do you avoid making decisions because you are afraid that it might upset others?
3. To what extent do you "pass the buck" rather than take responsibility for situations if you are afraid that people will become upset?
4. To what extent do you avoid giving others information that would be of help and value to them because you are afraid that they may become angry or upset at your frankness?
5. To what extent do you have an obsessive worry about how much others love you?[3]

Let's face it! It's a tough job. It is clear that no less than five different roles come into play almost every day that you report to work. You supervise and train the employees in your department; you are responsible for implementing ideas that you have generated or that have originated from the staff specialist; you have peer relationships with other supervisors; and you report to someone—you relate to your boss as your employees relate to you. Not the least of the roles you play is that of mediator, whether it be in a union shop where you interface with the union's steward or in a nonunion shop where you deal directly with the employees.[4]

MYTHS ABOUT SUPERVISION

In the past, supervisors were chosen on the basis of either strength or technical know-how. The biggest bully could well have moved into a supervisory position. Often a supervisor was selected because he or she was the best at whatever was being done mechanically, physically, or cerebrally. In the last several decades, however, research has indicated that there is not a one-to-one relationship between technical proficiency and supervisory skills. The "art" of supervision has been reshaped into the "science" of supervision.

Once the misconception that the best worker could become the best supervisor was dispelled, the misconception that "good supervisors are born, not made" had to be addressed. Most social psychologists and experts in communication agree on certain basic characteristics of leadership, and these experts have indicated that leadership qualities are not inborn. Environmental factors and training have a strong impact on the development of an individual's abilities to lead groups.

Loyalty and length of service are not the key factors in selecting individuals for leadership positions. Although loyalty is important, what is needed in addition is a sincere, energetic, and capable individual who has the motivation to assume a leadership role. One of the many myths of the effective leader is that only extroverts can hold such positions. This is not a universal truism. Some very fine quiet and reserved people exhibit tremendous leadership ability when given the opportunity. Still another myth is the typical appearance of a leader. Is there really a stereotype of leadership appearance? Absolutely not! Far more important than appearance are attitude and ability, specifically to motivate others. Leadership ability includes an interest in people. Although leadership does depend on the specific situation, those leaders who express a sincere interest in the people who work for them, and balance it with an interest in the work itself, are the most effective. There is little doubt today that almost every technique of supervision can be learned. These basic principles more often than not can be transferred from workplace to workplace. Indeed, the backbone of supervisory techniques is pure and simple common sense.

EFFECTIVE MANAGERS

Drucker tells us that there are essentially five practices or habits of mind that an individual must acquire to be an effective manager.

1. Effective executives know where their time goes. They work systematically at managing the little of their time that can be brought under their control.
2. Effective executives focus on outward contribution. They gear their efforts to results rather than to work. They start out with the question "What results are expected of me?" rather than with the work to be done, let alone with its techniques and tools.
3. Effective executives build on strengths—their own strengths, the strengths of their superiors, colleagues, and subordinates, and the strengths in the situation, that is, on what they can do. They do not build on weaknesses. They do not start with what they cannot do.
4. Effective executives concentrate on the few major areas where superior performance will produce outstanding results. They force them-

selves to set priorities and stay with their priority decisions. They know that they have no choice but to do first things first and second things not at all. The alternative is to get nothing done.

5. Effective executives, finally, make effective decisions. They know that this is, above all, a matter of system—of the first steps in the right sequence. They know that an effective decision is always a judgment based on "dissenting opinions" rather than on "consensus on the facts," and they know that to make many decisions quickly means to make the wrong decisions. What is needed are a few but fundamental decisions, the right strategy rather than razzle-dazzle tactics.[5]

The new breed of supervisors must master the art and science of consultation. Two-way communication with a feedback loop is the hallmark of today's successful supervisor. In communicating with your employees you must develop your ability to understand their motivations: learn how to speak their language, master techniques of introducing change in the face of resistance, and control subjective evaluation and determination and replace subjectivity with dependence on facts and logic.

The subordinate's perception of the supervisor plays a significant role in motivation. A supervisor who is seen as one who is interested in the subordinate's development, the subordinate's personal goals and the subordinate's problems, is far more effective than one who is perceived as disinterested. The subordinate views the supervisor through an acute lens, judging the ease in which he or she can approach the supervisor. If one has to be careful about choosing the time or place that such an approach is made, if a worker has to be concerned about the supervisor's mood, if the supervisor continually finds fault with the subordinate, then the worker will be poorly motivated. Such a worker believes that the supervisor neither trusts nor appreciates him or her. Study after study has indicated that poorly motivated employees believe that their supervisors did not trust them and had to control them, whereas highly motivated supervisors have a direct and positive effect on their employees.

Rather than get caught up in academic phrases and labels, most of the researchers involved in supervisor-subordinate relationships seem to address their studies to two diametrically opposed styles of supervision—employee centered and production centered.

At the Institute for Social Research at the University of Michigan, Likert conducted numerous studies in an attempt to find out what makes an organization tick and, more specifically, how the principles and practices of leadership bear directly on the productivity and job satisfaction of various groups. These studies made the following conclusions.

1. It is not necessarily true that a favorable attitude among employees toward the company will result in increased productivity.
2. When comparing people under general supervision (where the goal to be accomplished is clear and the employees are given leeway in accomplishing it) with persons under close supervision (where the supervisor is constantly in attendance and permits little leeway for the subordinates), those groups under close supervision tend to be associated with low productivity whereas those under more general supervision show higher productivity.
3. Supervisors of high-productivity groups more often report that they are kept informed of developments than supervisors of low-productivity groups.
4. When work groups with the highest and lowest morale were asked to describe what their supervisors did, workers in low-morale groups mentioned just as often as workers in high-morale groups that their supervisors performed such production-centered tasks as "enforces the rules," "arranges work and makes work assignments," and "supplies people with materials and tools." But the high-morale groups mentioned much more frequently than the low-morale groups such employee-centered functions as "recommends promotions and pay increases," "informs people about what is happening in the company," "keeps people posted on how well they are doing," and "hears complaints and grievances."
5. There is a marked relationship between worker morale and how strongly employees feel that their boss is interested in discussing work problems with the work group.
6. The high-productivity groups show greater group loyalty and greater group pride than do the low-productivity groups.
7. When supervisors were asked how their section compared with other sections in the way the workers help each other on the job, the answer showed a marked relationship to group productivity. Supervisors of high-productivity groups reported much more often than supervisors of low-productivity groups that their workers helped one another in getting the work done.[6]

In the Michigan Studies, Likert concluded that when a supervisor treats subordinates as human beings the result is greater group loyalty and pride. He stated that when supervisors stay sufficiently close to their workers to be able to see work-related problems through employees' eyes, they are better able to develop strong group loyalty. Supervisors who can empathize with workers can translate employee needs to top administration and thereby help arrive at policy decisions that are realistic and satisfactory to both the administration and the employees.

An effective supervisor must understand employee motivations and needs. Study after study has shown that supervisors and the people they supervise do not see eye-to-eye on what workers want most. The average supervisor replies that good wages, job security, and promotion are the worker's basic desires. On the other hand, workers consistently reply that their basic desires are full appreciation of work done, feeling "in on things," and sympathetic help with personal problems. Simply stated, there are two pay systems operative in every institution. The normal pay system is based on competitive wages and fair differentials within the institution, resulting in an adequate and satisfactory paycheck; the other pay system deals with employee motivation.

An interesting study by Herzberg revealed the duality of a person's nature. The study was designed to search out people's needs and to test the concept that a person has two sets of needs—needs as an animal to avoid pain and needs as a human being to grow psychologically. The participants in the study were engineers and accountants. They were asked to recall a time when they had felt exceptionally good about their jobs and the reasons for these feelings. They were also asked whether these feelings of job satisfaction had affected their performance, their personal relationships, and their sense of well-being. The study concluded that the strongest determinants of job satisfaction were achievement, recognition, the work itself, responsibility, and advancement. The last three factors were more important to a lasting change of attitudes than the first two factors. The major dissatisfiers were company policy and administration, supervision, salary, interpersonal relations, and working conditions. Thus, the satisfiers relate to what the person does and the dissatisfiers relate to the situation in which he or she does it. The satisfier factors were named *motivators*; the dissatisfier factors were named *hygiene*. Herzberg concluded that the motivators were effective in promoting superior performance and effort.[7]

To understand fully why appreciation, recognition, and consultation are far more important to employees than wages, let us review briefly Maslow's hierarchical structure of needs. Maslow points out that there are essentially five levels of need. At the lowest level are the physiological needs such as air, food, and good health. When these needs are reasonably satisfied, they no longer act as motivators to behavior. At the second level is the need for safety, protection against danger and threat, and fair treatment. If the employee is confident that his or her safety needs are met, these too are no longer motivators; but if he or she feels threatened or dependent, he or she is motivated to seek security. At the next level are the social needs. These needs are best typified by the drive to "belong," to be part of a purposeful group. We then move to the ego needs, which include the need for self-esteem, self-confidence, and status. These are rarely satisfied and have a far greater effect on motivation. At the fifth level is the need for self-fulfillment, that is, the need for realizing one's own potential.[8]

More often than not, the employees that you supervise have their lowest-level needs satisfied; this the organization accomplishes by paying adequate and competitive salaries. The second-level needs are also ensured by the institution's policies—when they are promulgated and implemented—providing for a safe workplace, a fair seniority system, a progressive benefit package, and due process guaranteed by a grievance procedure. It is at the third level, the social needs, that we face our major challenges and frustrations. The supervisor, more than the organization, must deal with these needs by bringing the employee into the work family and making the employee feel that his or her contribution is important. The fourth level needs are satisfied by recognition and appreciation for work done, by setting objectives and sharing plans with employees, and by reinforcing their confidence with positive feedback and rewards.

According to Zander, a good manager encourages participative management. This style emphasizes joint problem solving and decision-making by some or all persons who are relevant to the problem under study and tries to involve representatives from different levels of the hierarchy. The performance of an organization can be improved if those who do its work bring their experiences directly to bear in planning for this work. A wise manager recognizes that the motivation of subordinates is likely to be stronger if the members have a chance to influence decisions, particularly if these decisions serve the members' needs. Zander further states that a good manager treats a subordinate in a way that respects a member's dignity and desires. He or she has to be insightful, supportive, and helpful in dealing with his or her subordinates rather than aggressively assertive. Zander concludes with the basic assumption that an administrator's (supervisor's) major responsibility is to keep the organization functioning well. The successful managers have a stronger desire to work on behalf of the organization than those who are less successful. This results because:

1. the supervisor's duties involve him or her in the productivity of the unit instead of personal counseling
2. he or she has a role that is more responsible (or central) than less responsible (or peripheral)
3. he or she is more satisfied by the success of the organization than by his or her own achievements

4. he or she is usually competent in the tasks he or she must perform for the organization[9]

As a supervisor, you must accept the fact that by improved managerial practices and attention to the proper utilization of people and technology you can increase the satisfaction and productivity of the people who work for you. This is made clear by much of the theory and research on organizational motivation, satisfaction, and productivity. Such research indicates that people bring to the work area different mental and physical abilities. Supervisors must deal with various personalities and various levels of experience.

Need fulfillment or frustration produces either constructive or defensive behavior. How often have you noted tensions in employees who seem to be dissatisfied with their work? Such dissatisfaction produces behavior designed to relieve that tension. Employees whose needs are not met become defensive; they employ defense mechanisms such as withdrawal, aggression, substitution, or compensation. You must have seen employees who do very little talking; they seem withdrawn, and you have great difficulty in communicating with them. Other dissatisfied employees channel their frustration into constructive behavior by looking outside the work area for fulfillment. They join clubs, teams, or unions. Defensive behavior may work against the goals of the department and the institution. Dissatisfaction on the job exacts a high cost. It produces friction on the job, low productivity, high absenteeism, excessive turnover, and, of course, strikes. Many employees seek more satisfaction from their work than is available to them under present managerial structures. There is little question that employee motivation results in increased productivity and higher efficiency. Such motivation can be enhanced by a supervisory style that encompasses knowledge and appreciation of employee motives.

A relationship between a supervisor and workers that includes mutual understanding and agreement on goals and rewards is an ideally effective one. Supervisors must be willing to move from authority-obedience styles of supervision to involvement-participation-commitment styles. Supervisors are responsible for getting results from their work team. Therefore, they must demand such results. Demanding results, however, does not necessarily guarantee results. More and more evidence has been produced to indicate that the old authority-obedience approach is not result oriented. Yet the involvement-participation-commitment style of supervision is difficult and complex. The new approach involves reaching consensus on what is the real problem to be solved in any given case, listening for reservations and doubts rather than for signs of compliance, encouraging people to express their different views, and dealing with conflicts in an open and candid way.[10]

To repeat an earlier statement, research and experience clearly indicate that a supervisor is indeed able to meet the needs of employees and thereby make them more productive. Although there is no one sure way to make employees more efficient, there is a central theme that weaves through the mass of research and literature on this subject. This central theme, which found its way through the works of Herzberg, McGregor, and Mayo and was emblazoned in the singular study *Work in America*, points an accusing finger at the typical organization. Employees who start a new job bring with them a caring attitude and a high level of motivation. The subsequent lack of productivity and efficiency is usually caused by the organization, which by its inherent noncaring style destroys an employee's natural desire to care about work and to do it well.

It then falls to the supervisor to restructure the work situation for the employee. This restructuring includes an objective review of work content with an eye toward enrichment, redesign, and broadening of responsibilities. This is necessary because worker motivation derives from the task itself. In addition to the challenge of improving the job, attention must be directed toward improving the environment. Recognition is necessary at every level of the organization. Communication is just as important to the porter as it is to the surgeon. Everyone wants to know what is transpiring within the organization. Employees want to know what the supervisor is thinking and what management is thinking and planning. They want to feel that management knows that they are there—that they are not invisible. Alienation and frustration will develop if employees feel that nobody is listening or paying attention to their needs. The wise supervisor who directs his or her attention toward maximizing opportunities for effective work teams will keep these conclusions in mind and not be confused by long-ingrained beliefs and misconceptions that are counterproductive to getting the job done.

Brief summarizes various prescriptions for motivation that are key to the supervisor's interpersonal relationships with subordinates.

1. Managers should make sure that all employees thoroughly understand the performance objectives that they are expected to achieve. These objectives should be stated in as specific terms as possible and set at a high enough level to be challenging but not so high as to be discouraging.
2. All employees' performances in terms of the degree to which they have attained the specified objectives should be evaluated periodically and those analyses fed back to the individuals. Even though

these first two prescriptions are likely themselves to have a positive impact on employee motivation, they are viewed here as the necessary prerequisites for implementing any of the other recommendations.

3. Organizational policies should be implemented that allow employees who have attained the objectives specified above to acquire the extrinsic rewards they desire. The rewards to be covered by organizational policies include those whose distribution typically is governed by formal statements of policy (e.g., pay increases and promotions). The following prescription refers to rewards whose distribution typically is not formalized (e.g., recognition from supervisors and assignment to desirable tasks).
4. Managers should adhere informally to the intent of these reward policies by attempting to discriminate between high and low performers in allocating the other extrinsic rewards within the supervisors' control not governed by formally stated policies.
5. Managers should attempt to structure the jobs occupied by subordinates in a manner to make intrinsic rewards freely available.
6. Managers should attempt to reward themselves in public only when they clearly have achieved performance levels congruent with the goals of the organization. The preceding two prescriptions, enriching the jobs of employees, and serving as an appropriate role model represent some of the managerial activities associated with encouraging self-rewarding behaviors among subordinates contingent upon their attaining specified performance objectives.
7. In the case of employees breaking into new task assignments, performance objectives initially should be set low enough to allow the subordinates to experience success but not so low as to encourage them to view the tasks as easy.
8. Persons designated as coaches, trainers, and other role models should be interpersonally competent and should not exhibit aptitude levels far beyond the employees they are assigned to assist.
9. In the case of employees breaking into new task assignments, the task initially selected should approximate those already learned, and these similarities should be pointed out.
10. If managers identify reasons other than an employee's ability that may lead to the individual's failure on a task, these reasons should be communicated clearly to the person and, if possible, the performance obstacles should be removed. The preceding prescriptions all pertain to enhancing employees' task-relevant self-image.
11. Finally, managers must be willing to experiment and take risks when it comes to trying out new motivational strategies. A domi-

> nant characteristic of successful managers is flexibility. This last prescription reflects the need for health care managers to be somewhat adventurous in selecting alternative strategies for improving the operation of their units. This risky posture, however, must be tempered by the willingness of the manager (1) to investigate alternatives thoroughly before adopting them; (2) to evaluate the effectiveness of the alternatives implemented; and (3) in the face of failure, to try something different.[11]

Boyd and Scanlan offer four key factors that aid new supervisors moving into the world of management.

1. *Job knowledge.* Being technically equipped for the type of work you will supervise will be of immeasurable assistance in bolstering your confidence; your subordinates will recognize that you know what you are talking about.
2. *Assistance from others.* Don't be shy. Ask your superior or your peers for any support and advice that you need. It is not a sign of weakness.
3. *Good education.* Much of what you do involves communication, paperwork, and arithmetic. If you have educated yourself, you are a step ahead in the supervisory world. Remember, however, that what counts is the quality, not the quantity, of your schooling.
4. *Desire to succeed.* There is no substitute for the will to do a good job. You have been selected for the responsibility, and there is no reason why you shouldn't succeed if you try hard enough.[12]

The National Management Association made a study of 68 companies to determine why supervisors fail. Factors contributing to failure were:

1. poor general relations with workers or with other management people
2. individual shortcomings, such as lack of initiative and emotional instability
3. lack of understanding of management's point of view
4. unwillingness to spend the necessary time and effort to improve
5. lack of skill in planning and organizing work
6. inability to adjust to new and changing conditions[13]

The mark of the good supervisor is the ability to develop sound interpersonal relationships with workers and with other management people. To do this, the supervisor must respond to different types of organizational situations on the basis of differences in employee personalities. The successful supervisor is the people-centered supervisor. This type of supervisor understands the various needs of the employees under his or her jurisdiction.

The supervisor is often the only individual in the institution dealing daily with today's problems. He or she is often many people rolled up in one: counselor to employees, interpreter of the institution's policies, and implementer of the institution's programs. The supervisor must deal with staff people, medical people, top-level administrative people, union representatives, and often the public. This obviously requires a person who can deal with ambiguity and is able to adapt to new situations and a wide range of personalities.

First-line supervisors are the people on the firing line. Their prime responsibility is to develop their subordinates into an efficient production-oriented team while at the same time keeping friction at a minimum and satisfaction at a maximum and achieving optimum stability. There is probably no more difficult position in the organization than that of the first-line supervisor.

The supervisory role encompasses a broad range of responsibilities.

1. Supervisors are the immediate leaders of designated segments of the work force.
2. Supervisors are day-to-day decision-makers.
3. Supervisors must plan.
4. Supervisors must organize the work, the work area, and the workers.
5. Supervisors are responsible for setting up conditions that provide for maximum motivation of the work force.
6. Supervisors must counsel employees on job-related and other problems.
7. Supervisors must be communicators.
8. Supervisors are trainers.
9. Finally, most difficult, and possibly most important, supervisors must be agents of change.

A PRESCRIPTION FOR CURING "INVISIBILITY"

There are times when managers feel that they are the invisible people in the organization. They seem not to know what's going on. They often are not able to get the attention of their superiors when critical problems must be addressed. They often work for bosses who are too busy to relate to the day-to-day problems that most supervisors must deal with. That feeling of invisibility, however, need not be related to your potential effectiveness. *Possibility* is the watchword. In the words of Calvin Coolidge:

> Nothing in the world can take the place of persistence. Talent will not; nothing is more common than unsuccessful men with talent. Genius will not; unrewarded genius is almost a proverb. Education alone will not; the world is full of educated derelicts. Persistence and determination alone are omnipotent.

Grasping possibilities should be a constant goal of managers. One does not make progress by doing things by rote. In spite of the pressures—including difficult bosses—managers have been able to exert a leadership style that reflects directly on the willingness of their subordinates to contribute effectively to the overall goals of the organization and on developing a productive unit that demands recognition.

These managers display leadership traits such as the following.

1. They are willing to be risk takers. Those who play it safe (and there are legions of such managers in health care) may survive in the organization, but who will know that they are there?
2. They are decision-makers. This includes the need to make decisions even if they are unpopular. Decisiveness is a trait found in most successful leaders. Decisiveness and persistence are the hallmarks of those who move ahead in management. Passing the buck may well permit you to survive, but who will follow you?
3. They have a deep concern for the human aspects of management. Such managers believe that caring counts. It has been proved time and time again that employees will follow you to the ends of the earth if they feel that you care about them as human beings. Caring does pay off.
4. They are always sensitive to protecting the dignity of others. Shorris said "A manager who knows that his subordinates are his equals, becomes the equal of his superiors."[14] The manager who moves ahead, who is effective, and who has the most productive work team is the one who is constantly sensitive to the need for protecting the dignity of subordinates and, indeed, gets in return the protection of his or her own dignity. Support your people and they will support you; respect your people and they will respect you.
5. They have a "high touch" style of management. They are not reluctant to share credit and give rewards. There is an old oriental adage that says "If you wish your merit to be known, acknowledge that of

other people." They are the ones that Blanchard and Johnson suggested will "catch someone doing something right."[15]

6. They are willing to accept mistakes. To err is human; to admit that you make mistakes at times seems superhuman. People appreciate honesty. The "blame-throwers" of the world develop alienated workers.
7. They view development of subordinates as a priority responsibility. Effective supervision is based on the belief that people are not by nature passive or resistant to organizational needs. It is the manager's responsibility to enable the employees to fulfill their own needs and goals as well as those of the organization. The successful manager treats employees as resources that, if cultivated, will yield economic returns to the institution.

SOME TOUGH QUESTIONS FOR SUPERVISORY ASPIRANTS

It takes a great deal more than the obvious ingredients of desire, integrity, and technical know-how to be a supervisor. Black and Black list some questions designed to ascertain whether you really have what it takes to be a supervisor.

1. Are you able to take the loss of credit? You will be faced with the problem of your idea showing up as someone else's brilliant stroke of imagination.
2. Are you susceptible to the frustrations of communications breakdowns? Do you lose your temper when "you didn't get the word?"
3. Are you big enough to absorb the blame for a subordinate's mistake? You are going to have to be if you intend to put together a successful and efficient team.
4. Are you unable to cope with disappointment? There are going to be many disappointments ahead, but the "successful-unsuccessful supervisor" has to control resentment and move on to future successes.
5. Can you work for an unreasonable boss? This question is a real soul-searcher. Too often supervisors—those who do not succeed—undercut their superior. You often must look beyond your own agenda and attempt to understand actions of your superior that appear to be unreasonable.

6. Can you separate your life off the job from your life on the job? This may be the most difficult requirement for a manager, but it is the mark of the successful and experienced supervisor.
7. Can you keep pushing when there is no penalty for taking it easy? This is the test of true leadership; motivation to succeed comes from within.[16]

There is no question that supervisors face frustrating circumstances on a daily basis. Too often those at the top have lost touch with the problems and frustrations of the first-line supervisor. More often than not you find yourself in an organization reluctant to share decision-making, an organization that does not understand or appreciate your contribution, and an organization that does not seem to be able to differentiate between productive and nonproductive employees. It takes a great deal to succeed in the face of these obstacles, but successful managers seem to have the personality for the job.

THE SUCCESSFUL SUPERVISOR

There has been a great deal of research conducted regarding the desirable traits indicative of the successful manager. You find such words as decisive, informed, and creative, but more important is a general behavioral pattern that has emerged from opinions, observations, tests, and intensive research into the actual process of supervision. The following list of job behaviors seems consistent with that research. Successful managers:

1. manage work instead of people
2. plan and organize effectively
3. set goals realistically
4. derive decisions by group consensus but accept responsibility for them
5. delegate frequently and effectively
6. rely on others to help in solving problems
7. communicate effectively
8. are a stimulus to action
9. coordinate effectively
10. cooperate with others
11. show consistent and dependable behavior
12. win gracefully
13. express hostility tactfully[17]

Of course it is rarely possible to be all things to all people. The job of the supervisor is indeed broad in its demands and complex in its challenges. More often than not, the supervisor who has an efficient department is sensitive to three basic areas that affect the quality of employee performance. These areas are participation, communication, and motivation. Participation is accomplished by encouraging subordinates to offer suggestions about work flow and working conditions. It is enhanced by delegating responsibility. You maximize participation by setting up an atmosphere where subordinates can offer ideas, react to your ideas without fear of retribution, and participate in group decisions.

The hallmark of effective communication is the feedback loop. There must be two-way communication; that is, there must be a system that permits and encourages "checking" messages for understanding. Communication is enhanced by a permissive atmosphere where cooperation rather than competition is encouraged. Effective communication is built upon consultation and collaboration.

Motivation is at the heart of the modern manager's job. The successful supervisor needs to become conscious of three factors: (1) the needs and policies of the institution; (2) the needs and interests of the workers; and (3) the supervisor's own purposes and goals.

Here is a simple list of recommended supervisory practices.

1. Keep employees informed of work requirements.
2. Let employees know where they stand.
3. Obtain maximum participation and strive for maximum communication where changes are indicated.
4. Help employees improve and broaden their skills.
5. Compliment employees for a job well done.
6. Provide the opportunity for group and individual participation for solving operational problems.
7. Treat all members of the group as equals.
8. Delegate responsibilities and encourage the acceptance of such responsibilities by all members of the work team.
9. Understand each employee's job, and clarify the importance of each job in relation to the group.
10. Appreciate and attempt to solve and alleviate employees' problems, no matter how small.
11. Help the individual understand the basic reasons for management's thinking on tasks that he or she is required to do.

CHECKLIST FOR SUPERVISORS

To help you build more effective work teams, we will deal in subsequent chapters with interviewing skills, evaluating skills, communication skills, disciplining skills, and a review of measurement techniques. The following is a list of questions that require you to take a look at yourself as a supervisor and give you an advance look at what is ahead in the remaining pages of this book.[18]

1. Do you have a thorough understanding of the institution's goals and your part in meeting the objectives of the institution and budget goals for your department? Do you have full confidence in their attainment?
2. Do you avoid confusion with a clear understanding of what is expected and how to do it?
3. Do you offer suggestions or constructive criticism to your immediate supervisor and ask for additional information when necessary?
4. Do you build team spirit and group pride by getting everyone into the act of setting goals and pulling together?
5. Are you always submerged in operational emergencies, or do you schedule time for meetings with your subordinates and your superiors?
6. Do you encourage each of your employees to come up with suggestions about ways to improve the section's functioning?
7. Do you make it easy for your people to approach you with job or personal problems?
8. Do you keep your employees informed about how they are doing?
9. Are you too busy with operational problems to be concerned with your employees' personal difficulties?
10. Do you give your employees a feeling of accomplishment by telling them how well they are doing in comparison with yesterday or last week or a month or a year ago?
11. Do you build individual employee confidence and praise good performance, or are you afraid of being accused of sentimentality, coddling, and soft-soaping?
12. Do you use personnel records and close observation to learn exactly which skills each employee has so that his or her best abilities may be used?
13. Do you let your people know how jobs are analyzed and evaluated and what the job rates and progressions are?
14. Do you attempt to rotate people on different jobs to build up skills for individual flexibility within the group?

15. Do you train your people for better jobs?
16. Are you developing an understudy for your job?
17. Do you hold a good person down in one position because he or she may be indispensable there?
18. Do you take a chance on your people by letting them learn through mistakes, by showing a calm reaction and constructive approach to occasional failure, by encouraging them to stick their necks out without fear of the ax, and by creating an atmosphere of confidence?
19. Do you use every opportunity to build up in your employees a sense of the importance of their work?
20. Do you delegate responsibility to subordinates, or do you insist on keeping your hand in details?
21. Are you placing real responsibility on your subordinates and then holding them accountable?
22. Do you interfere with the jobs of subordinates, or do you allow them to exercise discretion and judgment in making decisions?
23. Are you acting in ways that discourage your subordinates?
24. Are you aware of sources of discontentment, discouragement, or frustration affecting your employees?
25. Do you listen to the ideas and reactions of subordinates with courtesy? If an idea is adopted or not accepted, do you explain why?
26. Do you usually praise in public but criticize or reprove in private? Is criticism constructive?
27. Are you aware that a feeling of belonging builds self-confidence and makes people want to work harder than ever?
28. Do you ever say or do anything that detracts from your employees' sense of personal dignity?

These are very difficult questions, but they must be reviewed. Your honest answers will give you a good picture of your present supervisory style.

KEY POINTS FOR EFFECTIVE SUPERVISION

1. Whether your boss acknowledges it or not, you have status deriving from your employees' acceptance of your position. You are seen as the boss.
2. Supervision is a complex and difficult job, but one that can be extremely rewarding.

3. To be effective you must be able to manage your time; do not let time manage you.
4. Effective supervision builds on employees' strengths; the supervisor is not a fault-finder but rather a strength-finder.
5. Supervision can only be productive through communication; you must master the art and science of consultation and communication.
6. Outstanding supervisors expect outstanding performance; when they see outstanding performance they give immediate credit and acknowledgment.
7. Supervisors of high morale groups:
   - recommend promotions and pay increases
   - inform subordinates about what is happening in the institution
   - keep subordinates posted on how well they are doing
   - hear complaints and grievances
8. Successful supervisors have a stronger desire to work on behalf of the organization than those who are less successful; the supervisor's major responsibility is to keep the organization functioning well.
9. Need fulfillment or frustration produces either constructive or defensive behavior; one of your major responsibilities is to provide fulfilling and meaningful work for your subordinates.
10. If you want your people to maximize their productivity, you must concentrate on ensuring that all employees thoroughly understand the performance objectives that they are expected to achieve; specificity, clarity, and mutual agreements are hallmarks of attainable performance standards.
11. Remember that there are two pay systems: the normal pay system built on competitive and fair differentials; and the other pay system, which includes appreciation, communication, and an opportunity for fulfillment.
12. Deal in possibilities; grasping responsibilities should be a constant goal of managers.
13. Productive units have managers who:
    - are risk-takers
    - are decision-makers
    - have a deep concern for the human aspects of management
    - are sensitive to the need for protecting the dignity of subordinates
    - have a "high touch" style of management
14. If you are to succeed in the modern and changed health care work arena—with its complex challenges due to rapid change, higher expectations of workers, and a more educated work force—then

you must give up a management style anchored in authority-obedience and take up a management style based on involvement-participation-commitment.

NOTES

1. W. Earl Sasser, Jr. and Frank S. Leonard, "Let First-Level Supervisors Do Their Job," *Harvard Business Review* 58 (March/April 1980): 116.

2. Earl Shorris, *The Oppressed Middle* (Garden City, NY: Anchor Press/Doubleday, 1981), 229.

3. Lawrence C. Bassett and Norman Metzger, *Achieving Excellence: A Prescription for Health Care Managers* (Rockville, MD: Aspen Publishers, 1986), 18.

4. Lester R. Bittel, *What Every Supervisor Should Know,* 2nd ed. (New York: McGraw-Hill, 1968), 4.

5. Peter F. Drucker, *The Effective Executive* (New York: Harper & Row, 1967), 23–24.

6. Rensis Likert, *Motivation: The Core of Management* (New York: American Management Associations, Personnel Series No. 155, 1953), 3–20.

7. Frederick Herzberg, *Work and the Nature of Man* (New York: World Publishing Company, 1966), 71–76.

8. A. H. Maslow, *Motivation and Personality,* 2nd ed. (New York: Harper & Brothers, 1970), chaps. 3–7 passim.

9. Alvin Zander, *Groups at Work* (San Francisco: Jossey-Bass Publishers, 1977), 92–95.

10. Robert R. Blake and Jane Srygley Mouton, *The Grid for Supervisory Effectiveness* (Austin, TX: Scientific Methods, 1975), 3.

11. Arthur P. Brief, "Theories of Motivation Applied to Health Care Personnel Management," in *Handbook of Health Care Human Resources Management,* ed. Norman Metzger (Rockville, MD: Aspen Publishers, 1981), 319–320.

12. Radford B. Boyd and Burt K. Scanlan, *Management Institute of the University of Wisconsin Survey of 215 First Line Supervisors* (Madison: University of Wisconsin Press, 1972).

13. Bittel, *What Every Supervisor Should Know,* 12–13.

14. Shorris, *The Oppressed Middle,* 373.

15. Kenneth Blanchard and Spencer Johnson, *The One Minute Manager* (New York: Berkeley Books, 1983), 102–17.

16. James Menzies Black and Virginia Todd Black, *The Front Line Manager's Problem Solver* (New York: McGraw-Hill, 1970), 8.

17. J. P. Campbell et al., *Managerial Performance and Effectiveness* (New York: McGraw-Hill, 1970), 8.

18. The author wishes to take special note of the contribution of Dr. Leslie M. Slote, Hartsdale, NY, who helped to develop checklists similar to those presented here.

Chapter 2

New Employees: New Challenges for Managers

> *What we all once thought of as "authority" is undergoing significant changes in our society. We are moving away from authority based strictly on power and status to authority based on knowledge and ability.*
>
> *Authority is granted by constituents to their leaders only so long as these leaders satisfy the needs and standards of the governed. This startling change applies equally to managerial authority.*
>
> *Thomas L. Quick*
> *Understanding People at Work*
> *(New York: Executive Enterprises Publications Co., Inc. 1976) p. vii.*

It is time to take inventory. We are not dealing with the same employees we have dealt with in the past. Some of them have been around for a while, but perceptions and needs have changed within the American work force. Let us look at the new breed of employee.

A survey was conducted recently to answer the critical question "Do employees feel that they make a difference where they work?"[1] The major finding of the survey was that a manager or supervisor who has a relaxed style and who invites employee participation in decision-making is more likely to have employees with a high level of organizational self-esteem than a more traditional manager. The managers whose employees have higher self-esteem show an interest in each employee's contribution, status, and well-being; show an interest in each employee's personal situation; and offer employees variety, a degree of autonomy, significant work experience, and a chance to use valued skills. A most important finding was that the extent to which an employee is permitted to participate in departmental decision-making is related to the employee's level of organizational self-esteem. Both experienced meaningfulness of work and experienced responsibility for work outcome correlate significantly with organizational self-esteem. Employees who could trust both their supervisor and the management of their organization in general had higher levels of self-esteem than those employees who found themselves working with supervisors or management (or both) that could not be trusted. Management's faith in the employee's capacity to direct himself or herself was related to level of employee self-esteem, and so was a show of satisfaction in the employee.

Research was conducted on the effective management of people. This research indicated the following trends.

1. Each employee group is less optimistic about its chances for advancement.
2. Feelings of security, although still high, are beginning to deteriorate.
3. Employees still like their jobs and most still find their employers credible, but there is evidence of a growing malaise, a gradual but persistent loss of optimism.[2]

Further findings indicate that work values, notably loyalty and commitment, are in decline because employees no longer feel that their employers are loyal and committed to them. The net effect is diminished commitment at all levels of the organization, even in some firms that are performing well.

THE NEW WORK FORCE

Many observers believe that there is a growing mismatch between the characteristics and aspirations of the work force and the ability of the workplace, as it is now constituted, to satisfy these new expectations. Kanter states "... promotion opportunities (one of the major sources of increase in pay, challenge and influence in a large corporation) were thought to be declining. Increased competition from a large number of aspirants, an aging work force postponing retirement, and a slower growth economy prevented the organizational pyramid from expanding to accommodate all those seeking the 'better' jobs."[3]

The new work force comprises employees who expect a greater voice in decisions at work and who want opportunities beyond those contained in their present jobs. They are more educated and, therefore, less fulfilled. More educated employees invariably come with elevated hopes of more attractive jobs, higher earnings, and greater opportunities for career advancement. This may well set the stage for worker disillusionment and discontent, since in many instances opportunities lag behind such expectations. Levitan and Johnson tell us:

> Job satisfaction surveys have identified the combination of longer schooling and low pay as one of the most potent formulas for dissatisfaction in the workplace, reflecting the belief that education credentials implicitly promise or guarantee future success. In sending them to school for longer stints, we prepare a veritable 'powderkeg' of expectations among new entrants to the labor force, who by virtue of youth and inexperience are most likely to suffer from the inadequacies of the labor market.[4]

The legitimacy of traditional systems is eroding, and foremost among the challenges to the traditional bureaucracy are the changing pay-for-performance systems, which reflect the new work ethic. Our employees expect greater meaning from their work and, indeed, want to feel that they make a difference. This feeling comes from a desire to innovate.[5] Innovation cannot take place in an organization that stifles employees' ability to contribute. This ability to contribute is based on an atmosphere in which risk taking is not only permissible but encouraged. Peterfruend believes that there is hardly an organization today where climate, culture, or management systems support and motivate risk-taking below the executive level. He states "The amount of risk individuals dare to take is adversely conditioned in most organizations by the belief (strongly entrenched as a result of past experience) that the rewards for successful risk-taking are *far* outweighed by the penalties for failure."[6] An organization that is innovative provides the wherewithal for its employees, at all levels, to take risks. Such risks are taken if employees believe that the rewards for success are in proper balance with the penalties for failure.[7] Inherent then in such an organization is the employee's ability to share in its successes. Equally important is the diminishment of the fear of ostracism and failure; there is a pervasive fear of criticism that employees evidence in traditional organizations. This stifles suggestions, contributions, and commitment. An employee must feel that there is freedom to make mistakes or to make "silly" suggestions. Finally, the employee must feel free to participate in problem solving and decision-making as a partner, and not as a junior partner.

It is time to turn our backs on the misconception that only top management is omniscient, that ideas worthwhile to the organization can come only from those presently in power. Ideas worth considering and implementing can come from people at all levels in the organization—professional, nonprofessional, high up in the hierarchy, low down in the hierarchy. Therefore, it is your responsibility to encourage employees to be innovative and to contribute. Through such innovation and contribution we can maximize employee commitment, thereby ensuring the excellence of the organization.

Brown and Weiner point out that today's young workers are immersed in a legacy of the late 1960s. Five overriding factors have developed since that era.

1. the introduction of two-wage-earner households
2. a broadened social awareness and search for "meaning"
3. the explosive growth of the service economy
4. the economic, demographic, and technological challenge to middle-management positions
5. a strong sense that now is a time of rapid change and that the future is uncertain[8]

WORKER ALIENATION

One of the results of these changing times is worker alienation. It is easy to recognize the symptoms of such alienation: low productivity, high absenteeism, lateness, and confrontational relationships. The key to understanding such alienation is that an alienated worker believes that his or her behavior cannot determine the outcome of what he or she seeks.[9] A Harris Survey[10] showed that the index of alienation of workers rose perceptively in the 1970s. Of the individuals surveyed, 64 percent answered affirmatively to the statement "Most people with power try to take advantage of people like yourself," and 59 percent answered affirmatively to the statement "What you think does not count very much anymore" (see Table 2-1). An alienated worker does not believe that his or her work can give fulfillment and meaning. Ruch and Goodman tell us that fulfillment and meaningful work experiences are characterized by four components:

1. *Knowledge:* employees want to know what's going on in the company and why certain actions are taken.
2. *Care:* employees want to know that management cares about what they are doing, and they themselves want to care about what they are doing.
3. *Respect:* such respect derives from one's humanity—indeed, it is the respect for people's humanness that makes people feel fulfilled at the job.
4. *Responsibility:* people want to have a feeling that they are responsible for something—that is, they want to be accountable.[11]

These four factors, K.C.R.R., are at the heart of the battle against alienation; they are the ingredients of fulfilling and meaningful work.

To deal with worker alienation you must communicate openly and frequently. The new breed of employee has an enormous appetite for information. We can no longer be gatekeepers of such information; rather, we must be expediters. We must let employees know what is going on; let them know how they will be affected by changes in the organization; let them share in our plans; and, indeed, let them share in the planning. People want to feel "in on things." It is essential that you facilitate that process. Being knowledgeable also means being equipped to face changing requirements. The new employee wants to grow, to improve skills, and to take on additional responsibilities. That again is your challenge. No matter how many times you have heard the expression "caring counts," it is a truism. The art of management is being reshaped. Old myths must be discarded. The key element of leadership is a genuine interest in people. Good people relations produce good patient care. If employees believe that we truly value their ideas, that we will consider their suggestions objectively, and that they are free to voice their concerns to us, then and only then will we have employees who are committed to the goals of the organization. Caring means that you have a primary concern for the human aspect of management, that is, as much respect for human capital as for economic capital. It also means that you have a belief in basic values: dignity, human fallibility, and human needs. Bettleheim made this profound observation:

> If we hope to live not just from moment-to-moment but in true consciousness of our existence, then our greatest need and most difficult achievement is to find meaning in our lives.[12]

It is your responsibility to make such meaning appear through the redesign of workers' responsibilities. Workers respond best and, indeed, most creatively not when they are tightly controlled by management, placed in narrowly defined jobs, and treated like an unwelcome necessity but instead when they are given broader responsibilities, encouraged to contribute, and helped to take satisfaction in their work.[13]

TRADITIONAL VERSUS CONTEMPORARY VALUES

As a supervisor and manager you will be exposed to a variety of employee values. Employees in general can be categorized as those with

Table 2-1 Results of a Harris Survey of Worker's Feelings of Alienation

Question: Now, I want to read you some things some people have told us they have felt from time to time. Do you tend to feel or not feel that (read each item)?

	1966	*1967*	*1968*	*1969*	*1971*	*1972*	*1973*	*1974*	*1977*	*1980*
The rich get richer and the poor get poorer.	45%	54%	57%	62%	64%	76%	78%	74%	77%	76%
Most people with power try to take advantage of people like yourself.	x	x	x	33	39	55	58	56	60	64
What you think doesn't count very much anymore.	37	42	38	44	50	61	57	58	61	59
The people running the country don't really care what happens to you.	26	36	35	41	45	55	56	56	60	48
You're left out of things going on around you.	9	12	13	20	24	29	32	40	35	41
Index of alienation	29	36	36	40	44	55	56	57	59	58

Note: When more than one study was conducted in one year, the figures for that year have been averaged (1972, 1974, 1976). Index of alienation is average for all questions combined.

Source: The Harris Survey, ABC News; latest survey, December 11, 1980.

traditional values and those with contemporary values. Those with traditional values are usually best supervised by managers who express a high locus of control, high self-esteem, low tolerance for ambiguity, low social judgment, low risk taking.[14] Such managers believe that advancement depends on achievement and that he or she has a great deal of control over subordinates' behavior. They also place high priority on employee feedback, work best in structured and in unambiguous situations, tend not to let personal feelings interfere with work, and are stable and cautious. On the other hand many of your employees have contemporary values and are best supervised by those with a high tolerance for ambiguity (that is, the ability to function well in unstructured ambiguous situations), high social judgment (that is, sensitivity and good interpersonal relationships), and high risk-taking (that is, valuing change and excitement above maintaining status quo).

Knowing whether your employees' values are contemporary or traditional is very important. Knowing your own value system is equally important. More and more evidence indicates that the personal qualities most admired in the workplace are responsibility and honesty. This has not changed very much, although the composition of the work force has. Just a generation ago the typical worker was a man working full-time to provide complete support for his wife and children. Now two of five mothers of children aged six or younger work for pay. More and more of the work force hold college degrees, and we can expect these educational trends to continue. Such increases in the educational level of workers will have a serious impact on the work force and the workplace. The challenge will be to utilize such education, since surveys continue to show that more than half of all college graduates feel underutilized in their jobs; only one-third of noncollege graduates share this sentiment. This more educated work force is looking for better jobs. They expect equal treatment, and they expect to be listened to regardless of their job categories. They are less likely to accept differences in privilege and status.[15]

As the work force changes to represent the growth in the number of women employed and the number of workers who will be in the "prime age" years, we must reassess some of the old approaches to employee policies and supervisory techniques. Because the number of women with children is increasing in the work force, flexible work schedules should be considered. Innovative work schedules, including flexible hours, part-time employment, and job-sharing are likely to involve more than half the American work force by the beginning of the 1990s. At the beginning of this decade a report by the Work in America Institute concluded that changes in society and the composition of the work force, particularly the sharp increase in the number of working mothers, are providing an "irresistible force propelling employees in the direction of further experimentation with new work schedules." It states that the new work schedules "go beyond the employees' freedom to balance competing demands of work, family, and personal life. There are rewards for employees in increased productivity; for unions in fewer layoffs of members; and for the general public in less traffic congestion, energy consumption and air pollution." That study found that the single most important obstacle to flexible scheduling is "the autocratic tradition of supervision," developed by custom and practice under the theory that rigid work schedules are essential to efficiency.[16]

THE WORK ETHIC: DEAD OR ALIVE

There is a great fear that Americans have or will abandon work—that people are less committed to the work ethic. People do work for different reasons, but most truly want to work. Labor force data suggest that increased proportions of Americans are working more, not less, and are opting for leisure only when that step is consistent with the continuing identification of established work rules.[17] We are inundated with statistics on falling productivity levels, which are challenged by other statistics that indicate the contrary. Siegel has a clearer vision of the "true facts":

> Whatever the 'true facts' about the nation's productivity performance since the mid-1960s, and whatever the merit of anecdotal and other evidence and surmises regarding the flabbiness of 'the work ethic', it is more important to stress the improvability of both. It is also necessary to repeat that management, public as well as private, have ample scope and unavoidable responsibilities for upgrading both. Management has to recognize and respond strongly to the challenge and interest of maintaining customary living standards and maintaining competitiveness of American products in domestic and foreign markets.[18]

That, indeed, is the challenge. We can spend our idle hours bemoaning the loss of the work ethic. Continuing improvability is possible. Job commitment is necessary for such improvement; job commitment flows from understanding the need of the new breed of employee. It requires a restructuring of our present organizations: changing hierarchical relationships and moving from a management style anchored in authority-obedience and from organizations propelled by paper rather than by people to a management style based on involvement, participation, and commitment. Self-reliant, trusting, and decisive managers are able to develop self-reliant and efficient subordinates even if the work ethic has changed.

Many new employees do express a cynical view of work. Yankelovich documented that an overwhelming 84 percent of all Americans feel a certain resentment due to a belief that those who work harder and live by the rules end up on the short end of the stick.[19] Our employees are less content and less likely to be trustful of managements' intentions, but our response has to be a broadening concern with aspects of people's lives, a broadening attempt to include employees in the deliberations as to how to provide the services of the institution and how to satisfy their needs. Indifference and frustration result from employees being excluded from the planning function and being overlooked in the communication network. You can change the organizational climate to a more positive direction if:

1. your employees feel that they can solve problems, and you will help them to do so
2. you help your employees develop a sense of independence, and you trust employees' judgments
3. you encourage your employees to take increased responsibility

You do this by helping your employees see that their rewards and recognition outweigh threats and criticism and that there is a promotion system that will enable them to move onward and upward. Most important, you must assure them that rewards are related to excellence of performance.

KEY POINTS ON HOW TO DEAL WITH THE NEW BREED OF EMPLOYEES

1. We are moving away from authority based strictly on power and status to authority based on knowledge and ability.
2. A manager or supervisor who has a relaxed style, and who invites employee participation in decision-making, is more likely to have employees with a high level of organizational self-esteem.
3. The new work force is made up of employees expecting a greater voice in work decisions and who want opportunities beyond those contained in their present jobs. It is up to you to meet those needs.
4. Our employees expect greater meaning from their work and want to feel that they make a difference; this feeling comes from a desire to innovate. Innovation cannot take place in an organization that stifles an employee's ability to contribute.

5. The workplace is full of employees with good ideas. Ideas worth considering and implementing can come from people at all levels in the organization.
6. Many of our employees are alienated; to deal with worker alienation you must communicate openly and frequently.
7. The new breed of employees responds best and most creatively when offered broader responsibilities, encouraged to contribute, and helped to take satisfaction in the work.
8. If you believe that "the work ethic" has deteriorated, it is important that you understand that it can be improved.
9. Even if the work ethic has changed, self-reliant, trusting, and decisive managers are able to develop self-reliant and efficient subordinates.
10. Involve your employees in goal-setting and assist them in recognizing that the goals of the organization and their own goals are not mutually exclusive.
11. To meet changing employee needs, you must help your people to develop a sense of independence and encourage them to take increased responsibilities.

NOTES

1. "The Management-Employee Climate and Its Impact Upon the Employees' Organizational Self-Esteem," in *The 1986 ASPA/CCH Survey* conducted by John L. Pierce, Ph.D. (Duluth, MN: Center for Organizational Management Research, 1986).

2. *Achieving Competitive Advantage Through the Effective Management of People, 1986–87,* research provided by Strategic Management Associates of the Hay Group and by Daniel Yankelovich and Clancy Shulman (Philadelphia: Hay Group, 1986), 1–14.

3. Rosabeth Moss Kanter, "The New Workforce Meets the Changing Workplace," *Human Resources Management* 25 (Winter 1986): 517–18.

4. Sar A. Levitan and Clifford M. Johnson, "The Survival of Work," in *A Critical Analysis, Work Ethic Series,* ed. Barbara D. Dennis (New York: Industrial Relations Research Associations, 1983), 21.

5. Kanter, "The New Workforce," 526.

6. Stanley Peterfruend, *Making Change: Risk-Taking,* an occasional paper prepared for New York Telephone (Closter, NJ: Stanley Peterfruend and Associates, 1986), 1.

7. *Ibid.,* 8.

8. Arnold Brown and Edith Weiner, *Supermanaging* (New York: New American Library, 1984), chap. 9.

9. Robert S. Ruch and Ronald Goodman, *Image At the Top: Crisis and Renaissance of Corporate Leadership* (New York: Free Press, 1983), chap. 4.

10. The Harris Survey, *ABC News* (New York, NY: December 11, 1980).

11. Ruch and Goodman, *Image At the Top,* 51–64.

12. Bruno Bettleheim, *On the Uses of Enchantment* (New York: Random House, 1976), 48.

13. Richard E. Walton, "From Control to Commitment in the Workplace," *Harvard Business Review* 63 (March/April 1985): 77.

14. This section was developed from Marck G. Mindell and William I. Gordon, "Employee Values in a Changing Society," *AMA Management Briefing 1981* 59 (1981): 57, 59–60.

15. Kanter, "Forces for Work Improvement in the Public Sector," *Quality of Work Life Review* 1 (1981): 3–4.

16. *New Work Schedules for a Changing Society* (Scarsdale, NY: Work in American Institute, 1981), passim.

17. Levitan and Johnson, "The Survival of Work," 24.

18. Irving H. Siegel, "Work Ethic and Productivity," in *A Critical Analysis, Work Ethic Series,* ed. Barbara D. Dennis (New York: Industrial Relations Research Association, 1983), 39.

19. Daniel Yankelovich, address to the National Conference on Human Resources, Dallas, TX, 25 October 1978.

Chapter 3

Empowering Employees

> *In effect, the self-oriented character says: "I can contribute more, if they listen to my ideas, if I am treated as an individual, neither as a child nor a machine, and the rewards are fair. Otherwise, I'll look out for myself."*
>
> *Michael Maccoby*
> The Leader
> *(New York: Ballantine Books, 1981) p. 49*

> If America is to win in the new global competition, we need to begin telling one another a new story in which companies compete by drawing on the talent and creativity of all of their employees, not just a few maverick inventors and dynamic CEOs. Competitive advantage today comes from continuous incremental innovation and refinement of a variety of ideas that spread throughout the organization.[1]

In the above passage, Reich recommends to us collective entrepreneurship. He further points out:

> In collective entrepreneurship individual skills are integrated into a group; this collective capacity to innovate becomes something greater than the sum of its parts. Over time, as group members work through various problems and approaches, they learn about each other's abilities. They learn how they can help one another to perform better, what each can contribute to the particular project, how they can best take advantage of one another's experience.[2]

Over the years employees in the health care industry perceived a security that remained for decades unthreatened by layoffs. Indeed, layoffs were virtually nonexistent in our industry. A dramatic change in the marketplace has developed on the basis of cost and revenue control measures. Many hospitals have and will experience dramatic staffing changes due to the impact of diagnosis-related groups (DRGs). "Downsizing" has become the order of the day. The new reimbursement formulas have created an incentive to get patients out of hospitals earlier than in the past and to reduce staffing. What does all of this mean in our quest for excellence in health care? The answer leaps out from the research of behavioral scientists that old traditional approaches are failing and will continue to fail. Management must move from seeking power to empowering others. There must be a new respect for the individual. It is clear that dissatisfied employees will not produce the excellence we so desperately need. We have become mired in an era that is hallmarked by the mesmerizing attention paid to charting, financial and strategic planning, and cost-benefit analysis to the exclusion of all else. We must pay more attention to people who breathe life into those programs. People who are respected and treated with dignity will be more productive. Good people care results in good patient care.

In the coming decade, the successful organization will address the changing environment. We must redirect our efforts to meet the challenges in the coming decade. We must somehow develop a climate in which one of two things occurs: (1) the individuals in the organization perceive their goals as being the same as those of the organization; or (2) the individuals perceive their goals, although different from those of the organization, as satisfied as a direct result of working toward the goals of the organization. It is clear that there is a rising clamor for acknowledgment among health care workers. To be acknowledged is to be validated. People who are respected and treated with dignity will be more productive. Roethlisberger,[3] who was involved in the original Hawthorne experiment, which we so familiarly discuss as the "Hawthorne effect," exquisitely identified that effect as "the big difference that the little difference of paying attention to people make to them." How do we pay attention to people? How do we bring them into the mainstream of productivity? It has been said that, to the extent that employees commit themselves to the goals of the organization because of their participation in its decisions, an organization is likely to have far more vivacious and far more productive people working together to accomplish common goals. There is increasing evidence that when employees are allowed to make some decisions about their work they are more productive. When employees are permitted to be collaborators rather than tools of management, they will, indeed, be less alienated. Let us understand that an alienated person believes that no matter what he or she does it will have no impact on the outcome. Health care employees must be permitted, indeed encouraged, to express themselves, and the critical nature of shared decision-making must be sold down the line to the organization. Plans must be developed to engender a spirit of cooperation and team work. Employees want more from their workplace than they have been getting. They want this in the form of increasing rights and responsibilities. They want "part of the action." What they are telling us is that they want some form of ownership and input into the job.

One can go back more than 50 years to the earliest work of Mayo.[4] In one of his first major studies, which took place from 1923 to 1924 at a Philadelphia textile mill, he addressed the excessive labor turnover in one of the departments of the mill. The workers were given an opportunity to schedule their own work and rest periods with dramatic results: morale improved, turnover rates fell, and productivity rose. Mayo's conclusion was that these positive results developed mainly from allowing employees to participate in the managing of their own work. He found that increased productivity resulted from giving all employees a major voice in deciding on the management of their own time. Study after study tells us that alienation is created in situations where nonsupervisory staff are not allowed to participate in the decision-making process and that inflexible bureaucratic systems tend to cause frustration and depersonalization of staff relations, causing loss of initiative.

Dickson, at the University of Texas at Austin, refers to the "empowerment of groups":

> True representation occurs only when groups have power to act upon their decisions. Without such power, groups become rubber stamps and are akin to formal suggestion programs. . . . The extent of a group's responsibility is less important than is clarity about what decisions a group can make and the level of support provided for the decisions that are made. . . . Since people tend to implement their own solutions more actively than the solutions others have worked out, often a net gain is achieved by supporting the decisions of others even if they are less "correct."[5]

What is happening out there—particularly outside the health care industry, unfortunately—is a new consensus. There is more attention being paid to relying on participation rather than intimidation. The preoccupation with technical ability is being replaced with the values of human skills.

Collaborative-participative management is extremely effective when the organization's end-product relies on technical expertise. The old organization chart, so pervasive in the health care industry, needs to be scrapped; at the very least it should be reconstructed. It is clear that employees become more integrated into the institution and committed to its goals when they work in a collaborative team. Employees want to be part of the act, as said before, instead of a part of a giant impersonal machine.

What does participation and collaboration really mean? What are the benefits? Let us list just a few.

1. The greater the number of competent judges, the greater the validity of their combined judgments. In our field too many cooks do not spoil the broth.
2. When participation and collaboration occur there is a tendency for participants to sharpen and refine an idea, to listen to another participant's ideas, and to change their opinions. Someone once said that if you could get into the castle of another person's skin you would be liable to see things the way he or she does; you are then liable to change.
3. Tasks that are performed through cooperation as opposed to competition are more efficiently accomplished, and the persons involved exhibit a higher degree of motivation and morale.
4. Group discussions and deliberations where the participants are collaborators and where a democratic approach is used are more likely to alter opinions; conversely, attitudes are less likely to change when an authoritarian approach is used.
5. Participation increases the likelihood that a goal will be set that is congruent with group-perceived values.
6. As a result of discussion and collaboration involving the establishment of a goal, the collaborators are more likely to have adequate knowledge of the nature of the goal, its worth to themselves, and its true attainability.

What is being suggested here is the development of a strategy to reshape the technical health care organization, to rebuild it around the following premises:

1. emphasis on organization informality and fluid flexible lines of communication in reporting relationships
2. the sharing of managerial prerogatives with line-supervisors and workers on a systematic institutional basis
3. encouragement of innovation and decentralized initiative at the line level
4. a broad collaboration between hospital administration and all members of the health care team for the provision of quality patient care

Collaboration and participation is the order of the day. To paraphrase Dangen:

> Participation is not a program nor a technique—neither is collaborative management. It is an almost mystifying philosophy of change for helping people to fulfill themselves. What we must do is to change our approach from an adversarial one to a collaborative one. We must be willing to share power.[6]

FROM CONTROL TO COMMITMENT

Walton, in discussing managers' beliefs, tells us:

> Only lately have they begun to see that workers respond best—and most creatively—not when they are tightly controlled by management, placed in narrowly defined jobs, and treated like an unwelcome necessity, but, instead, when they are given broader responsibilities, encouraged to contribute, and helped to take satisfaction in the work.[7]

Here Walton is describing a plant where participatory management approaches are used compared to one where the "control" strategy is pervasive. He says of the former that its employees are actively engaged in identifying and solving problems. That organization operates with fewer levels of management and fewer specialized departments compared to the latter plant. The latter plant, much like most health care institutions, has its traditional—or control-oriented—approach to work force management. Very little regard was paid to employee voice unless the work force was unionized, and in that case it was only the labor relations department that paid attention (in order to protect "management's prerogatives"). In the plant where commitment is the order of the day jobs are designed to be broader than before, to combine planning and implementation, and to include efforts to upgrade operations, not just to maintain them. Individual pay is linked to skills and mastery over the job. Employee participation is encouraged on a wide range of issues. The role of the supervisors is dramatically different from the traditional "control" strategy organization. Supervisors are facilitators rather than directors of the work force. They have as a priority responsibility assisting workers to develop the ability to manage themselves. In effect, supervisors in such "commitment" strategy organizations are delegating away most of their traditional functions. Of course, this is a major problem, and one to which we must all be sensitive. What voice will supervisors in organizations that practice participatory management have? What recognition and dignity will they have? Only the brave and secure supervisors can operate in such an organization. Such supervisors must have a level of interpersonal skill and conceptual ability often lacking in the supervisory work force. Walton does well in directing our attention to such a need.

GAINSHARING

In moving from the "control" strategy to the "commitment" strategy, several approaches are worth our attention. Among those approaches is gainsharing. Gainsharing incentive programs have been around for more than four decades. Simply stated, if a work unit or "team" exceeds some set level of production or quality, its members receive higher pay for that pay period corresponding to the excess productivity. It is critical to understand that this is a "team" program rather than an individual one. Initial installation of gainsharing programs in the health care industry follows the "Improshare" model.[8] Improshare, like other gainsharing programs, puts muscle behind the oft-repeated hospital organization statement that "people are its most important resource." In this type of program the hospital shares with employees the financial gains realized through improved productivity as direct acknowledgment that the employee is the expert at the particular job being performed. The goal of such a program is to reward employees for productivity gains while improving the quality of patient care and patient services. This program is a group incentive program, encouraging team work in making effective use of supplies and equipment and sensitivity toward labor hours expended as well as encouraging creative solutions to interdepartmental production problems.[9] These goals are realized by development of department measures to ensure quality care as well as productivity improvement objectives.

Generally, the first step in a gainsharing program is the creation of a mixed employee and supervisor group, which will be representative of all or most constituencies in the hospital, to act as a sounding board, problem solver, sales team, and communication link for the program. The committee, which includes a management engineer, works with individual cost centers to create the group measure (standard). When met or exceeded, this standard leads to a group incentive payment. In many cases the measurement basis for calculating improvement is set at the average productivity level of a work group, based on total payroll and related costs together with supplies and material expenses. When a work group's monthly cost per unit service level is lower than a six-month's average cost per unit of service, the work group is eligible to share in gains made by the hospital in that month.

Improshare Program Profile

The Robert Wood Johnson–University Hospital in New Brunswick, New Jersey, has been reviewing for installation a gainsharing program entitled Improshare. In this program, the hospital shares with employees the gains realized through improved productivity. Management believes that as employees reduce the cost of providing health care they should receive a share of the gains that are made.

The plan covers all employees except per diems, employees working fewer than 32 hours in a pay period, and employees still in their introductory period. This profile documents other aspects of the program.

The Goals of Improshare

The goals of the program are to reward employees for productivity gains and to improve the quality of patient care and patient service. These goals are achieved by:

1. promoting quality care
2. ensuring maximum employee productivity
3. ensuring effective use of supplies and equipment
4. more effectively using hospital services and resources

How the Program Works

The program reaches its goals by:

1. developing department measures that provide quality as well as productivity improvement objectives toward which employee work groups will cooperatively work
2. creating monetary incentives that result from meeting those objectives

What the Results Are

The results of the program are that:

1. quality care is maintained or improved while labor expenses remain cost effective through decreased use of overtime and total hours paid
2. supplies and equipment expenses decrease

How Maintaining and Improving Quality is Measured

As the program was being developed, staff at all levels in the hospital emphasized that cost reduction could not be at the expense of patient care. The program should reward departments for successful attempts at quality enhancement while reducing cost. On the basis of this concern for demonstrated quality enhancement, each month every work group will determine a quality target. This target can come from the Quality Assurance program, current quality review practices, feedback from patient evaluations, employee feedback, or management feedback. Meeting this quality target is the first step for qualification.

How Productivity is Measured

The measurement based for calculating improvement is set as the average productivity level of a work group based on total payroll and related costs and supplies and material expenses. The actual expenses and unit of service of each month are compared to those for the first six months of 1986. This six-month average is the cost–unit of service qualifier. When the work group's monthly cost–unit of service level is less than the six-month average cost–unit of service qualifier, the work group meets the second step for qualification.

When a Work Group Qualifies for Gains

A work group qualifies for gains when it achieves its quality qualifier and meets or beats its cost-unit qualifier. Eligible employees of these work groups will share in gains made by the hospital for that month.

How Gain or Loss is Calculated

Each month the actual adjusted net operating result for the hospital will be compared to the adjusted budgeted net hospital result. The adjusted net operating result is the excess or deficit from operations, excluding faculty and resident physician fees, depreciation and amortization, and interest expense. When the difference between the actual adjusted net operating result and the adjusted budgeted net hospital result is positive, there is a gain that is shared with employees. If the difference is negative, there is a loss and no gainsharing can occur that month.

How Employee Share is Calculated

Gains are shared equally (50 percent) with employees except when previous months' losses within the most recent 12 months are outstanding. When a loss from a previous month exists, the employee group share is at least 25 percent of the positive adjusted net operating result variance. The employee group share remains 25 percent until the loss is recouped, then the share percent becomes 50 percent. In this way, the hospital and employees share in the gains and losses.

The individual share percentage for each employee is determined by dividing the employee gain by the paid worked hours for qualifying employees. This percentage is the percentage of productive pay an employee will receive as a bonus. This includes shift premium and overtime but excludes pay for time not worked, such as vacation, holiday, and sick time. For example, if the employee gainshare is $30,000 and the payroll for qualifying departments is $750,000, each eligible employee in qualifying departments will receive 4 percent of their salary for that month, excluding pay for time not worked, determined as follows:

$$\frac{\text{(Employee gainshare)}}{\text{(Qualifying payroll)}} \quad \frac{\$\ 30{,}000}{\$750{,}000} = \begin{array}{l}\text{4.0\% share for each}\\ \text{eligible employee}\end{array}$$

Example of a Department that Qualifies

An outpatient department acknowledges a problem where patients wait for a treatment and then are discovered to be missing all necessary paperwork at the time of the treatment. This requires additional time spent by them in filling out forms or returning to another department. This department chooses 9 percent "checked papers" at a time of patient arrival as its quality qualifier. This same department has a cost-unit qualifier of $50 per visit.

In the first month of the Improshare program, this is how the department performed.

Quality qualifier: There were 250 patient visits. Ten patients were found to have incomplete paperwork at the time of treatment; however, there was a 96 percent success rate. This work group met its quality qualifier.

Cost-unit qualifier: Expenses for the month were $12,125 for 250 patient visits, averaging to $48.50 per visit. This is less than their cost-unit qualifier of $50 per visit. This work group met its cost-unit qualifier.

In this example, this department met both qualifiers and, therefore, qualified for participation in any gain that occurs in that month.

The hospital gain for that month was $80,000. Fifty percent of $80,000, or $40,000, is shared by employees since there were no losses carried over from previous months. The total payroll of all qualifying departments equals $900,000. The individual share percentage equals 4.4 percent ($40,000 divided by $900,000).

Eligible employees in qualifying departments will receive 4.4 percent of their productive pay. Productive pay excludes pay for time not worked, such as vacation, holiday, or sick pay.

How Payment is Made

Employees may elect to receive their share of Improshare gains monthly in cash or as a deposit in their Tax Sheltered Account (TSA). Monthly cash distributions are subject to state and federal withholding and Social Security taxes and are added to the employees' regular paycheck once per month. Monies deposited in the TSA are subject to federal and state withholding taxes.

When Qualifiers are Changed

Improshare measurement standards will be changed to allow for capital equipment changes or additions made by the hospital that directly result in improved productivity.

Why Have the Program?

The program is being promoted at this time in response to employee-articulated desires for its development. The hospital benefits from Improshare through employee-driven attempts at quality enhancement, cost reduction, and productivity. The program creates an incentive to maintain a long-standing employee quality and productivity improvement effort. Finally, it sets up a condition to place a more controllable, long-term "cap" on costs, which everyone—employees, consumers, and providers—supports as a worthwhile goal.

Goldstein and Spivak point out the multifaceted benefits of gainsharing.

> While productivity improvement, cost effectiveness or revenue enhancement can be termed the first-order benefit of the gain-sharing incentive model, the claim is being made that there are additional, second-order benefits, including:
>
> 1. stimulation of employee involvement programs
> 2. improvement in employee behavior, attitude and morals
> 3. minimization of adversarial relationships between management and workers

4. increased acceptance of change
5. building a more effective organization and culture[10]

Fein, the developer of Improshare, tells us:

> As workers' interests shift towards management's, the rationale for traditional management fades. When workers become concerned with final outcomes, they will also be more interested in how operations proceed throughout the plant and in the many details and production impediments that occur around them, which in the past they ignored or even encouraged. Since productivity gains are shared, whether innovated by workers or by management, then conceivably industrial engineers, who are now disparaged by workers, will instead be welcomed because workers will gain from engineers' improvement efforts. That would indeed signal a significant change in the attitude of workers and managers towards each other's interests and needs.[11]

The three major elements of gainsharing are management know-how, employee participation, and shared reward. The outcome should result in increased productivity, a significant portion of which will be in that portion of an employee activity under management's control. Yankelovich and Immerwahr define that process as follows.

> [The worker controls what is termed] discretionary effort . . . the difference between the maximum amount of effort and care that an individual could bring to his or her job, and the minimum amount of effort required to avoid being fired or penalized; in short, the portion of one's effort over which a jobholder has the greatest control. Put another way, discretionary effort focuses our attention on that portion of effort that is controlled by the jobholder, rather than by the employer or the inherent nature of the work.[12]

The discretionary effort concept not only helps explain the effect workers have on productivity but emphasizes an area of employee activity that largely cannot be managed or controlled effectively: the individual's will to work. A properly conceived and structured gainsharing program will, as one of its outcomes, achieve productivity gains in the area of discretionary effort.[13]

QUALITY CONTROL CIRCLES

Quality circles use participatory management to its fullest. Such a process has the following objectives.

1. reduction of errors and enhancement of quality
2. creation of problem-solving capabilities among broad-based groups
3. promotion of job-involvement
4. optimization of employee motivation
5. movement of the supervisor-employee relationship from an adversarial one to a cooperative and harmonious one
6. development of problem-prevention techniques
7. promotion of personal and leadership development
8. promotion of cost reduction

It has been said that a quality circle is a deceptively simple concept. A small group of workers (usually six to ten) from the same department voluntarily meets each week to identify and solve problems affecting the department. The members address a range of topics, including product quality, productivity, cost-containment, and quality of work life. They use simple statistical tools and group problem-solving methods to analyze each problem objectively. They present recommendations to management and help implement the solution that management accepts. Karatsu states:

> We have a quality control circle program in Japan. After work hours, without being paid overtime, workers get together to discuss ways of improving quality in their operations. People from other countries ask why we do not pay overtime for this. But these Japanese workers are serious. They are engrossed in their work. They can find improvements that even their lead engineers cannot discover—so they contribute to the company. They enjoy the process of working together . . . they enjoy work as much as they enjoy sports.[14]

It is clear that quality circles are used by participatory management to its fullest. The theory is that an organization's workers are closest to the problem, indeed may be part of the problem, and therefore are best equipped to increase the output and improve the caliber of work or service. Such a mechanism gives a broader base of employees the opportunity to speak up in an atmosphere where management is listening.

What Is A Quality Circle?

A quality circle is a voluntary group of workers who have a shared area of responsibility. The process starts with problem identification, either from members of the circle, management, or staff. They meet together weekly to discuss and analyze the proposed solutions to quality problems. Simply, the process includes the following.

1. *Problem identification:* typically several problems are identified. Problem selection is the prerogative of the circle.
2. *Problem analysis:* the problem is analyzed by the circle with assistance, if needed, by appropriate circle experts.
3. *Problem solutions or recommendations to management:* the circle makes these directly to the manager using a communication technique described as the "management presentation."[15]

The following concepts form the cornerstone of quality control circle programs.

1. A quality circle is initiated only on the decision of senior management.
2. Initial meetings for a quality circle are held with all union management and supervisory personnel.
3. Participation in the circle is voluntary.
4. The managers who decide to try a circle then make presentations to the hourly workers, and again participation of the hourly workers is voluntary.
5. Participation of management in the circle is voluntary.[16]

Group members are taught a group communication process, quality strategies, and problem analysis techniques. Circle leaders go through training in leadership skills, adult learning techniques, motivation, and communication techniques. Circle meetings are held on company premises. Where companies have unions, the union members and leaders are encouraged to take an active role in the circle, to attend leader training, and to become fully aware of circle principles.[17]

The quality circle concept provides an opportunity for maximum participation. Although many organizations pay lip service to participatory management, they cling to outdated management models. The unquestioned right of management to direct the work force, assign work, change methods, and exercise other managerial prerogatives is guarded jealously. To circumvent such control, workers take informal measures and, at times, openly confront management. We must accept the fact that decision-making is not solely a management activity. It is the process of choosing between alternatives, and the extent to which individuals are free to exercise discretion is the extent to which they participate. The critical question is not whether there should be participation but how far it should be extended—that is, not *if* but *how much*.[18]

Concepts and Principles of Quality Circles

Cole presents to us basic principles that can be applied regardless of whether an institution adopts quality circles or not.

1. Trust your employees. Expect that they will work to implement organizational goals if given a chance.
2. Build employee loyalty to the company. It will pay off.
3. Invest in training, and treat employees as resources that, if cultivated, will yield economic returns to the firm. This means developing employee skills. Implicit in this perspective is aiming for long-term employee commitment to the organization.
4. Recognize employee accomplishments. Symbolic rewards mean more than you think.
5. Decentralize decision-making.
6. Regard work as a cooperative effort, with workers and managers doing the job together. This implies consensual decision-making.[19]

Yager presents certain behavioral science concepts with application to quality circles.

1. People should have control in deciding about or changing work elements close to them.
2. Individuals should not be coerced to change.
3. Work should have intrinsic motivation and be enriching.
4. Any change effort should be monitored and measured for impact.
5. Workers need opportunities to meet higher motivational needs through their jobs.
6. Managers will be more effective as they work toward developing a team or consensus style of leadership.
7. Employees need feedback on their performance to be reinforced.[20]

Quality circles offer management an unusual opportunity to obtain employee involvement beyond that achieved by some of the old mechanisms, which have been less than successful over the years. It has been shown over and over again that this participation results in higher motivational levels. For this process to succeed, however, the key is the willingness of supervisors to permit, indeed encourage, employee involvement. Such commitment derives from a basic trust of employees by supervisors, which constitutes a dramatic change from the distrust that is pervasive in most of our organizations. Autocratic, tightly controlled work forces are "bossed" by supervisors who rarely take risks. The converse is represented by organizations where trust is the order of the day and where there is an openness and a belief that group solutions can produce effective answers to problems. Such a process has as its basis the importance of the individual; therefore, the supervisor must treat employees as individuals. By such treatment the employee's self-esteem is increased, and consequently the employee will be more open and not fear such a display of openness. It is to the supervisor's benefit that employees be permitted to discuss, suggest, and set quality goals and methods for reaching those goals. An employee who participates in a quality circle is more likely to be concerned about the effectiveness of the recommendation springing from that activity and would be more effective in monitoring the group's activities.

Bennis predicted an organizational form for the future in the following terms.

> The social structural organization of the future will have some unique characteristics. The key word will be "temporary"; there will be adaptive rapidly changing temporary systems. There will be problem-oriented "task forces" composed of groups of relative strangers who represent a diverse set of professional skills. The groups will be arranged on an organic, rather than a mechanical model; they will evolve in response to a problem rather than to program rote expectations. The "executive" thus will become a coordinator or "linking pin" among various task forces. He must be a man who can speak the diverse language of research, with skills to relay information and to mediate between groups. People will be differentiated not vertically according to rank and status, but flexibly and functionally according to skill and professional training.[21]

Such "executives," whether they are women or men, must display their willingness to share problem-solving responsibility; they will be part of a more flexible organization for optimum coordination and task evaluation. They will be more concerned with performance and productivity than with personal power.

Some three decades ago, Schwab presented a report on shared decision-making at the Detroit Edison Company. It is well to note how long we have been looking at and experimenting with participatory management programs. In Schwab's report, evidence was presented to show that group-sharing decisions displayed reasonable and often high production standards. These groups working together as decision-makers set high-quality goals, and the decisions were characterized by acute judgments. It was interesting to note that the workers introduced facts that supervisors might have overlooked. The following factors directly related to motivation were evidenced in work groups such as those described in the report who shared in decision-making.

1. There is increased satisfaction. The groups derive satisfaction from solving problems.
2. Attitudes and objections can be voiced and receive recognition.
3. Cooperation results in constructive use of social pressure within the group.
4. Each individual in the group feels responsible for the success of the decisions.
5. The individuals do not feel ordered about. They do unpleasant tasks more willingly.
6. In participating, each individual feels that he or she is part of the company.
7. Goals are specified by the group, and progress toward goals is experienced by each member.[22]

Hayes points out the benefits of shared decision-making.

> . . . To the extent that free men commit themselves to the goals of the organization because of their participation in its decisions, we are likely to have organizations of spirited vivacious people working together to accomplish their common goals—not bossed—not "hired," but free committed men.[23]

Employees as Partners

There is a continuing and heavy temptation to move along in familiar ways, to accept things as they are. We must be ready to move off the path that others have taken. The successful health care organization of the coming decade must address the changing environment and therefore be willing to change itself. There is a crying need for flexibility and participatory management techniques. We must develop systems to maximize the opportunities for employees to express their innate motivation to contribute. We must develop a style of health care delivery that is collaborative in nature. There is a need for all of us to pull our noses out of statistical bases, out of long-range planning tomes, and out of personnel policies and procedures; all are necessary but not mutually exclusive with people-building efforts. With our ears clear there is a chance that we will hear the voice of the people. That voice cries out for a chance to participate and rails against powerlessness; that voice must be considered along with the voice of the boardroom, the senior administration, and the medical board.

Incentive plans allow employees to share productivity gains, thereby encouraging productivity. Quality circles allow employees to participate in decision-making and problem solving, thereby giving them a "piece of the action." We must accept that an organization's workers are best equipped to increase the output and improve the caliber of the service. Even if the solutions arrived at by employees who are permitted to participate in problem solving are no better than those arrived at by supervisors and technical personnel, such workers will be more enthusiastic and more likely to make things work.

KAIZEN

Kaizen has been described as the key to Japan's competitive business success.[24] *Kaizen* means gradual unending improvement, doing "little things" better, and setting and achieving ever-higher standards. This continuing improvement involves everyone—managers and workers alike. Imai states that *Kaizen* starts with the recognition that any corporation has problems. *Kaizen* solves problems by establishing a corporate culture in which everyone can freely admit their problems. This atmosphere of trust, where employees are neither embarrassed nor frightened of admitting that they have problems, produces a joint-effort at problem solving, that is, a systematic and collaborative approach to cross-functional problem solving. *Kaizen* emphasizes process. It has generated a process-oriented way of thinking and a management system that supports and acknowledges people's process-oriented efforts for improvement. This is in sharp contrast to the Western management practice of reviewing people's performance strictly on the basis of results and not rewarding the effort made.[25] Everyone is involved in the process. In the hierarchy of

Kaizen involvement, top management allocates resources and establishes policies and cross-functional goals; middle management establishes, maintains, and upgrades the standards, makes employees *Kaizen*-conscious through intensive training programs, and helps employees develop skills and tools for problem solving; supervisors provide guidance to workers, improve communication with workers, sustain high morale, support small group activities (such as quality circles), and the individual suggestion system; workers engage in *Kaizen* through the suggestion system and small group activities, practice discipline in the workshop, and engage in continuous self-development to become problem solvers; finally, they enhance skills and job performance expertise with cross-education. It is a pervasive process, based on cross-functional management. It is a humanistic approach, because it expects everybody to participate in it. It is based on the belief that every human being can contribute toward improving the workplace, where he or she spends one-third of his or her life.[26]

Once again the Japanese present us with a clear message: whether it is through quality circles or *Kaizen* programs, employee participation is the key to quality and productivity.

KEYS TO EMPOWERING EMPLOYEES

1. The collective capacity to innovate enables an organization to become greater than the sum of its parts.
2. People who are respected and treated with dignity will be more productive.
3. To the extent that employees commit themselves to the goals of the organization because of their participation in its decisions, an organization is likely to have far more vivacious and productive people working together to accomplish common goals.
4. Alienation is likely to occur in situations where nonsupervisory staff are not allowed to participate in the decision-making process.
5. Group problem solving provides each individual in the group with an unprecedented feeling of responsibility for the success of the group's decisions.
6. The sharing of managerial prerogatives with line supervisors and workers on a systematic institutional basis will bring us the excellence we so desperately need in the health care industry.
7. A primary responsibility of the modern health care manager is to assist workers to develop the ability to manage themselves.
8. It is essential that we develop programs that reward employees for

productivity gains while improving the quality of patient care and patient services.

9. It is time to trust your employees. Expect that they will work to implement organizational goals if given a chance.
10. Employees are more and more concerned with their powerlessness; it is time to empower our employees.

NOTES

1. Robert B. Reich, "Entrepreneurship Reconsidered: The Team as Hero," *Harvard Business Review* 87 (May/June 1987): 77.

2. *Ibid.*, 78.

3. F. J. Roethlisberger, *Management and Morale* (Cambridge, MA: Harvard University Press, 1941), 7–26.

4. Elton Mayo, *The Social Problems of an Industrial Civilization* (Boston, MA: Harvard Business School, 1945).

5. Nancy Dickson, "Participative Management: It's Not as Simple as it Seems," *Supervisory Management* 3 (December 1984).

6. Richard Dangen and Harley Shaiken, *Work Transformed: Automating Labor in the Computer Age* (New York: Holt, Rinehart & Winston, 1984), xii.

7. Richard E. Walton, "From Control to Commitment in the Workplace," *Harvard Business Review* (March/April 1985): 77.

8. "Improshare" is the registered service mark of Mitchell Fein, Inc., copyright 1986, Mitchell Fein, Inc.

9. Special recognition is given to the contribution of Fred W. Graumann, Senior Vice President, Human Resources, Robert Wood Johnson–University Hospital, New Brunswick, New Jersey, who helped to develop the description given herein of "Improshare."

10. Jeffrey Goldstein and Julius Spivak, "Gainsharing in Hospitals: Organizational Impacts," Speech given at the 1987 Annual Health Care Systems Conference of the Institute of Industrial Engineers-Health Services Division and Health Manpower Systems Society, Norcross, Georgia, February 9-13, 1987.

11. Mitchell Fein, *Improshare: Alternate to Traditional Managing* (Hillsday, NJ: Mitchell Fein, Inc., 1982).

12. Daniel Yankelovich and John Immerwahr, *Putting the Work Ethic to Work* (New York: Public Agenda Foundation, 1983), 1.

13. Goldstein and Spivak, "Gainsharing in Hospitals," 84.

14. Hajime Karatsu, *New York Times*, (10 July 1987) All.

15. The Quality Circle Institute, California.

16. E. P. Yager, "Quality Circle: A Tool for the '80s," *Training and Development Journal* (August 1980): 60.

17. John S. McClenahen, "Bringing Home Japan's Lessons," *Industry Week* (23 February 1981): 62.

18. John E. Hebben and Graham A. Shaw, *Pathways to Participation* (New York: John Wiley & Sons, 1984), 100-102.

19. Robert E. Cole, *Work Mobility and Participation: A Comparative Study of American and Japanese Industry* (Berkeley: University of California Press, 1979).

20. Yager, "Quality Circle," 60.

21. W. G. Bennis, "Changing Organizational Behavioral Science," *Journal of Applied Behavioral Science*, no. 2 (1966): 247-63.

22. Robert E. Schwab, "Motivation: The Core of Management," *Personnel Series no. 155* (New York: American Management Associations, 1953), 32-33.

23. James J. Hayes, *Memos for Management Leadership* (New York: AMACOM division of American Management Associations, 1983), 14.

24. Masaaki Imai, *Kaizen* (New York: Random House, 1986), passim.

25. *Ibid.*, xxxiii.

26. *Ibid.*, 227.

Chapter 4

The Supervisor's Role in Positive Reinforcement

> *The worst sin towards our fellow creatures is not to hate them, but to be indifferent to them; that's the essence of inhumanity.*
>
> *George Bernard Shaw*
> The Devil's Disciple
> *Act II*

> Management has no choice as to whether it will have a program of performance evaluation. It has a program . . . and the results of the evaluations are continuously used. . . . Employees are transferred, promoted, demoted and fired on the basis of the opinions of management.[1]

Positive reinforcement should have been the goal of performance evaluation programs in the past. Alas, it turned out to be an "also-ran." Too often performance evaluation has resulted in negative feelings and defensive postures. Most employees resent criticism. Nevertheless, all of us understand the need for feedback, for knowing how we are doing. The critical point of departure for this chapter is that *immediate positive recognition is a necessary stimulus for continued efficiency.*

The average employee wants to feel "in on things," to know what is going on in the department and in the institution in general and, more specifically, how it affects his or her job and how he or she is doing in the eyes of the supervisor. Too often the process of communicating appreciation or criticism is institutionalized in a once-a-year performance evaluation program. It is usually so formal as to be off-putting. Several years ago an article appeared on the Op Ed page of the *New York Times,* in which the writer bemoaned his fate as a result of being "reviewed."

> . . . This is a bad time of the year. It's review time. That means I have to go before my boss and have him evaluate me. . . . I didn't get one "outstanding." Not for "initiative." Not for "creativity."

> Not for "productivity." Funny, I used to think I was creative and productive. I even used to think of myself as cooperative and attractive. All I am, it turns out, is "punctual."
>
> I didn't show up for work today. I'm home. Should I go on living? My wife says yes. She thinks I'm at least average. She thinks I ought to go back to work and tell him off, my boss. I can't do that, of course—and that's no way to get even. What I can do tomorrow is review my secretary. I'm small, but I'm bigger than she is.[2]

This jocular commentary on performance evaluation shows how we have failed in communicating to employees how they are doing.

The opposite of the approach of counter-productive ticking off of boxes on a once-a-year basis, which pretends to communicate positively about employees' performances over the past year, was contained in a little anecdote in *In Search of Excellence.*

> Late one evening a scientist rushed into the president's office with a working prototype. Dumbfounded at the elegance of the solution and bemused about how to reward it, the president bent forward in his chair, rummaged through most of the drawers in his desk, found something, leaned over the desk to the scientist, and said "Here!" In his hand was a banana, the only reward he could immediately put his hand on.[3]

This is the essence of positive reinforcement! Of course not everyone will appreciate a banana, but in this anecdote it was the act itself of attempting to show gratitude that is important. It is your responsibility to find the "fruit of choice" and hand it out to those who excel. One person's banana is another person's tangerine.[4] Indeed, if one of your employees makes a contribution—if you have caught him or her doing something right—an immediate reward (it need not be money) will make it more likely that such behavior will be repeated. The higher the value of the reward, of course, the more likely the behavior will be repeated. Skinner, the behavioral scientist, made this very clear to us.

Performance evaluation programs in their formal design are one of the most complex and controversial areas of supervisor-subordinate relationships. There have been many failures in attempting to attain satisfactory performance evaluations. Smith and Elbert list some.

1. High levels of education and professionalization germane to health and medical care stimulated a demand for improved personal performance evaluation.
2. Revised definitions of effective performance that include both cost-effective resource allocation and high-quality patient care have added to the need to achieve more sophisticated methods of evaluation.
3. Ancillary personnel are demanding fair assessments of their performance.[5]

The dilemma resulting from these pressures creates a major problem for you as a supervisor.

THE GOALS OF PERFORMANCE EVALUATION

Managers who acknowledge the contributions of their subordinates often gain acknowledgment for themselves. Full appreciation of a job well done is still one of the most important needs expressed by workers. The primary purpose of performance evaluation is the improvement of job performance by:

1. communicating specific standards to employees and gaining acceptance of those standards
2. measuring the employee's performance against the agreed-upon standards
3. developing with the employee a plan of action to assist the employee in overcoming obstacles to developing and strengthening his or her capabilities
4. encouraging reactions, facing and resolving differences, and reaching a mutual understanding of the implications of the review
5. offering constructive suggestions and tangible assistance to the employee working toward personal development

Your key responsibility in performance evaluation is to meet the need of your subordinates to know what is expected of them on a day-to-day basis and to inform them when they are meeting your expectations. Kessler lists some of the most important points in the critical management process of performance evaluation.

1. Work performance is improved appreciably when the employee knows what results are expected. Work planning and review sessions provide the individual with information as to the results expected,

the methods by which they will be measured, the priorities and the resources available.

2. Work performance is improved appreciably when the employee knows that it is possible to influence the expected results. The process is sufficiently flexible to permit the individual to have some say about the results expected, the methods by which they will be measured, and the priorities. The degree of influence the employee exercises will vary according to the situation.
3. Knowledge of results may be as precise and as specific as possible. Work review allows the subordinate and the manager to review the results against the goals.
4. Knowledge of results must be immediate and as relevant as possible.
5. Knowledge of results that comes from the individual's own observations is more effective than that obtained from someone else's.[6]

People want to know where they have been, where they are now, and where they are going. Unfortunately, which area requires improvement is often not clearly communicated to employees. If such information is presented properly—that is, with an eye toward reinforcement and improvement rather than punishment—it can be far more effective than the often-perceived punitive nature of negative evaluation. You, as a manager, are responsible for the performance of others. Therefore, you must systematically communicate to others how they have done. You must develop performance standards so that an employee knows what is expected of him or her, and, indeed, such standards should be high enough for the employee to grow in the position. You must measure performance against those standards. The first-line supervisor must inspire improvement and must develop a plan to help individual workers become more efficient. In the arena of performance evaluation, half the battle is won when the employee understands your expectations, how well he or she is meeting those expectations, and where improvement is needed.

MANAGEMENT BY OBJECTIVES

There have been many variations of performance evaluation, including management by objectives. Such programs include a well-defined goal stated as a result to be achieved by a specified time and deemed to be worthy of the effort, difficult but obtainable, essential to the organization, and involving a commitment to do it. A well-thought-out, logical, and realistic plan of action designed to produce the desired results, plus free exchange in a dialogue involving understanding, support, and sharing of information, are the ingredients that foster growth, trust, and competency when effective coaching skills are practiced.[7] Such programs have three important requirements.

1. *self-commitment.* Employees are neither ordered to do something, nor simply handed a set of goals, nor treated as puppets. Rather, individuals commit themselves to accomplishing the goals and work plans.
2. *self-analysis.* Individuals perform work related to the commitments, and, when there is a variance from the intended result, they are the first to know and act accordingly.
3. *self-motivation or self-discipline.* Individuals have a strong desire to succeed. Negative variances from the intended result are a challenge.[8]

This excellent review of the requirements points out a critical element of successful performance evaluation. Whether it is accomplished by management by objectives or any other form, a successful evaluation of results must include the subordinate not as a receiver but as a participator. Self-motivation and self-discipline are the strongest forces for a plan to obtain excellence. The role of the supervisor is to inspire improvement and to develop a plan to help individual workers become more efficient. When you reinforce acceptable or exceptional behavior by verbal recognition, you serve to extend such behavior and produce more acceptable or exceptional behavior.

KEEP YOUR EYE ON THE PURPOSE OF EVALUATION

Thirty years ago McGregor succinctly presented three basic purposes of the evaluation process.

1. letting people know where they stand and providing them with performance feedback
2. identifying an individual's training and development needs in terms of correcting deficiencies as well as helping that person develop his or her potential to the fullest extent possible
3. providing accurate performance data for organizational decision-making, both microdecisions (such as an individual's pay increment) and large-scale decisions (such as long-term hiring and development plans)[9]

What McGregor was talking about was feedback, development, and assessment. The key to effective performance appraisal is refining the feedback mechanism. Sashkin offers us six principles that will aid us in making feedback more productive.

1. Use description rather than evaluation. Evaluation, positive or negative, creates automatic blocks to effective communication. The more you describe how you feel about your subordinate's performance, the more he or she will understand.
2. Be specific. The goal is to tell the subordinate what he or she should do to correct mistakes if there have been any as well as what successes the employee has had.
3. Consider the receiver's needs. Remember, employees continue to express full appreciation for a job well done as a primary need. There are times when you must communicate evaluations that are not favorable. This is very difficult, but by stating the plan for improving a particular behavior of a subordinate you can frame it in a positive way.
4. Know the difference between asking and imposing. Bring the subordinate into the plan for improvement by asking for suggestions. An employee is more likely to change if he or she has participated in a discussion of the change and in framing the method for the change.
5. Be timely. One of the criticisms of performance evaluation is that it is often done once a year and goes over material that is "old hat." Recognition and reinforcement should come as quickly as possible after the relevant performance or behavior is observed.
6. Don't ask for the impossible. Although it is essential that you state goals that will stretch the employee's performance, remember that it is best to move ahead in an incremental fashion. Don't set up a plan that will result in failure.[10]

Focus your attention again on the purpose of the appraisal process. It is essential that it be a mutual goal-setting process and a mutual focus on those goals by you and the subordinate. This includes a plan for progress. A plan for progress is a realistic action plan for attainment of goals mutually agreed on by supervisors and subordinates.

A DEVELOPMENTAL STYLE OF APPRAISING PERFORMANCE

Many supervisors and managers would rather say nothing than subject themselves to the time-consuming and potentially adversarial nature of performance evaluation. Some will comment that it is easier to terminate a subordinate's employment than to do the distasteful work of improving his or her performance. That is why so many performance evaluation programs are "packaged" and reduce the possibility of dialogue, which is so essential to the successful use of such systems. Merrihue states:

> The supervisor who obtains the best from his employees is the one who creates the best atmosphere or climate of approval within which his work group operates; he accomplishes this through the following methods:
> 1. he or she develops performance standards for the subordinates and sets them high to stretch the employees
> 2. he or she measures performance against these standards
> 3. he or she consistently commends above-par performance
> 4. he or she always lets employees know when they have performed below par[11]

A developmental style of appraising performance can be surprisingly effective and free from the difficulties that many supervisors and managers anticipate if it is used with reasonable judgment. A work group tends to elicit an employee's loyalty to the extent that it satisfies the employee's needs and helps the employee to achieve goals. The worker tends to feel committed to a decision or goal depending on the degree to which the worker has participated in determining that goal. The employee must understand why the goal has been set. Each group is able to improve its operation to the extent that it consciously examines its processes and their consequences and experiments with improved processes. This is called the feedback mechanism, a process originally used with guided missiles to correct any flight deviations by feeding back into their control mechanisms data collected by sensitive instruments. In the same way, the first-line supervisor must set high standards for the group and communicate them to each individual employee. This feedback mechanism is intended to keep the work group "on course."

SENSITIVITY TO THE PSYCHOLOGICAL EFFECTS OF PERFORMANCE EVALUATION

Henderson gives us some reasons to be sensitive to the psychological effects that performance appraisal has on both the appraisers and the appraisees.

Appraisees

1. Identifying me as an average performer will limit my promotional opportunities in the organization, and a below-average appraisal is a stigma that will stay with me for the rest of my career in the organization.
2. Recommending additional training and development may identify me as a marginal employee.
3. Validating hiring, selection, and promotional criteria from my performance appraisal against those of others makes me feel that my qualifications are borderline.
4. Appraising my performance as superior will identify me as a "rate buster" and cause other members of my work group to be uncooperative and unfriendly.

Appraisers

1. The great majority of my employees feel that their performance is at least average, if not above average.
2. Appraising the performance of any employee as below average will cause that employee to dislike me; will result in reduced, not better, performance; and, although unlikely, could result in some physical harm to me or damage to my career.
3. Appraising employee performance consumes an inordinate amount of time and results in few, if any, positive organizational actions.
4. Identifying differences in performance among employees will cause jealousies, rivalries, and hostilities within work groups and dysfunctional organizational intrigue.[12]

These problems may well be inherent in most performance appraisal systems, but sensitivity to them directs our focus to better communication throughout the year rather than the normal once-a-year programs that are in effect in most of our institutions. If we communicate on an ongoing basis to employees, if we communicate and exchange perceptions, answer questions, and redirect efforts, most of the negative effects given above can be ameliorated.

COMMUNICATING THE APPRAISAL

Sashkin offers the following appraisal interview outline.

1. *Establish rapport.* Engage in a bit of small talk, at least briefly. Explain what the meeting is about and why it is being held, and see

whether the employee is really prepared. If not, you may wish to discuss setting a different time after the employee has had a chance to think carefully through step 2.

2. *Get the employee's views of his or her own performance.* Do not permit avoidance, that is, do not allow the employee to present you with a filled-out form and a "Here it is." Insist on verbal detail and explanation. Ask open-ended questions, such as "Can you tell me more about that?" or "Why do you see it that way?"
3. *Present your own views of the employee's performance.* Cover everything that the employee mentioned and any other performance elements that you believe are important. You should have filled out the form, if there is one, in advance (though perhaps in pencil) and made yourself some notes to guide you in this presentation.
4. *Let the employee express feelings and reactions.* Do not disagree. Do not get upset, even if the employee is upset (or, actually, *especially* if the employee is upset). If you have trouble controlling yourself—say, if the employee curses you—say nothing at all. Usually the employee will cool down and apologize. If at all possible, try to summarize and reflect to the employee what his or her feelings were as you heard them expressed. This lets the person know that you heard and understood (not necessarily that you agreed).
5. *Discuss the areas of agreement and disagreement.* After the employee has vented his or her feelings, you can get down to a careful review of each evaluation area. Explicitly point out where you agree and where you disagree. Discuss how to resolve any differences.
6. *Summarize and conclude the discussion.* Review the areas of agreement. Define the areas of continuing disagreement. Again, be as explicit and detailed as you can. Make explicit, in writing, any commitments to action by either party. Plan specific steps to be taken next, such as another meeting, a group conference, and so on.[13]

Critical to the appraisal interview is an exchange of views. This requires a great deal of openness and must be considered a two-way street. You must present your own views of the employee's performance and permit, in fact encourage, the employee to express his or her feelings and reactions. After obtaining areas of agreement and disagreement, work out a plan for the future. Remember, the purpose of performance evaluation is feedback. The appraisal interview is a feedback mechanism requiring you to:

1. let employees know where they stand
2. help employees do a better job by clarifying what is expected of them
3. plan developmental and growth opportunities

4. strengthen the supervisor-subordinate working relationship by developing a mutual understanding of expectations
5. allow subordinates to express themselves concerning performance-related issues[14]

The employee should come to anticipate an appraisal interview as an opportunity to learn how the supervisor perceives his or her work accomplishments and to share his or her perceptions with the supervisor. In order to do this the interview must be held in privacy and without interruptions. Do not rush such meetings. The key to the successful interview is open communication. The objective is to set goals mutually agreed on as the result of a review of past performance and future expectations.

PITFALLS TO BE AVOIDED: HAVING A PLAN

Stoner focuses our attention on pitfalls that supervisors must avoid for the successful implementation of a performance appraisal program.

1. *Shifting standards.* Some managers rate each subordinate by different standards and expectations. To be effective, the appraisal method must be perceived by subordinates as being based on uniform, fair standards.
2. *Rater biases.* Personal biases of supervisors may tend to distort the ratings given to subordinates. Documentation is most important, and an explanation for ratings is essential.
3. *Different rater patterns.* Managers differ in their rating style. Some are tough, some are easy. There should be precise definitions of each item on a rating form.
4. *The "halo effect."* There is a tendency to rate subordinates high or low on all performance measures on the basis of one of their characteristics. The critical element here is that rating employees separately on each item is essential. Guard against going down the center of the page on ratings.[15]

Henderson has developed a description of "guilt-rationalization–blame the organization syndrome." He describes that process as follows.

1. The appraisor tells the appraisee that he or she is performing well or acceptably.
2. A guilt feeling arises because the appraisee feels that he or she is not performing to self-assessed potential.

3. Initial embarrassment concerning demonstrated behavior gives way as the employee rationalizes the reasons for such behavior. (i) no one performs any better, or (ii) others perform not nearly as well, yet receive more or better rewards.
4. The employee internalizes the rationalization and does not change workplace behavior that would lead to improved performance.
5. The individual continues to harbor deep-seated frustrations based on a lack of motivation to perform to the level of his or her capability (self-actualization).
6. Continuing good and acceptable performance rating energizes this dramatic experience.[16]

In many instances the need to know which areas require improvement is often suppressed by employees because of the way in which such information is communicated to them. It is critical that the approach be one with a view toward improving rather than punishing. Indeed, most supervisors dislike having to criticize subordinates' work. Managers must inspire improvement and develop a plan to help individual workers become more effective. In that jocular commentary on performance evaluation given earlier in this chapter, the author talked about it being "a bad time of the year . . . review time." Human values are at the core of efforts to obtain excellence from your subordinates. As a manager you must be genuinely interested in the people who perform the work in your department. Displaying interest and obtaining positive results can be institutionalized in a plan for excellence, which is another way of viewing performance evaluation. Such a plan includes the following elements:

1. Getting your employees to see the end results of purposeful, consistent effort on their parts, as it relates to the advancement of their own careers.
2. Showing your subordinates how they fit into institutional goals; giving them deserved praise and meaningful recognition.
3. Giving the workers in your department an opportunity to achieve, recognizing that achievement in itself is a great motivator.
4. Knowing what your subordinates' personal goals are, and tieing [sic] these in with the goals of the institution.
5. Helping your employees to set and achieve self-improvement goals.
6. Providing public acknowledgment of the accomplishments of your subordinates, to satisfy the key need for recognition and for feeling important.
7. Being continuously sensitive to the need to have your employees

believe that they are accepted and approved by the institution and by their bosses.

8. Showing your employees how and why they are doing useful work.
9. Communicating to your employees about their progress.
10. Listening with interest to your subordinates' problems, their ideas and their grievances.
11. Never neglecting, nor forgetting your subordinates.*

Performance evaluation forms seem to take as many shapes as the number of institutions using them. Many of you have been exposed to Rating Scales, which present you with the choice of an appropriate rating along a scale with such terms as "below average," "average," and "above average." Rating is often done for various traits, such as ambition, character, cooperation, responsibility, attendance, and punctuality. Checklists are similar to rating scales except that, instead of providing a quantitative measurement of traits (by numbers or letters), each trait is followed by descriptive statements that offer the rater an opportunity to select an appropriate description of the employee's job performance. With Employee Comparison Systems, the supervisor is asked to compare the employee with other employees being evaluated. The rating is done on a factor-by-factor basis. Many supervisors find that this method forces them to make ratings and that it makes performance evaluation an easier process. Finally, goal-setting is part of management by objectives, which is a goal-setting process.

Each of these systems has its advantages and disadvantages. It does not matter which system is used. The essence of performance evaluation is positive reinforcement. Your institution may use any of the methods described above, but it is your commitment to discussing performance openly with your employees that will make a system succeed. Once again, be warned that once-a-year evaluations are not as productive as ongoing, immediate evaluations. The primary purpose of the evaluation process is to set up an interchange of ideas, where you are a coach and you are coaching for performance.

Blanchard and Lorb tell us "feedback is the breakfast of champions," "achieving good performance is a journey—not a destination," and finally, "people who produce good results feel good about themselves."[17] It is well to repeat, in conclusion, the advice from Blanchard and Johnson: "Help people reach their full potential. Catch them doing something right."[18]

---

*Reprinted by permission from *Hospitals,* Vol. 50, No. 14, July 16, 1976. Copyright 1976, American Hospital Association.

KEY POINTS FOR APPRAISING THE PERFORMANCE OF EMPLOYEES

1. Behavior that is rewarded will be reinforced and therefore is more likely to be repeated.
2. Recognition and reinforcement should come as quickly as possible after the relevant performance or behavior is observed.
3. Subordinates crave recognition from their supervisors.
4. Recognition should fit the employee's achievement.
5. Behavior you approve of, and want, should be rewarded; behavior you do not want should not be rewarded.
6. The performance appraisal process offers an opportunity to discuss past successes and past deficiencies, but it also offers an opportunity to plan, counsel, and coach for future improvement.
7. Employees will be better motivated if they know precisely what is expected of them, if they have the opportunity to obtain assistance as needed, if they know exactly how their supervisor feels about their performance, and, finally, if they receive appropriate recognition when it is deserved.
8. Supervisors who do a good job in communicating their evaluation of an employee's performance will encourage reactions, face up to and resolve differences, and reach mutual understanding of the implications of the review. The successful supervisor is able to communicate to employees who perform below standard and is interested enough to commend those whose performance is above standard.

NOTES

1. R.S. Barrett, *Performance Rating* (Chicago: Science Research Associates, 1966), 1.

2. Jack Engelhard, "The Company Man," *New York Times,* 6 February 1982, Op Ed section.

3. Thomas J. Peters and Robert H. Waterman, Jr., *In Search of Excellence* (New York: Harper & Row, 1983), 70–71.

4. Portions of this chapter were excerpted from Lawrence C. Bassett and Norman Metzger, *Achieving Excellence: A Prescription for Health Care Managers* (Rockville, MD: Aspen Publishers, 1986), chap. 3.

5. Howard L. Smith and Norbett F. Elbert, "An Integrated Approach to Performance Evaluation in the Health Care Field," in *Handbook of Health Care Human Resources Management,* ed. Norman Metzger (Rockville, MD: Aspen Publishers, 1981), 173.

6. Theodore W. Kessler, "Management by Objectives," in *Handbook of Health Care Human Resources Management,* ed. Norman Metzger (Rockville, MD: Aspen Publishers, 1981), 184–86.

7. Kessler, "Management by Objectives," 183.

8. Kessler, "Management by Objectives," 183.

9. Douglas McGregor, "An Uneasy Look at Performance Appraisal," *Harvard Business Review* 35 (May/June 1957): 89 and 94.

10. Marshall Sashkin, "A Manager's Guide to Performance Management," in *AMA Management Briefings* (New York: American Management Associations, 1986), 21–23.

11. Willard L. Merrihue, *Managing by Communication* (New York: McGraw-Hill, 1960), 122.

12. Richard Henderson, *Performance Appraisal: Theory to Practice* (Reston, VA: Reston Publishing Co., 1980), 7–9.

13. Sashkin, "A Manager's Guide," 43.

14. Robert L. Lazer and Walter S. Wikstrom, *Appraisal Managerial Performance: Current Practices and Future Directions* (New York: Conference Board, 1977), 30.

15. James A.F. Stoner, *Management,* 2nd ed. (Englewood Cliffs, NJ: Prentice-Hall, 1982), 548–49.

16. Henderson, *Performance Appraisal,* 10–11.

17. Kenneth Blanchard and Robert Lorb, *Putting the One-Minute Manager to Work* (New York: William Morrow & Co., 1984), passim.

18. Kenneth Blanchard and Spencer Johnson, *The One-Minute Manager* (New York: Berkeley Books, 1985), 39.

Chapter 5

Communication Skills: The Supervisor As a Change Agent

> *If language is not used correctly, then what is said is not meant; if what is said is not meant, then what ought to be done remains undone; if this remains undone, morals and art will be corrupted, justice will go astray and people will stand about in helpless confusion.*
>
> *A Chinese Adage*

Communication is behavior that results in an exchange of meaning that produces action. Some years ago participants at a conference for supervisors were asked to write down their personal definition of the word "communication." Many replied that communication is a process of sending messages.[1] This definition emphasized the sending aspect of communication and overlooked the importance of the need for a receiver (listener). Too often we believe that if we send out a message it will be received or listened to. Good communication requires the time and effort to listen to and understand what has been said.

Other supervisors at the conference defined communication as a process for "sending" and "receiving" messages. They had a clear understanding that to ensure good communication there must be deliberative listening that evolves into interaction, exchange of information, and understanding. There must be a focus on the receiving or listening aspects of the communicative act.

Cancelliere focuses our attention on listening as a key to productivity.

1. Studies show that on the average people listen at about 25 percent of their capacity.
2. One of the major problems that managers face is that they do not know how to create the type of environment that will encourage people to make their maximum contribution. Managers can help to

accomplish this goal by learning to LISTEN to their employees as well as to their peers and superiors.[2]

Supervisors often must initiate changes. Such changes touch the organization's structure, personnel policies and procedures, equipment, techniques, technologies, and, in general, the way that health care is delivered. There is an inherent obstacle to effecting change, however: change implies a move from the old, comfortable, and mastered way to an unknown and perhaps threatening way. To be successful, an organization requires managers and supervisors who can recognize the need for change, who can initiate change, and who can adapt to change. You do this through communication. The supervisor who does not communicate properly will often have an unproductive group. Essentially you implement change and get work done through other people, and to accomplish this you must communicate effectively with them. Half the process of communication is listening—not just sitting back and listening, but sitting up and listening. The better listener a manager is, the better listening the manager will inspire. Communication is a joint effort: someone talks and someone listens, not just passively but actively. Effective communication springs from an environment that encourages rather than discourages trust. We fail in communication when there is fear or suspicion. We fail when we view the listener as invisible. Your skill as a communicator is essential to your success as a manager and to the productivity of your subordinates. Productivity stems from an understanding of goals and of the processes needed to obtain them. This understanding is dependent on your skill as a communicator. No matter how varied your activities, how important your responsibilities, and how specialized your other skills, in the final analysis your success as a manager is related to communication.[3]

THE ESSENTIALS OF CLEAR COMMUNICATION

Fulmer offers us the "five C's" of communication.

1. *Clarity.* A message needs to be straightforward and as logically stated as possible. Very often a lack of clarity is due to an attempt to include too many ideas in the same sentence.
2. *Completeness.* Part of a message is sometimes more harmful than no message at all.
3. *Conciseness.* The communicator must delineate the specific message he or she wants to transfer. Most communications are enhanced

when a few well-chosen words replace a verbose, carelessly worded effort.

4. *Concreteness.* Communicators usually revert to abstraction and generalizations when they are unsure about actual concrete facts. Choosing concrete terminology is of great importance.
5. *Correctness.* Flawless use of communication techniques is all in vain if the message is incorrect.[4]

Because it is difficult to convey meaning, and because the full meaning of any message is affected by the total personality and the experience of the employee receiving the message, feedback is important. You cannot possibly know what you have communicated until you receive feedback. Often what you mean to say is not what the other person hears. Feedback is a way of giving assistance. It is essential information supplied by others to help people discover their effectiveness as communicators. It can be either corrective or confirming; an employee needs both. With the continual flow of reliable feedback, supervisors can determine whether they are on target and can make any necessary changes. Feedback is not evaluative. It is focused on specific behavior, not on the quality of the person. By avoiding personal evaluation there is no need for the individual to act defensively. Because each person's perception of other people is somewhat distorted, feedback from one person should always be checked against feedback from others. It is well to note that a little feedback is better than none at all, but the more feedback the better. The supervisor should not limit the employee to simple yes or no responses but rather encourage open responses and questions.[5]

Fleishman offers us some check points to assist us in gaining cooperation through communication from subordinates.

1. Do you tell your people what the job is and why it needs to be done?
2. Do you give them a chance to feel that they are part of something important, no matter how small their job seems to be?
3. Do you ask or do you order people?
4. Have you cultivated the "asking questions" technique to get cooperation and team work?
5. Do you give your people a chance to make some decisions themselves in doing the job, listen to their suggestions, and make them feel a sense of responsibility?
6. Do you make people feel, given an especially tough job, that you are asking them to do it because it takes people with real ability to get it done?

7. Do you give credit and recognition to an employee or a member of the staff who comes up with an idea or suggestion?
8. Can you let other people complete their thoughts or statements without interruption?
9. Can you talk about an event with an employee without the discussion reflecting on his or her personality?
10. Are you aware that words are just about the most important tool a supervisor has?
11. Are you aware that words affect people's "guts," their nervous system? Are you aware that what you say and how you say it has a lot to do with how they react to you or hear you?[6]

THE SUPERVISOR'S ROLE IN "URBAN RENEWAL"

Shaiken tells us "the ways in which the workplace is revamped . . . are not a mandate or even simply a byproduct of the technology but a result of conscious choices."[7] There is a need, in considering your role as a change agent, to understand that conscious choices must be made by your subordinates. For them to be able to make such choices you must communicate openly, freely, and honestly. Change is the order of the day in most of our institutions. When you are given the responsibility to be a change agent in a time of "urban renewal" in the health care industry, it is up to you to be the spokesperson for your employees.

Often such communication is met with resistance. It is necessary to understand that resistance is behavior intended to protect the individual or group from the effects of real or imagined change. These perceptions are important. Facts alone will not alter the concern of your employees when the organization dictates the need for change. The most important factor in initiating change, and in overcoming resistance to change, is to build a relationship of trust among managers, supervisors, and employees. To do this you must be sensitive to employee needs. For one, employees express a need to be involved. A key, then, to this process of effecting change is establishing a plan toward ameliorating the effect of the change on the person involved. This is done by presenting reasons for the change in detail. Essential to the promotion of change is the encouragement of an exchange of concerns and information, including the setting up of situations in which employees will ask questions and in which such questions will be answered.[8]

Imundo alerts us to barriers to effective communication.

1. *Sentiments.* These include biases, prejudices, values, feelings, attitudes, experiences and beliefs. They act as filters.

2. *Language.* Whether it is spoken, unspoken or written, in communication we rely heavily upon the use of language. There is a need to simplify the use of language throughout the organization, and compel people to work together towards solving common problems or achieving common goals.
3. *Position, role and importance in an organization.* Organizations are environments of inequality. Differences in position, role and importance in an organization are evident in all communications. Accurate upward communication is difficult to achieve because people will act or react in light of their perceptions of the information's possible effect on their power and prestige.
4. *Failure to understand personal motives.* Motives play a very important role in communication. There is a need to understand the personal motives of the people involved.
5. *Protection of one's prestige.* This is a critical element in effective communication. If an individual's prestige is threatened then he or she will not hear what is being communicated.
6. *Being distrusted.* Trust is at the heart of effective communication. If an employee does not trust you he or she will not *hear* you.*[2]

The most critical barrier to effective communication is poor listening habits. The better listener a supervisor is the more effective his or her communications will be. How can you improve your listening habits? Here are some warnings and some advice.

1. *Most of us talk too much.* Silence is a great way to motivate the other person to speak. Try to time your periods of silence; the use of judicious silence is an effective mechanism in communication.
2. *Most of us phrase questions to get the answers we want to hear.* Try to use open-ended questions. Your questions should be an incentive for the receiver to respond. Allow enough time for the other person to finish his or her thoughts.
3. *Most of us set up communications in a counterproductive atmosphere.* Haste and impatience have no place in effective communication. Try to select the time and place that provide minimum distraction and maximum comfort. Most important, protect the dignity of all parties to the communication process.

---

*Reprinted by permission of the publisher, from *The Effective Supervisor's Handbook* by Louis V. Imundo, © 1980 AMACOM, a division of American Management Association, New York. All rights reserved.

4. *Much communication is done on an ad hoc basis with little advance preparation.* Be prepared! Get as much information as possible in advance of a meeting. Investigate facts ahead of time.
5. *Many of us let emotional filters get in the way of understanding.* We must recognize that we have certain biases. When you feel strongly about a subject be particularly careful.
6. *Most of us listen only for facts.* There is more to communication than facts alone. The way one says things is as important as what is said. Perfect your listening skills to perceive feelings by deliberately putting aside the facts and details of the presentation and listening for the overall approach.

Barriers to the achievement of effective communication can be overcome by considering the receiver's frame of reference. As we have said, and will say again, if you can get into another person's skin and see the way he or she sees, you are liable to understand his or her point of view and, therefore, liable to change. You may then be able to change both the content and form of the communication. It is essential that you deal with the many barriers to effective communication that are thrown up each day. Remember that what you mean to say is not always what you actually say and certainly, in many instances, not what the other person hears. McMurray tells us "It is assumed that as long as the message, whatever its content, is clear, concise, well illustrated and dramatically presented, its reception will be satisfactory."[9] This, unfortunately, is not always true. There is much more to communication than merely the cogent presentation of a message. If the communication is not understood, believed, and regarded as having a positive value for its recipient, it will fail in its mission.

GAINING COOPERATION: A NECESSARY INGREDIENT IN EFFECTIVE COMMUNICATION

Much of what we communicate reflects the need for change. Change requires cooperation. An essential part of the supervisor's job is convincing subordinates to change work habits, work methods, and work responsibilities. Lateiner many years ago offered an excellent outline of the skills necessary to create a spirit of effective teamwork.

1. *Avoid arguments.* Criticizing your subordinates often results in counterproductive behavior. It is best to move from small points of consensus to overall and final agreement on the totality of the change.

2. *Admit your errors.* The hallmark of the effective supervisor is an open and willing admission of mistakes. It can gain you immeasurable respect from your subordinates.
3. *Establish a receptive frame of mind.* This is best done by clearly indicating the essential role that the subordinate plays in implementing change and by soliciting the employee's ideas and suggestions on moving from present methods to new methods. This will ensure a receptive frame of mind on the part of your subordinates and, therefore, a cooperative effort in effecting the change.
4. *A sympathetic "no" is better than a hard "yes."* You may well have to say "no" at times. It can be communicated in a sympathetic and understanding way so as to ameliorate negative reactions. It is best to explain the reasons for your "no" and to express your appreciation of the other person's point of view.
5. *Dramatize ideas or suggestions.* The sense of sight is one of the strongest. Use diagrams, charts, and films: it is not a waste of your time.
6. *Set a fair challenge.* Most employees are dying to make a commitment, and most will rise to challenges. Performance is immeasurably improved when employees are presented with a challenging goal and have participated in a free discussion of methods to attain that goal.
7. *Praise in advance.* Again, the worth of recognition and praise cannot be overestimated. Praise should not be bestowed grudgingly. Find the time to "catch someone doing something right." The successful supervisor is able to find something to commend, even in the least competent person.
8. *Don't demand cooperation.* It just won't work. Volunteerism is the order of the day.[10]

ACTIVE LISTENING

Active listening—sitting up and listening—plays an important role in supervisor-employee relationships. This means paying attention to the total presentation, including body language, eye contact, vocabulary, and voice volume. To be effective, the supervisor must actively listen for feedback. The supervisor must be able to listen to all meanings in what has been said and, in some cases, what has been left unsaid. The supervisor should remember that even silence can be communication. When employees refuse to communicate with their supervisors or co-workers, they are sending all kinds of messages. We cannot *not* communicate.[11] You must be prepared to listen with understanding and to see the other person's point of view. An active listener is an empathetic one and expresses empathy by the following behavioral patterns.

1. facing the other person squarely
2. adopting an open posture
3. leaning toward the other person
4. maintaining good eye contact
5. being relatively relaxed
6. reflecting attention through facial expressions
7. attending with vocal cues

What is recommended is that you become a deliberative listener. You should have, as a prerequisite, the desire to understand the speaker's point of view. This requires intense concentration. You cannot be passive. Weaver tells us that listening "is an active, not a passive process. We cannot just make sure that our ears are alert or open and let the rest come naturally. Because active listening involves both emotional and intellectual inputs, it does not just happen. We have to make it happen. It takes energy and commitment."[12] You must actively listen for feelings. You must want to listen. Rogers and Farson state that the good listener must meet four prerequisites to experience a mutually beneficial interaction.

1. The listener must *want to listen.*
2. The listener must *be willing to suspend judgment;* this means accepting the other person. This does not mean that the listener must approve of all the behaviors or attitudes of the other person; it means, however, that such approval or disapproval must be suspended throughout the interaction. If the other person is to deal with the problem responsibly, the listener cannot make judgments or offer advice.
3. The listener must *allow and encourage a statement of feelings* by the other person. To solve problems successfully, the listener must acknowledge and accept such feelings.
4. The listener must *be aware of personal feelings* during the interaction and must be prepared to integrate them into the interaction when appropriate.[13]

It is well to remember that no matter what form communication takes there is a sender and a receiver. There can be no communication without a receiver. Here are some principles to ensure the effectiveness of your communication.

1. Communication is the essence of organized activity and the basic process from which all other functions derive.
2. Communication should be thought of as directional, that is, upward, downward, or horizontally outward from the center.
3. Ineffective communication can mean wasted time and resources and, therefore, can result in lower productivity and higher costs.
4. Communication is not only verbal but nonverbal as well. We communicate through gestures, facial expressions, body postures and movements, tone of voice, and dress. Most of all we communicate by our actions.
5. People tend to hear, read, observe, and choose to understand only those parts of a message that relate to their own interests, desires, and needs.
6. One cannot *not* communicate. Silence communicates fear, stubbornness, or uncooperativeness. Our choice is not between communicating or not communicating but between communicating effectively or ineffectively.
7. Repetition is an important element of communication.
8. Feedback enhances the communication process. Without feedback the sender cannot know what effect the message has had on the receiver's behavior, nor can the sender know how to achieve better communication the next time. Feedback is a two-way communication.
9. Communication does not occur merely because a message is sent; it must also be received with reasonable fidelity.[14]

COMMUNICATING VISIONS

Zierden focuses our attention on a view of the communication process that is often overlooked: "To communicate a vision is to portray through words, media and exemplary behavior a view of what the organization is to become, such that employees can transform that view into their own mental image of the future."[15] Much of this is done by developing answers through a democratic or participatory approach. Zierden reminds us that leading can be viewed as any act on the part of the manager that serves to provide employees with answers.

The four basic questions to which most employees desperately seek an answer are:

1. Where am I going?
2. How am I going to get there?
3. Who will I be when I arrive?
4. Can I feel good about myself in the process?

If you, as a supervisor, can answer those questions, then employees will be less alienated and more committed. Again, if we are to build a relationship of trust, we can ill afford to be the gatekeepers of information. We must be the conduit to the people who breathe life into programs, processes, and services. To do that employees must know the answers to the foregoing four questions. Zierden reminds us that an employee understands and accepts a vision when, in the face of a perplexing decision, he or she can say "I know what the manager would have me do and that is what I will do."

KEY POINTS ON HOW TO COMMUNICATE THE CHANGE

1. To be successful an organization requires managers and supervisors who can recognize the need for change, who can initiate change, and who can adapt to change.
2. There is a direct relationship between communication skills and a group's productivity.
3. Successful communication is not a one-way street; it requires a sender and a receiver, both tuned to each other.
4. People do not hear what another person says when they do not trust that person.
5. Feedback is an essential part of communication. The feedback loop ensures that you are on target. Often what you mean to say is not what you actually say. Feedback is a mirror; look into that mirror often.
6. Understand resistance: it is behavior intended to protect the individual or group from the effects of real or imagined change. Individual perceptions are very important.
7. Half the process—the better half—of communication is listening. The better listener the supervisor is, the more effective his or her communication will be.
8. Gaining cooperation is a necessary ingredient in effective communication. You cannot demand cooperation; you must win it.
9. Keep in mind that there are four basic questions to which most employees desperately seek answers:

   - Where am I going?
   - How am I going to get there?
   - Who will I be when I arrive?
   - Can I feel good about myself in the process?

NOTES

1. From the author's notes taken at the 7th Annual Hospital Topics, Supervisor/ Management Conference, October 9, 1979, Chicago, Illinois.

2. Frank Cancelliere, *Listening Key to Productivity* (Rockville Center, NY: Listening Dynamics, 1980), readings 1-1 through 1-3.

3. Lawrence C. Bassett and Norman Metzger, *Achieving Excellence: A Prescription for Health Care Managers* (Rockville, MD: Aspen Publishers, 1986), 45–52.

4. Robert M. Fulmer, *The New Management* (New York: Macmillan, 1983), 272–73.

5. Harry E. Munn, Jr., and Norman Metzger, *Effective Communication in Health Care* (Rockville, MD: Aspen Publishers, 1981), 7–8.

6. Alfred Fleishman, *Commonsense Management: Hints for Communication in Business* (San Francisco, CA: Alfred Fleishman, 1984), 4–7.

7. Harry Shaiken, *Work Transformed: Automation and Labor in the Computer Age* (New York: Holt, Rinehart & Winston, 1984), xii.

8. Bassett and Metzger, *Achieving Excellence,* chap. 10.

9. Robert V. McMurray, "Clear Communications for Chief Executives," *Harvard Business Review* 43 (March/April 1965): 131–32.

10. Alfred R. Lateiner, "Modern Techniques of Supervision" (Stamford, CT: Lateiner Publishing, 1968); originally published in Lateiner, *Techniques of Supervision* (New London, CT: National Foreman's Institute, 1954), 28–29.

11. This section was developed from Harry E. Munn, Jr. and Norman Metzger, *Effective Communication in Health Care* (Rockville, MD: Aspen Publishers, 1981), chap. 4.

12. Richard Weaver, *Understanding Interpersonal Communication* (Glenville, IL: Scott Foresman & Co., 1978), 100.

13. Carl R. Rogers and Richard E. Farson, "Problems in Active Listening," in *Communication Probes,* eds. B.D. Peterson, G.M. Goldhaber, and R.W. Pace (Chicago, IL: Scientific Research Associates, 1974), 30–34.

14. Training, Research and Special Studies Division of the United Hospital Fund, *Improving Employee-Management Communication in Hospitals, A Special Study in Management Practices and Problems* (New York, NY: United Hospital Fund, 1965), passim.

15. William E. Zierden, "Leading Through the Follower's Point of View," in *Organizational Dynamics* (New York: AMACOM Division of American Management Associations, 1980), 38.

Part II

Maintenance Functions: Supervisory "How-To's"

Chapter 6

How to Interview: First Step to Better Placement

An interview has four major purposes:
1. to get information
2. to evaluate the applicant
3. to give information
4. to make a friend.
Although making a friend is listed last, it permeates the entire interview and should be considered throughout the interviewing process.

Arthur R. Pell
Recruiting & Selecting Personnel
(New York: Regent Publishing Co., Div. of Simon & Schuster, Inc.) p. 102

How often have you asked yourself "How can I be sure that the candidate for an open position in my department is the right one to whom to make the offer?" When a position falls open in your department, it is your responsibility to hire the right employee since it is your function to strengthen the effectiveness of the work team. It is in the selection mechanism that you are afforded the challenge to judge the applicant's qualifications and match them to your needs. Given the importance of the employment interview, it is disturbing to note that most supervisors are not equipped to handle interviewing because of little understanding of and minimal training in interviewing techniques. To complicate the issue further, most supervisors are pressed for time and find interviewing a distraction rather than a target of opportunity. It is through the interview, however, that the supervisor obtains information from the candidate, which must then be evaluated. In the interview the supervisor must also give information and act as a public relations representative of the institution.

THE EFFECTIVE EMPLOYMENT INTERVIEW

It will help to review some key steps to follow in the employment interview. The supervisor who wishes to be effective in the employment interview should do the following.

1. Set a plan. Structure the interview to obtain maximum information and cover all necessary areas.
2. Review the job specification or job description. There is nothing more fatal to positive results than to enter the employment interview with little knowledge of the job requirements. If the personnel department has not provided you with a written description of the job, then write one yourself.
3. Don't begin the interview until you have reviewed the job application. Have the applicant wait outside your office while you review the application form, any tests administered by your personnel department, and any reference checks made in advance.
4. Pick the right place for an interview; it should be held in private. Limit phone calls, which can disturb the applicant and interrupt your train of thought. Ensure that you have enough time for the interview (30 to 45 minutes).
5. Familiarize yourself with the five logical segments of the employment interview (warm-up stage, applicant talking stage, question stage, employer information stage, and wind-up stage; see below).
6. Keep in mind that it is not necessary for you to impress the applicant with the importance of your position. This means that you are going to have to control the amount of time you talk compared to the amount of time for the applicant to speak.
7. Watch the level of your language. Speak to the applicant in terms easy to understand, not above or beneath his or her level.
8. Watch your biases; don't let them get in the way of your ability to select the best-qualified candidate.
9. Don't be hesitant about making notes; make a record of essential facts and judgments during and after the interview.

As Pell has written (see the epigraph to this chapter), an interview has four major purposes: to get information, to evaluate the applicant, to give information, and to make a friend.[1] In many interviews one or two of these purposes are satisfied and the rest remain uncovered.

If you are going to make an intelligent placement decision, you must obtain the maximum information from the applicant. This requires sensitive listening skills. The ratio of interviewer talking to interviewer listening is critical. In the average 45-minute interview, the applicant should talk more than half the time. Since it is equally important for the applicant to judge you and your firm or institution, it is essential that the applicant receive basic information about the job, the institution, and career opportunities.

The evaluation process is just as important as eliciting and giving information. Often, the supervisor's personal bias can intrude on the effective evaluation of a candidate. Biases can be favorable or unfavorable. We often like certain things about people and, therefore, are impressed when an applicant shows one of those favorable traits. Some of us are impressed by the way an applicant dresses or combs his or her hair. Still others are sensitive to speech mannerisms (how often have you been impressed by someone with a British accent?).

Some interviewers rely on pseudoscience (a pretense at scientific validity) and popular misconceptions. For example, too many interviewers believe that they can detect "the criminal type," or they harbor prejudices against fat people (they are jovial or they are lethargic) or against redheads (they are always unintelligent). The "natural" judges of character are as unreliable as the content of such judgments. Needless to say, appearance is not a reliable predictor of personality traits.

The intrusion of personal bias and pseudoscience has produced an alarming proportion of "quick sets." Very often interviewers allow their initial impression of a candidate to influence their final decision. One researcher found that most personnel interviewers made their decisions after just 4 minutes of a 15-minute interview.[2] This is unfortunate because very often an initial impression is positively or negatively affected by intensive exploration of the candidate's qualifications over a much longer period. It would be well to recall the silent screen star whose good looks and swashbuckling manner produced an aura of masculinity but whose high-pitched voice doomed his career when talking movies were introduced. The opposite is often true as well: an individual who may not look the part may very well be just the person for the part.

Some supervisors are reluctant to vary their approach to interviews. Stereotyping interviews—that is, falling into a comfortable routine—often are nonproductive because of the different types of people who present themselves for interviews. The successful interviewer is flexible in approach and tries to be aware of the applicant's personality and needs.

According to Pell, one purpose of the interview is to "make a friend." Keep in mind that every unsuccessful applicant is often a member of the community served by your institution. Impressions made in the interview are lasting ones. Common courtesy, a dignified approach, and a sympathetic rejection will be remembered even though the job was not offered.

For the applicant who is successful, first impressions of the institution—usually obtained in the initial interview—are brought into the work area and can aid in developing an efficient and dedicated employee. When you interview an applicant for employment, you are functioning as a public relations arm of the institution. A dignified interview, with ample opportunity for the applicant to present his or her credentials, will be of immeasurable encouragement to the new employee in a new institution.

THE USE OF THE APPLICATION FORM

The personnel department is responsible for attracting as many qualified applicants as possible. Although recruitment, which is the responsibility of the personnel department, is a positive mechanism designed to bring in as many applicants as possible, selection, which is the supervisor's responsibility, can be considered a negative mechanism. A proper selection program lets only the qualified applicants through the sieve. You, as a supervisor, must perfect the sieve to improve your selection abilities. It is in the selection process that the supervisor attempts to appraise qualities that the institution feels are indicative of success on the job. It is critical that you define those qualities. The entire selection process necessitates the making of a value judgment, a forecast as to which applicants will turn out to be productive employees. Mandell tells us "the application form plays a simple and important role in selection. Its content can discourage unsuitable applicants and its design can reflect the company's dignity, reduce to a minimum the time needed to fill it out and simplify its review. Its wording and its comprehensiveness affect the efficiency and validity of the selection process."[3]

It is imperative that supervisors analyze their institutions' application form and make constructive suggestions as to its design. If the application form is properly designed, it will greatly reduce the time required for the interview. Does your institution's application provide definitive indicators that you can quickly interpret? Keep in mind the primary objective of the application form: to compare the applicant's qualifications with the qualifications required for the available job. Your institution's application form is the primary written record to prepare you for the interview.

Pell offers us some advice about the use of the application form.

1. Use the application form to provide you with the necessary information to evaluate an applicant.
2. Use it as a guide to the interview.

3. Read the application form before you start the interview; review it carefully and compare substantive material with job specifications.
4. From the application form, evaluate the applicant's progress in his or her career with relation to his or her age, education, earnings, and work experience.
5. Remember that the résumé or the application form (or both) are written to present the applicant's background favorably, so read between the lines. Keep in mind that what the applicant presents to you on those forms is important but that what he or she has omitted is equally important.
6. Do not assume that an applicant is a job-hopper solely on the basis of his or her work record; check the reasons for job changes.
7. Do not be overly impressed by superficial aspects of the résumé or application form.
8. Do not eliminate an applicant solely on the basis of the application form; the interview will tell you a great deal more than the application form does.[4]

THE FIVE STAGES OF THE INTERVIEW

The Warm-Up Stage

It is essential that you establish rapport with the candidate, who is often apprehensive about the interview. Diving into a cold pool can be quite a shock; it is often best to wade slowly into cold water. Remember this when the applicant comes in and identifies himself or herself to you. Most applicants are tense, and tension will affect the productivity of the interview. It is essential that you invest the time to put the applicant at ease.

This can be accomplished in many ways. Make an effort to establish a proper setting for the interview. If you seem harried and give the impression that this interview is a necessary evil, then the applicant will be defensive and often unresponsive. Talk about the weather. Talk about transportation; ask whether the applicant found it easy to get to the institution or found your office without difficulty. Don't have the applicant sit and wait while you look over the application; review the form before the applicant comes into the room. Don't open the interview with a caustic or insensitive question.

The warm-up period should take as long as is required to put the applicant at ease and in a nondefensive frame of mind. Sometimes you may be able to base your warm-up question on an item that appears in the application form. Move on to the next stage when the applicant is talking and freely exchanging information with you.

The Applicant Talking Stage

To begin this stage, once again refer to the application form and ask an open-ended question. Questions that can be answered with a simple "yes" or "no" are not effective. An example of a good opening remark is "I see that you worked at Metropolitan General Hospital for 3 years. Can you tell me about your job and what you did there?"

Now is the crucial test: can you keep your mouth shut? The idea is to let the applicant talk and set the pace. The extent to which you may have to ask questions and guide the interview will depend entirely on the applicant. There will be enormous pressure on you to keep the conversation flowing; almost all inexperienced interviewers have difficulty in handling periods of silence. Resist the temptation to step into the breach. The applicant will eventually move on and very often will reveal critical points about his or her character or experience.

The Question Stage

Remember, there is no set combination of questions that will be satisfactory for every interview. Pell gives us a helpful review of the types of questions applicable in most situations.

1. *"W" questions:* The "W" questions—"what?" "when?" "where?" "who?" and "why?"—coupled with "how?" are useful in most interviewing situations.
2. *Leading questions:* Too often these questions move the applicant to give the answer that he or she thinks the interviewer wants. Leading questions are discouraged, but they may be used to control the interview or to stop digressions.
3. *Probing questions:* These are incisive and specific questions used to obtain more detail about a specific activity or area. When a probing question is asked, the interviewer should be quite familiar with the area being examined.
4. *"Yes"-"No" questions:* This type of question should be used sparingly. A yes-no question cannot stand alone, since the form of the question does not give the applicant the opportunity to expand the answer.
5. *Situational questions:* With these the interviewer poses hypothetical problems and encourages the applicant to answer. In so doing, the applicant reveals knowledge and understanding of a subject. This type of question can be effective if the hypothetical problem is close to reality.

6. *Clarification and reflection questions:* This type of questioning essentially "mirrors" the interviewee's answers. It is used to get a fuller understanding of a question previously answered.[5]

It is a good idea to prepare your questions in advance of the interview. It is nonproductive to overload the applicant with a series of rapid-fire questions so that he or she is forced to remember the three or four questions posed in succession. Again, remember that the successful interviewer speaks far less than the applicant, even when giving information about the job. This often gives the applicant an opportunity to ask questions and make comments that can be evaluated.

In the questioning stage you should give the applicant the impression that you are genuinely interested in his or her background. This can be accomplished by putting yourself in the applicant's position (remember the strain of an interview when you were on the other side of the table?). Beware of being argumentative in this "drawing out" stage. If you disagree with an answer, it is not essential for you to correct the applicant or argue. If you feel that the applicant is holding back information or not telling the complete truth, it may be best to avoid a confrontation and to assume a sympathetic posture. This can result in finally arriving at the complete and true story.

The Employer Information Stage

Supervisors often forget that there are two decisions to be made in an interview. First is the supervisor's decision as to the match: Does the applicant fit the job? Should an offer be made? The second decision is one that falls to the applicant: Do I want to work for this institution?

It is essential that the supervisor provide the applicant with all pertinent information concerning the job itself and the institution in general. Tell the applicant the what, why, how, and when of the job, and answer any questions. This can be a most revealing part of the interview since the applicant's questions often are indicative of his or her value system. Too often this part of the interview is rushed or underrated. Too many times newly hired employees state that the job to which they are assigned is quite different from the job explained to them in the interview.

A vital tool in the informational stage of the interview is a job description and, if one is available, a job specification. The job description often contains a job summary section that gives the applicant (and, most important, the interviewer) an overall concept of the purpose, nature, and extent of the task to be performed. It also shows how the job differs generally from others in the organization. The job specification is also invaluable, as it contains the personal requirements, necessary skills, and the physical demands of the job. The job specification form commonly includes the requirements for education, experience, initiative, and ingenuity. Physical demands, working demands, and unavoidable hazards are outlined. A job description and a job specification are thus indispensable to the interview and placement process.

It is incorrect to assume that a supervisor and a subordinate are in fair agreement about the nature of the subordinate's job when they are discussing some plan or decision affecting the subordinate's work. A study conducted on superior-subordinate communications in management concluded:

> . . . if a single answer can be drawn from the detailed research study (presented in the report) into superior-subordinate communication on the managerial level in business, it is this: If one is speaking of the subordinate's specific job—his duties, the requirements he must fulfill in order to do his job well, his intelligent anticipation of future changes in his work, and the obstacles which prevent him from doing as good a job as possible—the answer is that he and his boss do not agree or differ more than they agree in almost every area.[6]

This kind of misunderstanding too often starts at the original placement phase. Applicants should be absolutely certain about the duties and requirements of the job for which they are being interviewed; this is the responsibility of the immediate supervisor who will make the placement choice.

In either this stage or the previous one, there are questions that can be extremely helpful in revealing the applicant's life-style, personal philosophy, and general character. Here are some sample questions in that area.

1. What books have you read during the last 6 months?
2. Looking back over the last several years, what is the most important way in which you have changed?
3. Where do you want to be—as far as your work is concerned—in the next 3 years, 5 years, 10 years?
4. What are some of the things you do when you are not working? What are your hobbies and outside interests?

The Wind-Up Stage

Knowing when and how to conclude an interview comes with experience. The inexperienced supervisor will often end an interview abruptly and many times on a less-than-positive note. Be careful not to abort an interview on the basis of a very quick, surface evaluation of the applicant. It may well be that you will cut down the amount of time spent in the interview because it is obvious that the individual being interviewed is not up to the standards of the job. It has been the author's experience over many years of interviewing at all levels that intuition and initial feelings are not the best guides for proper placement. Sometimes an applicant takes a long time to warm up, and initial negative vibrations change much later in the interview. It is your duty to give the applicant a fair chance to reveal a complete picture of his or her qualifications, motivations, and aspirations. It is also important that you not let the interview drag on, that you close at the right time, that you end on a positive note, and that you leave the applicant with a positive impression of your institution.

DOs AND DON'Ts IN JOB INTERVIEWING

At this juncture it is helpful to list those factors that make an interview successful and productive and those that are counterproductive to sound placement.

1. Do not stereotype your interview.
2. Do not allow the interview to assume the character of a comfortable routine.
3. Do not fall back on selecting only those candidates who show previous experience similar to that of the job in question.
4. Do not overhire. That is, do not select someone whose ability far exceeds that required by the job.
5. Do not be overly formal. Getting the applicant to relax is essential for a productive interview.
6. Do not give advice to the applicant. This is a pre-employment stage, and your only responsibility is to select a candidate appropriate for the position.
7. Do not be impatient. Let the interview run as long as necessary to develop a proper evaluation of the candidate.
8. Do maintain control over the interview. If the conversation is wandering, bring the applicant back on track. If his or her responses are too general, ask for relevant details.

9. Do familiarize yourself with the job specification and job qualifications.
10. Do prepare in advance for the interview, permitting yourself enough time and enough privacy.
11. Do not speak more than the applicant does. A good gauge is to limit your talking to one-third of the time (anything less than half the time will do).
12. Do leave the applicant with a favorable impression of the institution.
13. Do not set inappropriate standards for the job—either too high or too low.
14. Do not judge the applicant by one favorable or unfavorable attribute (the "halo" effect is detrimental to overall evaluation).
15. Do know your biases, and do not let them interfere with the evaluation process.
16. Do not reach a conclusion before the interview has started (this happens more often than we are willing to admit) or before the interview has been completed.
17. Do not reveal by either word or expression that you are critical of the applicant's responses.
18. Do not interrupt the applicant unless he or she is wandering or not being specific.
19. Do review, in advance of the interview, the application form and any personnel tests or references.

In any list of "don'ts" it can be helpful to review some of the mistakes that inexperienced interviewers make. Arthur Witkin, an industrial psychologist, discusses six classic mistakes.

1. The interviewer "telegraphs" the answer expected on each question. This results in a "yes-no" response.
2. The interviewer tries to scare or intimidate the applicant by setting up traps. Very little will be revealed about the applicant's real self since he or she is too busy defending to reveal any relevant information.
3. The interviewer does all the telling—about the company, about the job, about his or her own work, about his or her own family, and so on. The interviewer is in love with the sound of his or her own voice.
4. The interviewer is so busy writing down every word the applicant utters that there is no time for listening, looking, and reacting. After the interview, the interviewer really doesn't know what kind of person the applicant is.

5. The interviewer is busy filling out "an application form." That is, the interview consists of getting references, statistics, salaries, dates.
6. The interviewer believes in intuition and is a "star-reader." He or she sees qualities in the applicant that no one else is able to see.[7]

THE SCREENING INTERVIEW

In situations where a great number of applicants apply for an open position, it is important to conduct a screening of the candidates as quickly as possible to save time for the supervisor and the applicants. In many instances the personnel department is responsible for the preliminary screening, but there may be occasions when this is the supervisor's responsibility. Here, briefly, are the objectives of the screening interview:

1. to determine whether the job applicant is generally qualified for a specific job opening
2. to determine whether the job applicant is qualified for other present or future openings in the department or in the institution
3. to make a favorable impression on the job applicant (it is essential to create a favorable public relations impact on all applicants who contact the institution for a job).

The screening interview is designed to limit the number of applicants given a placement interview. Although recruitment is a magnet, its prime objective being to attract as many candidates as possible, screening is more like a sieve that lets through only those candidates who might well qualify for the job. It is important that the applicant feel that his or her candidacy has been reasonably considered. Therefore, although the screening interview is short it should not be uncomfortably rushed.

One of the best ways to expedite the screening interview is to identify those elements in the candidate's qualifications most crucial in determining his or her possible suitability for the job. For example, the nature of the position may require the employee to work overtime or to work unusual hours. If the interviewer spends 30 minutes determining the applicant's technical knowledge and experience and then finds out that he or she is unwilling to work the required hours, valuable time has been wasted.

It is important to recognize that the screening interview is merely an opportunity to determine in a rather general way whether or not the applicant is qualified for the job opening. Intensive consideration of technical qualifications and personality should be left for the latter stages of the interview or for the placement interview. The primary objectives of the screening interview are to put the candidate at ease and to determine as rapidly as possible whether he or she meets the basic requirements. The purpose of the placement interview is to determine specifically and in depth whether the applicant's work habits, attitudes, and personality are compatible with the job and with the institution.

AFFIRMATIVE ACTION

You and the applicant are not alone in the employment interview; sitting in are unseen but still powerful participants: the federal government and its partner, the state government. Various legislation affects the employment interview and, more important, circumscribes behavior that was possible before the enactment of such legislation.

It is now firmly established, if not finally interpreted, that employers must make a special effort to hire individuals who are deemed to be in a protected class. The law defines a protected class as one of several minorities that have been subjected to discrimination in hiring and promotion in past years, including Blacks, Spanish-surnamed Americans, Asian Americans, Native Americans, and women. Special emphasis is placed on the several areas of the employment process where rejection is possible. These sensitive areas are:

1. in the general prescreening of applicants through replies to ads, walk-in candidates, and any other system of applying for a job
2. in the most controversial arena of testing (which has been criticized as racially biased)
3. in the two forms of selection interviews—screening and placement
4. in any checks, such as security checks, reference checks, or physical examinations, that may result in rejection

Affirmative action is mandated by federal, state, and local laws in addition to presidential executive orders and court decisions. It is most helpful for the supervisor to be provided with the operative legislation in the area of equal employment opportunity, such as the following.

1. Title VII of the Civil Rights Act of 1964 as amended by the Equal Employment Opportunity Act of 1972. Chances are great that your institution is covered by this Act, since it applies to organizations engaged in interstate commerce, employing 15 or more persons; all educational institutions, public and private; state and local govern-

ments; public and private employment agencies; labor unions with 15 or more members; and joint labor-management committees for apprenticeship and training.

2. Executive Order 11246 as amended by Executive Order 11375. This covers all contractors and subcontractors who do more than $10,000 in government business. Only those with 50 or more employees and $50,000 in contracts with the federal government need have a written affirmative action plan, however.
3. The Equal Pay Act of 1963 as amended by the Education Amendments of 1972 [Section 6(d) of the Fair Labor Standards Act]. This specifically requires that organizations pay their female employees, both those exempt and nonexempt from the Fair Labor Standards Act, the same salary that their male employees receive for doing basically similar work.
4. The Age Discrimination and Employment Act of 1967 as amended in 1978, which specifically prohibits discrimination against persons between the ages of 40 and 70.
5. The Rehabilitation Act of 1973 as amended in 1974. Again the employer is required to maintain an affirmative action program, in this case ensuring the hiring and promotion of qualified handicapped people.
6. The Vietnam Era Veterans Readjustment Act of 1974. This extends the protection of affirmative action on behalf of disabled veterans and veterans of the Vietnam era by contractors holding federal contracts of $10,000 or more.
7. State Equal Employment Opportunity Acts. Your state may well have passed legislation modeled on Title VII. You should become familiar with it.

Health care organizations have been the subject of court action in the area of equal pay for men and women. In the past several years a federal district court ruled that an institution had violated the Equal Pay Act by paying its male attendants 30 cents an hour more than its female nursing aides[8]; another court decided that there was no distinction between the aides[9]; and another court declared that the job duties in a hospital for male orderlies and female nursing aides did not differ and that the higher pay scales for orderlies was unjustified.[10] In another case, California's Fair Employment Practice Commission ruled that a hospital discriminated against a minority worker, a Native American, when she was not rehired as a laundry worker after a leave of absence even though the hospital then employed other people for similar laundry jobs.[11]

As a supervisor doing the actual hiring, you may find yourself in the "hot seat" because of recent court decisions and settlements involving reverse discrimination. In one hospital a suit was brought by a male private-duty nurse against the hospital for not referring him for duty with female patients. The court decided that the hospital was unfairly discriminating against the male nurse and ordered administration to reach a satisfactory agreement with the nurse regarding future assignment policy.[12]

Members of groups not included in the protected classes listed under various acts are beginning to test the morality of affirmative action and to question systems of quotas for protected classes. As a supervisor you must be up-to-date on the requirements of affirmative action laws. If your institution has an affirmative action plan, review it, specifically for hiring and promotion goals, to identify areas of underutilization of protected classes.

MAKING THE RIGHT CHOICE

The final decision to hire or not hire a particular candidate should be based on a battery of assessments. It helps to work from a planned checklist of interviewing findings, covering the following criteria.

1. *Previous experience.* Although it may not be necessary for the applicant to have exactly the same experience outlined in the job description, you should consider similar job duties, similar working conditions, and same degree of supervision exercised or received on previous jobs.
2. *Education and training.* You should review the candidate's formal education, major fields of study, and specialized training.
3. *Manner and appearance.* Consider general appearance, speech, nervous mannerisms, self-confidence, and aggressiveness.
4. *Emotional stability and maturity.* Consider friction with former supervisors, relationships with peers, reasons for leaving previous jobs, and job stability. Consider the candidate's sense of responsibility and attitude toward work and toward family.

Still another checklist separates interviewing impressions into two areas.

1. *Personality factors.* You should determine what the applicant liked best and least about his or her previous job. The answer may reveal attitudes or patterns of behavior that may be useful in evaluating the applicant's suitability for the present opening. Perhaps the candidate will indicate a preference for jobs that are closely supervised or those

that require independent action. Does the applicant want a job that does not demand too much or one that involves more routine? Your questions should allow the applicant to reveal plans for the future. Does he or she see this job opening as temporary or as a career commitment? Did the applicant understand each question and reply directly to the point? Was the applicant communicative, or were replies responsive? Was the applicant spontaneous or more thoughtful in response to questions? Consistency is most important. Was there internal agreement between the various answers and descriptions given by the candidate?

2. *Nonpersonality areas.* The candidate's educational background is important to any evaluation. Is the applicant's education adequate for the position, more than adequate, or less than adequate? Will the applicant need specific training? References should be reviewed before final evaluation. References completed by the applicant's former direct supervisors are usually the best and most accurate. It may be possible to obtain such references by telephone checks planned in advance and handled by your personnel department. Specific attention should be directed toward verifying the job held by the applicant, the job duties described by the applicant, and the reasons for leaving that job. Ask former employers whether they would rehire the applicant. In general, two specific areas should be checked out through references:
   - the applicant's performance
   - the applicant's work habits, personal habits, and ability to get along with supervisors, subordinates, and fellow workers

Pell has some cogent recommendations for evaluating an applicant and making an offer. He lists areas of "do" and areas of "do not."

1. *"Do"* be specific in letters requesting references; use the telephone where possible in checking references; plan the reference interview in advance; understand the advantages and limitations of using outside investigative agencies; have realistic physical and medical standards for each position; make the job offer in person or by telephone; confirm the offer by letter.
2. *"Do not"* pay much attention to letters of reference carried by applicants; forget to ask a former employer why an applicant left his or her job; forget to ask whether the company would rehire the applicant; make the job offer before reference reports are completed; accept a bad reference without question (the reference may be based on a personal dislike of the applicant by someone in the company, so

check it against other sources if it does not appear to be consistent with all other factors).[13]

Here is still another breakdown of the essential factors that make the interview effective and more scientific:

1. Limit the interview to areas that cannot be measured by other methods. Tests, the application form, and reference checks augment the interview. Remember that the interview is a public relations opportunity in which you are marketing the worth of your institution.
2. Train yourself in interviewing techniques. Ask your personnel department to develop an interview training seminar, or attend a seminar given by a local college, hospital, or nursing home association.
3. The primary purposes of the interview are to ascertain whether the applicant would fit in with your work group and be content with the work and whether the applicant has the qualifications to do the assigned duties.
4. In the best selection programs the interview will only be one of a number of selection methods used.
5. To be successful, the interviewer should have complete knowledge of job requirements, working conditions, and supervisory preferences before beginning the interview.[14]

SOME RECENT FINDINGS

Is the structured interview, where the interviewer follows a set procedure, more effective than an unstructured interview, where the interviewer has no set procedure and follows the interviewee's lead? Recent findings suggest that the structured interview, where the interviewer knew what to ask and what to do with the information received, was more valid. In the less-structured interviews, supervisors may receive more information but it is often difficult to evaluate.[15]

Do interviewers become more effective through experience? Findings reveal, on the contrary, that interviewers benefit very little from day-to-day interviewing experience. Systematic training is needed, and some form of feedback mechanism must be built into the selection procedure for supervisors to learn from their experiences.[16]

How much effect does appearance have on the supervisor's decision to hire or not hire an applicant? It was found that personal information was given twice as much weight as appearance when both were favorable or both were unfavorable. Appearance had its greatest effect on the interviewer's final rating when it complemented the information on the application form and personal history elicited in the interview.[17]

How accurately can supervisors recall what an applicant says during an interview? Results indicate that recall is poor except in the case of supervisors who had been following an interview guide and took notes. Those interviewers who did not have a factual record of information assumed that the interview was generally favorable; those who had notes and could refer to factual information rated interviewees lower.[18]

The Life Insurance Agency Management Association, which conducted this research on interviews, drew two major conclusions from the findings.

1. The selection interview should be made an integral part of an overall selection procedure that makes use of a comprehensive, structured interview guide along with standardized evaluation and prediction forms.
2. An intensive training program for interviewers is necessary.[19]

The Woods Group offers advice to applicants for a managerial position (see Appendix 6-A). It may be helpful to those supervisors who are being considered for promotion or for a managerial position in an institution other than their present one.

KEY POINTS FOR THE INTERVIEWING PROCESS

1. Become knowledgeable about affirmative action regulations and laws.
2. To match the person to the job, know in advance what the job is. Review the job description, the job specifications, and profiles of employees who have successfully held similar jobs.
3. Assemble all the information about the candidate before you start the interview. Use the application form, the résumé (if available), references, and other information obtained before the interview.
4. Plan the interview in advance. Don't stereotype the interview, but remember to establish rapport and to communicate to the applicant complete information about the job content and institutional policy.
5. Permit time for an exchange of information, including the answering of all questions.
6. Keep in mind that there are two decisions in every interview: your decision to hire or not hire the candidate, and the candidate's decision to accept or not accept the position.

7. Look for potential. Don't be misled by the popular notion that "previous experience is always the best qualifier." Look for transferable experience.
8. Never forget that the candidate is under unusual stress. Understand the role that tension plays in affecting the quality of the interview. Try to help the applicant relax.
9. Accept the fact that you are a representative of the institution and perform a public relations function in all interviews. You have an opportunity to make friends even though you cannot make offers.

NOTES

1. Arthur R. Pell, *Recruiting and Selecting Personnel* (New York: Simon and Schuster, 1969), 102.
2. E.C. Webster, *Decision-Making in the Employment Interview* (Montreal: Industrial Relations Center, McGill University, 1964), 13–14.
3. Milton M. Mandell, *Choosing the Right Man for the Right Job* (New York: American Management Associations, 1964), 158.
4. Pell, *Recruiting and Selecting Personnel,* 101.
5. Ibid., 105–106.
6. N.R.S. Maier et al., *Superior-Subordinate Communications in Management, Report No. 52* (New York: American Management Associations, 1961), 9.
7. Arthur Witkin, "Which Interviewer Are You?" (New York: Personnel Psychology Center of New York), pamphlet.
8. *Hodgson v. G.W. Hubbard Hospital of Meharry Medical College,* 351 F. Supp. 1295 (D.C., Md., Tenn., 1971).
9. *Hodgson v. Brookhaven General Hospital,* 470 F. 2d 729 (C.A.5, 1972).
10. *Brennan v. Prince William Hospital Corporation,* 503 F. 2d 282 (C. A. 4, 1974).
11. *Northern Ioyo Hospital v. Fair Employment Practice Commission,* 38 Cal. App. 3d 14 (1974).
12. *Sibley Memorial Hospital v. V. Wilson,* 488 F. 2d 1338 (C. A. D.C., 1973).
13. Pell, *Recruiting and Selecting Personnel,* 150–51.
14. Milton M. Mandell, *Recruiting and Selecting Office Employees, Research Report No. 27* (New York: American Management Associations, 1956), 73.
15. Robert E. Carlson et al., "Improvements in the Selection Interview," *Perspectives on Personnel/Human Resource Management* (Homewood, IL: Richard D. Irwin, Inc., 1978), 143.
16. Ibid., 144.
17. Ibid., 145.
18. Ibid., 146.
19. Ibid., 148.

Appendix 6-A

The Corporate Interview*

Although this chapter is offered as assistance to supervisors and managers in making more informed decisions in the selection of applicants for employment, I add this excellent advice to some of you who will be on the other side of the interview: As an applicant for a managerial position.

BE ENTHUSIASTIC

One of the most important ingredients for a successful job search is enthusiasm. People enjoy interviewing others who have a certain vitality and aliveness and who appear to be genuinely interested in the position being discussed.

Interview each and every time as though *this* is the position you want. Give every interview your full attention and enthusiasm. Even if you may have decided that the job is not one you want to pursue, still attempt a very positive meeting. It's always a point in your favor to leave a company feeling impressed with you and wanting to speak to you again—immediately or at some future date.

BE WELL MANNERED

The obvious good manners always apply: Be on time. Dress professionally and in good taste. Smile. Be polite—listen carefully, do not interrupt or dispute what is said. Maintain good eye contact. Answer all questions directly—do not go off on tangents.

---

*This appendix was developed by The Woods Group, 275 Madison Ave., New York, NY 10016 in a brochure entitled "The Corporate Interview." Reprinted with permission.

BE LIKEABLE

Try to develop rapport with the person interviewing you. An initial informal discussion will put you both at ease. Try to find something about the other person to like. If you make a real effort to like someone, you will be surprised to find out that they will usually like you, too. And people want to hire people that they like. Very often a candidate does not get a position, in spite of outstanding credentials, if the "chemistry" is not right. Make this phenomenon work *for* you. It really is possible to get others to like you.

BE POSITIVE

Present everything about yourself and your background in a positive light. Highlight your skills and accomplishments, describing them in a natural relaxed manner. Be ready to sell yourself and all your attributes, but do not brag. Never bring up *anything* that is negative. If some lack is pointed out, try to diffuse it by subtly going back to your strong points. Maintain a confident "can-do" attitude.

BE SMART

Never be critical about your current or previous employer. Even if you have been in a very difficult situation, *do not* bring it up. If you complain in an interview you may make the impression that you are chronically dissatisfied and probably would be in this company as well. More than likely, you would lose the opportunity to interview with them any further.

BE PREPARED

Have all the information you need. Make sure you know what position you are interviewing for, who you will be meeting with and their role. If you can, find out more about this individual: what kind of personality they have, how they conduct an interview, the types of questions they ask, their likes and dislikes, etc. Be knowledgeable about the company itself. Do your research. Read their annual report or check out sources at your library. If you have an opportunity, talk to people who work there.

BE READY

Have ready answers to the typical questions that come up in an interview. Consider practicing them so your responses come easily and sound perfectly natural. Some likely questions are: What are your strengths? Your weaknesses? Never actually admit to a weakness; instead turn it into a positive statement like: "I have limited experience in the use of database, and I have recently started a course called Leading Database Design Concepts." Why do you want to leave your current job? Remember to be positive here; say you are looking for more challenge or a better career path. Certainly never say you want more money or don't like your boss or anything else that could be construed as negative. What is your long range goal? Even if you don't have a goal, have a ready, plausible answer for this question.

BE SAVVY

When asked about your salary requirement, do not start to discuss it prematurely. Say you are making a move for a better opportunity and need to evaluate the entire situation before you can respond. Say you will give it some thought and get back to them. The secret here is not to demand too much too soon. If you mention a figure that is considered too high, you may be eliminated as a candidate right away. If they get to interview you fully, and you have a chance to sell yourself, they may see that you do indeed warrant a higher salary. At the same time, if you ask for too little money, you can never be sure that they did not have a higher figure in mind for you. It is also wise to avoid asking about benefits and vacation at this time. Remember that you must make them *want* you first before any serious negotiations begin.

BE NICE

Write a brief note to the person who interviewed you. This accomplishes a number of things. First, it shows you are genuinely interested in the position and very often, the person who seems to *really want the job* gets the offer. Also, a note will help keep you visible after the interview. A nice reminder when they are seeing a lot of other candidates. Besides, it will win you points for being a thoughtful, polite, professional person—just the kind of individual anyone would want to work with.

Chapter 7

How to Avoid the High Cost of Turnover: Getting the New Employee Started

> *Few things affect employees more than the way they are first introduced to their job, to their workplace, and to their co-workers. If new employees are treated with indifference, left to wait interminably "til people get around to you," loaded down with incomprehensible policy and procedure manuals, given sketchy introductions to the people and things they encounter, left with their questions unanswered and curiosity unslaked,* they are likely to be far less than fully productive new employees. *(emphasis added)*
>
> *Gordon F. Shea*
> Introduction and Orientation in Human Resources Management and Development Handbook, *ed. William R. Tracey*
> *(New York: AMACOM, Div. of American Management Associations) p. 591*

> More can be done to make or mar the employee's future during his [her] first few days than in weeks at any other time.[1]

There is general agreement among management experts that a large proportion of turnover occurs with new employees, especially during their first month. Supervisors play a critical role in getting the new worker started on a job and often must act as vocational guidance specialists. The first days on a new job can make the difference between a productive, efficient employee and one who may soon become dissatisfied and leave.

Angelo Patri, a specialist in child development, was once asked by a mother "When should I begin teaching my 6-month-old son the way to behave?" "Madam," he replied, "you are already 6 months too late!" The first few days and few weeks on the job are difficult ones for the employee and for the supervisor. Both must make an adjustment. The supervisor has the responsibility of balancing the employee's abilities and personality against the requirements of the job. The prompt integration of the new employee into the work force can yield optimum efficiency in minimum time. The cost of turnovers is not a small one. When one considers the time, effort, and salaries expended in recruiting, interviewing, checking references, and processing and training new employees, it is easy to understand the urgent need to reduce turnover during the probationary period.

Placement refers to the assignment of new employees to specific jobs and their melding into the larger work teams; induction is the process by which placement is made effective. If one were asked, "When should I start inducting and orienting my employees?", the answer should be that induction and orientation begin on the very first day of employment.

THE INDUCTION AND ORIENTATION PROGRAM

> If the supervisor attempting to orient others and those others are to succeed in this endeavor (seeing to it that the new employee adjusts to the work situation, at least partially through an attempt to resolve the needs conflict), the organization's wants and desires must be carefully determined.[2]

For an induction and orientation program to succeed, its objective must be clearly stated and communicated to all supervisors and employees. There are four general objectives of a successful induction and orientation program.

1. *Reinforce the employee's confidence in his or her ability to cope with a new work assignment.* Despite the fact that applicants often present a positive view of their ability to handle the job, on the first day of work they are faced with a myriad of doubts. Most individuals fear criticism. Even when criticism is judiciously applied it is often a threat to self-confidence, and at no time is there a greater need to feel worthy than that first day on a new job.

   First impressions remain with an employee for many years. He or she will approach the new assignment with some apprehension, with many predetermined attitudes carried over from home, school, church, and previous jobs, and certainly with the sense of not belonging. These new employees are not all the same and thus react differently to criticism: some are aggressive, some are shy, some get angry quickly, and some are introspective. They think differently, and their ability to "catch on" differs. It is the supervisor's task to understand these basic differences among people and to alter the induction and orientation program to meet different needs.

Differences notwithstanding, most new employees want to be a member of a purposeful group; they want to be accepted into the work team as quickly as possible. Some of them may have done a similar job in other institutions, "but not quite the way you do it here." Once people do a job in a certain way, they form habits and become resistant to change. To change habits, you must change attitudes. Offer a complete explanation of "why" things are done in a certain way.

2. *Communicate complete and detailed conditions of the person's employment.* Although this should have been covered in the placement interview, the applicant may have been under tremendous pressure during that interview and perhaps did not absorb all that you and the personnel interviewers communicated. Thus there is a need for further communication at a more receptive time—after placement, during the induction period. An employee who knows what must be done and why it must be done in the prescribed way and also understands why his or her contribution is important to the total institution is likely to be more efficient and loyal.
3. *Inform the person of the rules and regulations surrounding employment.* In the first day or week of employment, the new employee has not formed any strong opinions and is far more receptive to an explanation of the rules and regulations of the institution, the "laws of the shop." The basic purpose of induction is to help employees become adjusted to their role as members of the work team. In addition to understanding the team's objectives and how they are attained, the new employee must know what constitutes acceptable behavior for the work team.
4. *Instill in the employee a feeling of pride in the institution.* Although it is true that the modern work area and work system are routinized and that standardized techniques have robbed the worker of much of the emotional reward and sense of ownership that early craftspeople felt, it is equally true that with proper opportunity and encouragement employees will gain a sense of the purpose of their work on whatever level it may be performed. Everyone's job can be important if there is an understanding of the interrelationship and interdependence of various jobs in the work team. It is difficult for individuals today to find satisfaction in their work compared to the days of the handicraft system. Special attention must be directed to the employee's desire to gain satisfaction from work and to take pride in the end product.

POLICY

The supervisor must develop in the new employee an understanding of the ultimate goals of the institution and how the new employee contributes to the success of these goals, whether they relate to patient care, teaching, or research. As a supervisor you should be aware of your institution's policy, which is a clear statement of philosophy regarding the institution's approach to employees. Here are some key statements as to that commitment of the induction process.

1. Human resources are our most precious asset and require both our understanding and our empathy.
2. Each new employee who joins the institution must be convinced that he or she is welcome and needed.
3. All information necessary to acquaint the new employee with the job, the institution, and his or her fellow employees must be communicated at the very onset of employment.
4. The ultimate objectives of the institution and the role the new employees play in attaining these objectives must be communicated. This communication does not end with the completion of the probationary period.
5. Induction is the first-line supervisor's responsibility. It is an ongoing process and may well make the difference between average, below average, or exceptional performance.

THE SUPERVISOR'S RESPONSIBILITY FOR EMPLOYEE ORIENTATION

There are several areas of responsibility that fall to the supervisor in the induction of a new employee into a department.

1. the establishment of a cordial and positive atmosphere
2. the communication of orientation and training programs to the new employee
3. the communication of the organizational structure of the department and, specifically, how the department functions in relation to the rest of the institution
4. the review of the job description and job specifications
5. the introduction of a new employee to fellow workers
6. a tour of the department, the work area, and the institution

7. communication of the rules and regulations of the institution and an explanation of the benefit programs available to the new employee
8. the assignment of the new employee to a "sponsor"
9. an evaluation program that follows up periodically on the new employee's progress

These responsibilities can be incorporated in a specific induction program designed to meet the following overall objectives.

1. to make the new employee feel at ease with the institution, the new job, and new associates and to give the new employee a proper first impression that will be positive and lasting
2. to assist the new employee in understanding the total function of the institution and to relate the ultimate function of the institution to the new employee's job
3. to assist the new employee in understanding completely the conditions of employment and the rules and regulations of the institution
4. to assist the new employee in knowing and understanding the employee benefits and services available[3]

STAFF AND LINE INDUCTION

The two main steps of an orientation program are staff induction, usually performed by the personnel department, and line induction, always performed by the first-line supervisor.

Let us look first at the personnel department's responsibility. Induction starts during the hiring process. The first step in the hiring process is the interview, which may be viewed as the pre-employment phase of induction. The physical setting of the personnel department is an important factor in creating a favorable first impression. The next link in the induction process is the personnel interviewer. It is the responsibility of the personnel interviewer to ensure that every prospective employee is given all the information necessary to understand the demands of the job and the rewards of the job and to acquaint himself or herself with the working environment. The staff orientation phase is continued in the final placement interview conducted by the supervisor. The supervisor's responsibility does not end with the placement interview, however. The employee's first day in the new department is a difficult one and should be a day of good staff induction and good line induction.

Line induction is the responsibility of the first-line supervisor and is not made unnecessary by the supervisor's role in the interviewing process. The supervisor must introduce a new employee to fellow workers.

Although this is the first-line supervisor's primary responsibility, it can be delegated to specialists.

Some of the techniques to consider in fulfilling the institution's obligation for proper induction are as follows.

1. *Notice of employment in writing with complete details.* Every new employee should receive in advance of reporting to work a written statement of the actual job offer. This statement should include the title of the position, a brief description of the position, the supervisor's name, the pay rate, and the reporting time and place. The supervisor is vital to the induction procedure, and therefore the new employee should be directed to report to the office of the immediate supervisor. It is the supervisor's responsibility to escort the new employee to the work area and to introduce him or her to fellow workers.
2. *Institutional tours.* Many successful induction programs feature institutional tours to key areas. This gives the new employee a broader sense of the purpose of the organization and an opportunity to see areas that may be off-limits during subsequent employment with the institution.
3. *Employee handbooks.* Almost all successful induction programs include the distribution of an employee handbook. These handbooks contain a statement of policy, conditions of employment, obligations, and benefits. The purpose of an employee handbook is to provide the new employee with a complete overview of the institution's personnel administration so that policies and procedures approved by the institution's board are clearly understood. The handbook, therefore, is a natural offshoot of the personnel policy and procedures manual. Most good employee handbooks start off with a section on "getting started," which details the organization's selection policy, deals with proper induction of new employees, and explains the probationary period. A summary of the obligation of employees is included in a separate section and is a concomitant to the benefits and opportunities available to the employee. Employee manuals or handbooks are often illustrated and should attempt to present in a readable, informal, and understandable fashion information necessary to assist the new employee in acclimating to the new organization.
4. *Sponsorship or "buddy" system.* Sponsorship programs have found many adherents throughout the country. A senior employee is selected to be the "buddy" or sponsor of a new employee and to ease adjustment to the new work situation. The sponsor talks with the newcomer, is a companion during rest periods, helps interpret rules

Exhibit 7-1 Supervisor (Sponsor) Induction Checklist

Employee Name ____________________ Date Reported ____________________
Department ____________________ Supervisor ____________________

Each step is designed to ease the adjustment of the new employee. Do not skip any point. Please check (x) off the steps as you cover them with the new employee. Forward this completed form to the Personnel Department.

__________ *Welcome the employee*
Introduce yourself; put him or her at ease

__________ *Explain work schedule*
Communicate hours, days off, lunch hour, holidays, free days, and vacation

__________ *Tell him or her about the department*
What the department does; the importance of the work; how his or her job fits in

__________ *Pay*
Tell when pay day is, how much, chances for advancement, and review general dates for salary review

__________ *Rules and regulations*
Suggest the employee review the employee manual "All About Your Job," including rules and regulations

__________ *Illness or accident on the job*
Advise employee to go to health service or emergency room

__________ *Uniforms, lockers, parking, bathrooms, and rules of dress and cleanliness*
Explain, locate, and familiarize

__________ *Explain the job*
1. Prepare: Arouse interest, put at ease
2. Demonstrate: Tell, show, illustrate, ask
3. Try out: Have employees do; explain, and correct errors
4. Follow up: Tell employees where to get help; check frequently

__________ *Show department and introduce to coworkers*
Introduce employee to responsible supervisor with whom he or she may deal

__________ *Have someone accompany new employee to lunch*

__________ *FOLLOWUP:* At end of week, check progress, review employee manual; encourage questions

---

The above induction steps have been covered with the employee.

____________________ ____________________
Signature of Sponsor (if not supervisor) Signature of Supervisor

____________________ ____________________
Date Date

and customs of the work area, and in general attempts to make the new employee feel at ease in the new surroundings (see Exhibit 7-1)

5. *Informational lectures and films.* These are used widely in induction programs. All recently hired employees are invited to an orientation session, usually scheduled during the first week of employment. Most successful programs have mandatory attendance requirements. A staff specialist from the training department usually chairs the conference and provides a detailed and, in many cases, illustrated lecture on the nature of the institution and its policies, employment practices, safety programs, and employee services. Specialists in those areas may be called on to address the group and answer questions. A film may be shown. These films are usually obtainable from local or national hospital or home associations. It is possible to produce at low cost a film that deals with your institution's specialized situation, however.

WHAT THE NEW EMPLOYEE SHOULD LEARN ON THE FIRST DAY OF WORK

Here are some of the job aspects that a new employee should learn on the first day or certainly the first week on the job:

1. the routine of the job
2. the functions and workings of other parts of the organization
3. how to find one's way around the institution
4. how this job fits into the larger picture
5. the privileges of a new employee
6. who one's associates and fellow workers are
7. the history of the institution and how it services the community today
8. how most employees are interdependent
9. the channels for exchanging ideas and information

AN ALIEN IN THE NEW COUNTRY

Although many new employees have had experience in similar institutions, there will be some who must adjust to a completely foreign environment. A socializing process must take place to encourage good communication and behavioral patterns. Dubin offers the following explanation of the basic problems of orientation and induction.

Orientation and indoctrination of a new member are essentially processes of acculturation. He has to learn ways of behaving, a set of standards and expectations, and a point of view and outlook largely foreign to him in their specific details, although he may be generally familiar with them in their broad outline. A great deal of the new employee's time may be spent during the early weeks and months of employment simply becoming adjusted to the organization.

The adjustment process first involves becoming familiar with the language and its significant symbols that are used in the organization. In order for the new individual to understand how the organization operates, and his role in it, he has to understand the language by which communication is carried out. Accordingly, at the initial stage of orientation and indoctrination, a great deal of attention is paid, both by the new member and by those who are teaching him, to learn a vocabulary and a set of symbols that communicate significantly. In order to maximize understanding of what goes on, the new recruit has to become fairly familiar with the language of the organization.[4]

THE PROBATIONARY PERIOD

Most unionized institutions have labor contracts that contain provision for a probationary period. It permits the institution the unappealable right to terminate employment of new employees during either a 30-day, 60-day, 90-day, or 6-month probationary period. This period is a time for testing out the new employee. It is the supervisor's responsibility to evaluate the performance of a new employee so that a "go" or "no go" decision can be made before the expiration of the probationary period. It is critical to understand that, once the employee completes the probationary period, seniority protection plays an essential role; indeed, there is a moral obligation for the institution to live within the due process mechanism of the labor contract or of personnel policies in the area of termination. Therefore, it is essential for the supervisor to follow up on new employees at various points during the probationary period. These are appropriate points at which to review with the employee his or her performance to date. It would be well for you to have a checklist of critical points in your evaluation of new employees. An employee who displays poor work habits during the probationary period is a bad risk for productive and efficient employment. It is the supervisor's responsibility to ensure that those added to the work force are likely to be satisfactory employees.

A REVIEW OF THE PRINCIPLES OF INDUCTION

The cost of sound and formal induction and orientation is small when compared to the high cost of employee turnover and inefficiency. The following four principles of induction serve as the basis of a successful program and should be neither compromised nor neglected.

1. New members of a group or an institution must go through an extensive process of adjustment, during which they must learn new rules and adapt old habits to the new group.
2. This adjustment can be facilitated by providing new employees with facts relating directly to their specific jobs and to employment in the institution as a whole.
3. As with all other important responsibilities of a health care institution, the responsibility for induction and orientation must be delegated clearly to a capable member or members of the management team. This responsibility must be understood. Although the line is ultimately responsible for induction, the staff may be delegated a substantial part of this burden.
4. The process of induction does not end after the first week or month of employment. Orientation is a long process, and in the final analysis it is the key link between good selection and good job performance.

Induction and orientation are designed to provide a new employee with the information he or she needs to function comfortably and effectively in the organization. Typically, induction and orientation will convey three types of information.

1. general information about the daily work routine
2. review of the organization's history, purpose, and products and how the employee's job contributes to the organization's needs
3. a detailed presentation, perhaps through a brochure, of the organization's policies, work rules, and employee benefits[5]

KEY POINTS FOR THE INDUCTION PROCESS

1. Turnover is costly. The highest percentage of turnover occurs with new employees during the probationary period.

2. The supervisor has the main responsibility for induction and orientation of new employees. Although the personnel department, in its staff capacity, performs an essential function in the induction process, the supervisor is vital to successful assimilation and retention of employees.
3. Establishment of a cordial and positive atmosphere will make employees feel at home in an alien land. Mutual acceptance between the work group and the new employee is essential and must be expedited.
4. Good habits and bad habits are developed from the very start. The first few days and weeks on the job will be critical. Give the new employee a proper first impression that will be lasting and positive.
5. Ask the more responsible employees in your department to sponsor new employees.
6. Indoctrination is not a short, one-step procedure. It requires follow up and attention over a protracted period of time. Don't lose interest, and don't let the employee believe that you've lost interest. An early investment in this procedure will yield large dividends: an efficient employee, a long-term employee, and a loyal employee.

NOTES

1. George D. Halsey, *Training Employees* (New York: Harper & Brothers, 1949), 10.
2. John M. Pfiffner and Marshall Fels, *The Supervisor of Personnel,* 3rd ed. (Englewood Cliffs, NJ: Prentice-Hall, 1964), 300.
3. P. Ecker et al., *Handbook for Supervisors* (Englewood Cliffs, NJ: Prentice-Hall, 1959), 131.
4. Robert Dubin, *The World of Work* (Englewood Cliffs, NJ: Prentice-Hall, 1958), 337.
5. James A. F. Stone, *Management,* 2nd ed. (Englewood Cliffs, NJ: Prentice-Hall, 1982), 541.

Chapter 8

The Supervisor's Role in Training

> *Today, it is axiomatic to say that any training within an organization should be based on the assessed needs of individuals or groups. For an organization to function at a required level, workers need to perform at a given standard. When they fall short of the standard, they* may *need training, which, if effective, will enhance their performance.*
>
> *Kendrith M. Rowland and Gerald R. Ferris*
> Personnel Management
> *(Boston, Mass.: Allyn and Bacon, Inc., 1982) p. 310*

One of the responsibilities that most supervisors share and find time consuming is training. Its importance should be clear to you: it gives to the employee and to the supervisor what each desires without taking away anything from the other.

Let us begin by defining what training is. The training of employees is a process of aiding them to gain effectiveness in the performance of their duties as they are presently understood, or in any future assignment, through development of appropriate habits of thought, action, skills, knowledge, and attitudes. It is through the vehicle of training that attempts are made to communicate skills and attitudes.

PRECEPTS OF TRAINING

There are certain precepts that must be explored and understood before embarking on any discussion of the training function.

1. Training is an all-permeating function that goes on from day to day and cannot be considered an appendage or a necessary evil. It is a ubiquitious process directed toward maximizing employees' efforts

in the work arena and culminating in a more effective, cohesive organization.
2. Motivation is an essential part of training. It is important to consider the motivations of both the employees and the administration before developing a training program.
3. Training is a costly but productive undertaking.[1]

The keys to successful training are careful screening of the trainees and careful development of curricula. No matter how wide or narrow any applied program of training may be, it is essentially a method and a means of communication. Through training we communicate skills, methods, ideas, information, objectives, and last, but no means least, attitudes.

WHY SPEND THE TIME AND MONEY TO TRAIN?

As a supervisor it is well for you to recognize the advantages of establishing a formal training program.

1. The break-in time of new employees can be sharply decreased. Supervisors often demand longer probationary periods on the basis of a perception that it takes a long time to bring new employees up to acceptable efficiency levels. This time can be reduced by developing appropriate training programs.
2. Efficiency levels, once recognized, can be obtained through appropriate training. The training gives the employees an understanding of how to do the job and concurrently an understanding of what the job is all about. Given such awareness, the trainee must also appreciate what a fair day's work means at your institution. These efficiency levels, once established, must be communicated to the trainees.
3. Waste, spoilage, and accidents can be reduced with properly trained employees. Employees who are taught the right and efficient way to do a job will produce less waste and be involved in fewer accidents.
4. Research has clearly indicated that employee dissatisfaction expressed in absenteeism, tardiness, and turnover often results when employees are ill trained and ill equipped. Training programs, therefore, can immeasurably reduce such personnel problems. Employees become easily distressed and unhappy when they cannot do a job properly. Self-doubt results from poor workmanship. A key purpose of the training program is to reduce such dissatisfaction.
5. Employees can be prepared for higher positions and more responsi-

bilities through intensive training. Often participation in training programs is a reward for an outstanding performance.

6. Given the above, training can improve job satisfaction and morale and reduce the number of grievances.

SOME OTHER REASONS TO TRAIN YOUR EMPLOYEES

The high cost of hospitalization and the battle over scarce dollars to support health care clearly indicate a need to move from the acceptance of below-standard, marginal workers to an era of higher standards and formalized programs designed to produce more efficient work forces. The three following considerations make the investment in training urgent.

1. Wage and fringe benefits have reached new levels, and the "cheap" labor supply, once so prevalent in health care institutions, is disappearing. Unionization of health care workers produces higher and more competitive scales and broad fringe-benefits programs.
2. High levels of turnover are not acceptable. There is an obvious inefficiency inherent in short-term employment.
3. The cost of recruitment focuses our attention on retention. Retention is enhanced by training.

TRAINING OBJECTIVES

There are three basic objectives in any training program: (1) the acquisition of knowledge, (2) the development of skills, and (3) the development or modification of attitudes. As a supervisor you should be aware of the problems inherent in the training responsibility. Stokes lists some of these problems.

1. Training takes time. It is often in competition with the other activities (the central activities of the institution). Since it is time consuming, successful results must be highlighted by those sponsoring a training program. You've got to sell your administration on allocating the dollars necessary for this enterprise.
2. Training costs money. The trainee who becomes a highly skilled and productive worker must be considered worthy of a rather high hourly investment.
3. Employers want to retain trained help. One of the common protests against training programs is that "We don't want to train people for

other institutions." With a little extra effort and attention, it is possible to retain trained people, especially when area wage rates are quite similar and there is not much wage advantage in moving from one institution to another.

4. Small institutions especially need training. Although large institutions can have complete training departments that recruit trainees, set up professional programs, retain top-notch trainers, and spread the training course over a large budget, smaller institutions are limited in such matters. Once it is determined that training is necessary, regardless of the size of the institution, it is possible to run a successful program.
5. Training requires administrative time. Training is not an activity that can be isolated from other functions of the institution. Even though administration has assigned the conduct of the program to certain specialists, it must constantly support training, be aware of the results obtained, and be certain training is properly and effectively carried out.
6. Training must be done by specialists. The person who does the training must be chosen because of his or her technical skill and knowledge. Every technically competent supervisor must become an effective developer of people. It is one of his or her prime responsibilities to train his or her own people.*

RESISTANCE TO TRAINING

Many supervisors are often vehement in their resistance to the time and cost of training. It is not unusual to hear such supervisors complain about released time and the lack of immediate results of training. Often when the training is a vestibule program, given in advance of the new employee's assignment to the department, the supervisor will press for immediate release of the new employee to the work area. You must remember, however, that it is worth the wait. Training is truly the process of assisting employees toward becoming more effective in their present or future assignments within the institution. What you as a supervisor must understand is that every organization pays for a training program, whether it has one or not. If you cannot afford the time to release your employees, then you are probably accepting a level of performance below normal effi-

---

*Reprinted, by permission of the publisher, from *Total Job Training* by Paul M. Stokes, pp. 16-19, © 1966 AMACOM, a division of American Management Association, New York.

ciency. In addition, the lack of proper training results directly in a broad array of operating problems.

PLANNING THE TRAINING PROGRAM

The role of the supervisor in the planning of the training program has been given too little attention. The supervisor has to be involved in underscoring the need for training, in devising the training program around these needs, in actually executing the training in a professional manner, and, finally, in evaluating its effectiveness. These four responsibilities flow from four rules offered by Odiorne.[2]

An important responsibility of the supervisor, as well as the training department, in planning the training program is the conducting of a "needs analysis." A needs analysis is a process through which standards required of employees for a successful job performance are uncovered. Any training with an organization should be based on the assessed needs of individuals or groups. As Roland and Ferris have said, "For an organization to function at a required level, workers need to perform at a given standard. When they fall short of the standard, they *may* need training, which, if effective, will enhance their performance. In turn, this increased individual or group productivity results in desired organizational outcomes."[3] Such needs analyses must determine whether the problem is a training problem. Organizational analysis, operational analysis, and individual analysis are the three essential aspects of training needs analysis. Organizational analysis is a procedure that shows where training can be utilized within an organization; operational analysis attempts to break down a given job into a series of specific tasks and standards of performance for each task; and individual analysis determines how satisfactorily an individual is performing the tasks required to do his or her job and consequently areas where an individual's performances need to be improved.

Training needs should be clear to a supervisor and are indicated through the following day-to-day supervisory experiences.

1. manpower shortage or inadequate supplies of employees who are promotable
2. specific skill shortages within your department, which may reflect a shortage in the labor market in general
3. general employee dissatisfaction as expressed in large numbers of grievances, excessive turnover, and unacceptable levels of disciplinary problems

4. patient complaints about service
5. inability of your department to function within prescribed budgetary restraints
6. poor morale level
7. union activity, either expressed in new drives toward collective employee action or increased drives in already organized institutions
8. development of new policies or contractual agreements that must be communicated, understood, and implemented by supervisory groups
9. ineffective supervisory techniques

Programs must be developed on the basis of information that should indicate the desired areas of concentration. As a supervisor you are responsible for identifying those areas. You should assemble a reliable roster of actual skills and clearly indicate where there is a difference between potential skills and actual skills.

In assessing training needs you are asking two questions: (1) what don't employees know or do that they should know or do, and (2) what are employees doing that they shouldn't be doing? Defining the essential knowledge, skill, or in some cases attitudes needed by employees is a most important and preliminary step in the design of a training program. The design of such programs can be facilitated further by refining the needs into more precise learning or behavioral objectives. To be useful, behavioral objectives should involve three major elements:

1. *Performance*—What will the learner be able to do?
2. *Conditions*—Under what conditions (if any) should the learner be able to perform?
3. *Criteria*—What is considered acceptable performance?[4]

ON-THE-JOB TRAINING

Most training is done by supervisors and senior employees. This type of one-to-one training is conducted on the job and often informally. There is a perceptible tendency toward training of individuals rather than groups. An increasing proportion of all training done in health care institutions is conducted by supervisors or fellow workers rather than by members of a formal training department. The most successful approach to on-the-job training is the four-step method of instruction: preparation of the trainer, demonstration of the parts of the job, performance by the trainee, and follow up and review.

1. *Preparation of the trainer: setting an atmosphere of receptivity.* This is the most critical phase of the teaching job. Its main thrust is to establish a mood and general attitude in the trainee that will produce a willingness to accept the training that follows. Successful trainers spend more time preparing to train than in actual training. To facilitate properly this section of the basic training pattern, the trainer should have carefully reviewed the trainee's background. Prior training exposure should be ascertained. It is during this first step that the trainee's interest should be aroused. Key suggestions for the successful implementation of this step include establishing an atmosphere of informality, introducing both the trainee and the trainer, personal reviewing of past work assignments to establish a base of departure, and determining the importance of the job and how the trainee will benefit by being exposed to the training program.

   This latter point deserves careful attention. It is the "what's in it for me" syndrome too often underrated by so-called sophisticated trainers. The effectiveness of communicating the worth of the training in the short and long run of the employee's career often has a direct effect on how quickly he or she will learn and, in some cases, whether he or she will learn at all. If training is to be successful, it should be a challenge to the trainee; it should be something that the trainee really wants to do; it should be tied into the trainee's overall career aspirations; and it should be within the normal grasp of the trainee in terms of his or her understanding and ability to absorb the material.

   In review, this first step directs our attention to putting the trainee at ease and getting him or her personally involved and interested in the job, thus establishing a desire to learn.
2. *Demonstration of the parts of the job: tell and show.* Most learning results from seeing, and a lesser amount results from being told. The most effective training, therefore, results from telling and showing. In demonstrating the job, it is most important to plan the presentation in advance. This includes establishing a job breakdown sheet (see Exhibit 8-1). This sheet establishes the important steps and key points in the operation. A step is defined as a logical segment of the operation when something happens to advance the work. Alongside each of these steps, key points are outlined. A key point is anything in a step that might make or break the job or make the work easier to do. The trainer may pass over key points that he or she takes for granted. A job breakdown sheet can minimize such problems. Too often the

Exhibit 8-1 Job Breakdown Sheet for Training an Employee on a New Job

Operation ....Filling carton........

IMPORTANT STEPS IN THE OPERATION	KEY POINTS
Step: A logical segment of the operation when something happens to ADVANCE the work.	Key Point: Anything in a step that might make or break the job; injure the worker; make the work easier to do, i.e., "knack," "trick," special timing, or bit of special information.
Take carton from rack	Keep 4-section cover flaps well bent back.
Grasp six boxes at a time from drop feed.	
Place boxes in carton and repeat until filled.	
Insert instruction sheet.	
Insert excelsior packing. Close four-section cover flaps.	Grasp instruction sheet and excelsior at the same time. It saves time and makes sure both are inserted.
Remove full carton from table.	Slide, do not lift full cartons onto removing chute. This preserves strength and prevents accidents.

trainer instructs a trainee in the steps of a job in the order in which they are performed; it may be a great deal easier to break the job down into different segments (not necessarily in order), since some of the steps may be quite easy for the individual to learn while others may be difficult. In demonstrating, it is best to proceed from the known to the unknown and teach the simple first and lead up to the complicated. Too often the trainer thinks of the job in much larger units than can be absorbed by the trainee. The steps must be digestible. It is important to explain each step as it is being demonstrated and to explain why that particular approach is taken.

Tell and show incorporates a willingness on the part of the trainer to answer questions. Therefore, the trainee should be encouraged (by establishing that initial permissive atmosphere) to ask questions at any point in the demonstration.

3. *Performance by the trainee.* This is the first opportunity for the trainee to do the actual job alone. It can be done after all the job's parts are demonstrated or after a single part or a combination of several parts is demonstrated. The trainee should be required to explain what he or she will be doing before he or she does it. Do not permit the trainee to learn by error. If in his or her explanation he or she appears to be taking an improper approach to the job, he or she should be stopped, reinstructed on the procedure, and then permitted to perform. When the trainee performs, he or she should outline the key points. After successfully performing the job, he or she should be permitted to continue without interruption unless errors are obvious. Learning by repetition is a most important element of on-the-job training. As the trainee performs more efficiently, less and less time is needed in supervision.
4. *Follow up and review.* A formal program should be developed to check on the trainee's progress. The trainer should return at intervals to establish the effectiveness of the training. He or she must determine what additional training is needed to reinforce the trainee. The trainee should always be encouraged to call for help. Coaching is an integral part of this step and should be available as needed.

A modification of on-the-job training is the vestibule approach to instruction of employees. This self-contained vestibule training center is separated from the actual work area and simulates actual on-the-job working conditions. It offers the advantage of less pressure and remedies a common disadvantage to normal on-the-job training: the supervisor's impatience with trainees based on day-to-day needs in the work area. On-the-job training is often ineffective because of the pressures and needs of the daily operation. The vestibule approach minimizes such pressures.

CONFERENCES

Without a doubt the most widely used method of training in health care institutions is the conference. This method offers the participants the unusual opportunity to contribute ideas, exchange experiences, and solve problems by means of pooled judgment. Through peer pressure, participants often rethink previously untouchable positions within the context of the group. The essence of the conference is the drawing together of employees with various skills, experiences, and responsibilities so that group members can learn from each other rather than from a trainer. The success of the conference is largely dependent on the conference group's composition and the skill of the conference leader.

Who Shall Attend?

There are two basic methods in grouping employees at conferences. In one instance the group may be a homogeneous one. The participants come from the same area of operations in the institution but are at different levels of responsibility. For example, a conference of this composition (vertical grouping) in the nursing department includes participants at the head nurse level, supervisor level, and assistant director of nursing level. All group members are familiar with the operation of their department since they are all members of the same department.

A second method may offer a heterogeneous grouping (horizontal method). Here, although all the participants are in a similar level of authority in the organization, they come from different disciplines. A department head conference under this latter method would include the head of food service, the head of building service, the director of nursing, and so forth. The advantage of this horizontal grouping over the vertical grouping is the opportunities to exchange ideas from various vantage points in the institution and the absence of restraint inherent in a grouping that brings together superiors and subordinates.

Another key consideration is the size of the group. Too large a group (more than 20 people) does not afford all members the maximum opportunity to participate. Very often within the setting of a large conference, small numbers of participants dominate the group. The ideal number is somewhere between 12 and 15 people, although a skilled conference leader can deal with larger numbers.

Still another consideration is the time and setting of the meeting. In the health care institution pressures are diffuse, and the order of the day too often is crisis-oriented. Careful selection of dates, times, and places of conferences is necessary to minimize apprehension and interruption. Although it may at times be frustrating and, indeed, difficult to arrive at a consensus, it is advisable to survey the members of the group to establish the best day of the week, the best time of the day, and the best place for the conference to be held.

The Conference Leader

The ideal conference leader knows the topic, has planned the conference completely, and is fully aware of its goals. It is his or her responsibility to introduce the topic and to motivate the participants to obtain maximum input. He or she must keep the discussion moving and yet, to be effective, must be unobtrusive. His or her key roles are to keep the group on track, to summarize any conclusions that develop, and, of course, to strive to reach the goal or goals of the conference. The experienced conference leader must be able to deal with the overactive conferee who dominates the meeting. Conversely, he or she must encourage the timid participants to obtain balanced contributions from the group. Black and Ford suggest a checklist for effective conference management.

1. Make certain that the subject is worthy of a meeting.
2. Plan carefully.
3. Work out a plan of action.
4. Inspect the meeting room.
5. Know the participants.
6. Review your responsibilities.
7. Don't forget follow up.[5]

Too often conferences are called to discuss matters that can be handled in a more expeditious manner. Remember that time is valuable and that conferences "for conference sake only" are wasteful. Planning the agenda is essential to the success of the conference, and a timetable is helpful. In working out the plan of action, it is important to minimize time-consuming activities and to assemble and provide facts to establish a sound frame of reference for the conference. The meeting room should be large enough to hold the group, be well ventilated, and have appropriate training aids such as blackboards, charts, and pads. A U-shaped table is most suitable for conferences.

To get the meeting off to a good start, the conference leader must initially define the problem or problems precisely and clearly. He or she should be directing the conference to a consensus and should know the appropriate time to end the meeting. The follow-up procedure includes distribution of any summary of findings and careful attention to "for action" matters.

LECTURES

Where time is a factor and large numbers of trainees are involved, the lecture is often the preferred method for disseminating information and communicating new methods and policies. This is basically a "telling" method; the trainer or lecturer presents material in an authoritative manner. Interruptions are limited, and participation, unfortunately, is minimized. Often the lecture is an integral part of other methods such as the conference, role-playing, or even sensitivity training. By having facts presented in this fashion, the trainee or listener has time to digest them and to draw his or her own conclusions after the session. Although this method requires less preparation than any other method, there are some key considerations in maximizing the effect of lectures.

1. Set the goals and desired action in advance of the lecture. Keep them constantly in the forefront, build gradually toward full exploration of the problem, and direct the audience's attention to the goals.
2. Understand the group and consider the audience's needs. This is a difficult aspect of the presentation, since many groups are heterogeneous in make up.
3. Although notes are extremely important, actual reading of them should be limited. Move around as much as possible without affecting the ability of the audience to hear your presentation.
4. Opening remarks should be carefully planned to maximize listeners' interest and arouse their receptivity.
5. Use visual aids where possible. Intersperse reading of material with direct eye focus on parts of the audience, and make use of selected visual aids. In using such visual aids, limit the time during which the speaker's back is to the audience.
6. Prevent boredom by varying the tone and method of presentation; use handouts, blackboard, and, where possible, participants.

The chief disadvantage of the lecture is that trainee participation is minimized and, therefore, maintaining interest is difficult. This can be overcome by using more than one speaker, perhaps a panel of speakers. In addition, question-and-answer periods help to bridge the gap between the one-way communication of the lecture and the needed two-way exchange for effecting change.

MEASURES OF TRAINING EFFECTIVENESS

Nash offers excellent guidance about how to conduct effective training. He calls it the "ten commandments" for putting on a good training program.

1. Focus on behavior, not on the personality.
2. Train for results, not for the process.
3. Relate training to its context.
4. Remember that not all problems are training problems.
5. Have criteria and training objectives.
6. Match the techniques to the training need.
7. Break up the total training into successive stages.
8. Require that the learner produce some action during the training.
9. Give the trainee feedback, and make it fast, specific, and positive.
10. Measure training against goals.[6]

Some of the critical issues in determining the effectiveness of training include whether the training actually prepared the trainee to perform on the job and whether such training had a direct relationship to the institution's goals. Stark offers us an excellent three-way evaluation of training programs (see Table 8-1).[7]

LEARNING THEORY AND RESEARCH

Schneier offers us some principles and findings from learning theory and research.

1. Objectives and success criteria for the learning program should be specified and communicated to all learners before the program begins.
2. Tasks should be broken up into component behaviors that could be learned directly. The behaviors should be sequenced in order of increasing difficulty toward a final target behavior.
3. To measure learning, note observational changes in the frequencies of desired behavioral responses, not necessarily in the strength of responses, in intentions, or in attitudes. Baseline frequencies of behavior must, therefore, be established before the learning situation so that you can note the differential effects of learning.

Table 8-1 Three-Way Evaluation of a Training Program

Trainee	*Instructor*	*Management*
Reaction: How well was the program liked? How effective was the instructor?	Readiness of trainee for instruction in terms of background and experience.	Improvement in on-the-job performance that resulted.
Learning: What changes occurred in knowledges, skills, or abilities?	Extent of trainee's motivation and interest.	Degree of endorsement and support by supervision after trainee returned to job.
Behavior: How can concepts be applied? How may behavior have been influenced?	How content related to real-life problems. Extent of participation.	Whether the training program was worth the investment.
Results: Were the expectations satisfied and the objectives achieved?	Degree of application on the job.	Need for changes in organization, policy, compensation, or conditions.
Commitment: Will the new knowledges, skills, or abilities be applied?	Success or failure of follow up. Changes in program or instructions.	Need for additional training. How training program was planned and executed.

Source: Reprinted, by permission of the publisher, from "Conducting Training Programs" by Alexander T. Stark in *Human Resources Management and Development Handbook* by William R. Tracey (Ed.), p. 1423, © 1985 AMACOM, a division of American Management Association, New York. All rights reserved.

4. "Whole" presentation is usually better than "part" presentation; it gives the learner an initial sense of the total task.
5. Learning can and does take place in every context, not only in specified locations and informal programs. Undesirable and desirable behavior learned in these "informal" settings should be noted.[8]

Schneier goes on to indicate that people not only learn at different rates but that each person brings a different emotional state or temperament to a learning situation. It is, therefore, necessary to make an assessment of the temperament of the trainees. It should be understood that each trainee's prior conditioning or learning background will influence the amount, frequency, and type of reinforcement and punishment that is most effective as well as the method of the presentation. Schneier describes a series of processes in the human learning activity.

1. Interest and attention come from successful experiences, which in turn facilitate learning.
2. Attention and curiosity in learning are best facilitated by the use of moderate (not too high, not too low) levels of arousal, curiosity, or anxiety.
3. Learning can occur when a learner merely observes. Active participation is not always necessary unless motor skills are being taught.
4. Learners should not leave the learning setting after giving incorrect responses. Final responses should always be correct.
5. There are several ways to learn: trial and error, perception-organization-insight, and modeling other's behaviors. All are effective under certain conditions.
6. Learning usually progresses to a point, then levels off. This leveling (a "plateau" in a "learning curve") may be due to the fact that incorrect responses are being reduced or that small, simple steps in learning were learned rapidly and, now that the small steps are combined into complex tasks, learning slows. Incentives added at the "plateau" stage are helpful.
7. If motor responses are to be learned, verbal guidance, practice, and a favorable, supportive environment are helpful. If ideas or concepts are to be learned, active participation and the formation of meaningful associations between the new material and more familiar material are helpful.
8. Learning can be inhibited and proper responses decreased if too much repetition or fatigue is evidenced.
9. Avoidance learning occurs when fear is felt and a response is made to eliminate the fear. This fear (avoiding response) is often reinforced and has little chance of being eliminated because it is needed to avoid aversive stimuli. To eliminate avoidance behaviors the aversive stimulus must be removed.
10. Incidental learning is learning that remains dormant until the occasion for its demonstration arises (for example, when curiosity is stimulated or reinforcement is powerful enough to elicit a response).
11. Imitation requires that the learner be directly reinforced from a matching model's behavior. "Matched dependence" occurs when the learner imitates a model. "Same behavior" occurs when two learners respond to the same stimulus, not to each other. Vicarious learning is matching the behavior of a model without receiving direct or immediate reinforcement from the model.
12. Complex human learning includes a proper degree of discrimination and generalization. Discrimination is distinguishing between

quite similar stimuli that require different responses. Generalization is noting that similar but not exactly the same stimuli often require the same response.

13. Attitudes can be learned and reinforced in much the same way that behavior is reinforced.[9]

KEY POINTS TO THE SUPERVISOR'S ROLE IN TRAINING

1. Employees who are taught the right and efficient way to do a job will produce less waste and be involved in fewer accidents.
2. The supervisor's interest in training of employees derives from the fact that poorly trained employees have higher rates of absenteeism, tardiness, and turnover.
3. It is important for you to wait for a competently trained employee; don't rush the process, and don't accept a lower level of training because it will result in a lower level of performance.
4. A key part of training is the preparation of the trainee. This includes putting the trainee at ease and getting him or her personally involved and interested in the job.
5. Remember the three basic objectives in any training program:
   - the acquisition of knowledge
   - the development of skills
   - the development or modification of attitudes
6. The supervisor's role in developing training programs is that of identifying needs. You must point out what employees know and do not know and what they *should* know and do. You must also identify what employees are doing that they should not be doing.
7. It is the supervisor's responsibility to define what is considered acceptable performance.
8. Real education should not only be designed to improve competence on the job but should be directed to developing competence beyond the job now held.
9. The supervisor plays a critical role in the updating of training programs and employee skills.

NOTES

1. Blieck von Bleicken, *Employee Training Notebook* (Philadelphia: Chilton Company, 1953), 13.

2. George S. Odiorne, *Personnel Policy: Issues and Practices* (Columbus, OH: Charles E. Merrill, 1963), 244.

3. Kendrith M. Roland and Gerald R. Ferris, *Personnel Management* (Boston, MA: Allyn & Bacon, 1982), 310-13.

4. Henry C. LaParo, "Training," in *Handbook of Health Care Human Resources Management,* ed. Norman Metzger (Rockville, MD: Aspen Publishers, 1981), 281.

5. James M. Black and Guy B. Ford, *Front-Line Management* (New York: McGraw-Hill, 1963), 135-38.

6. Michael Nash, *Making People Productive* (San Francisco: Jossey-Bass Publishers, 1985), 86-87.

7. Alexander T. Stark, *"Conducting Training Programs,"* in *Human Resources Management and Development Handbook,* ed. William R. Tracey (New York: AMACOM Division of American Management Associations, 1985), 1423.

8. Craig Eric Schneier, "Training and Development Programs: What Learning Theory and Research Have to Offer," in *Personnel Administration Today: Readings and Commentary,* eds. Craig Eric Schneier and Richard W. Beatty (Reading, MA: Addison-Wesley, 1978), 327-33.

9. Ibid., 328-29.

Chapter 9

The Supervisor's Role in the Disciplinary Process: Progressive Disciplining

Only children and immature adults believe that life is a contest of strength, a win-or-lose situation. The battleground of health care management is strewn with the cadavers of managers who constantly practiced adversarial techniques to obtain cooperation. One does not mandate cooperation by punishing, by threatening, or by legislating.

Lawrence C. Bassett and Norman Metzger
Achieving Excellence: A Prescription for Health Care Managers
(Rockville, MD: Aspen Publishers, Inc. 1986) p. 76

As a supervisor, you are dealing with a complex new breed of employees who are far more assertive, far more knowledgeable about their rights, and far more certain about what they will do and what they won't do than employees of the past. They tolerate less, they trust less, and they seem to want more. The big stick of punishment does not work when dealing with this new breed. The goal of positive discipline is to salvage the employee and to correct the behavioral pattern that is either antisocial or anti-institution.

Some years ago Yankelovich stated that in a study he had conducted an overwhelming 84 percent of all Americans expressed resentment over their impression that those who work harder and live by the rules end up on the short end of the stick.[1] The real challenge to managers is to turn this cynicism around. This cannot be done by the use of the old punishment tools.

TAKING INVENTORY OF YOUR PRESENT VIEW OF DISCIPLINE

What is your present view of discipline? Here is a set of statements your response to which will give you a clear picture of where you stand.

1. My role is to get employees to toe the line.
2. Most employees are trying to "beat the game."
3. Most employees are shirkers.
4. A major part of my role is acting as a policeman.
5. Often I find it easier to turn my back on poor performance than to meet the problem head on.
6. Realistically it is better to accept employees' poor attendance and lateness records than to face up to the reality that I may have to discipline them or terminate them (or both).
7. I will more often than not accept surface explanations for misbehavior rather than delve into an employee's hidden agenda.
8. I am a blood-and-guts supervisor: I believe that discipline should be strict and severe.

If most of your responses are positive, the only comfort you can take is that you are in the mainstream of leadership styles in our country. What you believe is similar to the beliefs of most Theory X managers.[2] Such supervisors start from the premise that employees are basically lazy, indolent, need to be led, need to be carefully monitored, and—of course it follows—need to be punished for their transgressions. Very often this turns out to be a self-fulfilling prophecy.

TWO CASE STUDIES: INEFFECTIVE-EFFECTIVE DISCIPLINARY ACTION

"You just can't fire anyone here. The union won't permit it." A physician at a large medical center voiced this complaint to the personnel director. The physician referred to the "good old days" when the hospital was run by the doctors and administrators. Now she felt that it was run by the union.

The physician was talking specifically about an employee in her department whom she felt was "beyond redemption." Since she had concluded that she could not terminate him, she offered a proposal to the personnel director that in effect would "neutralize" the unsatisfactory employee. Instead of releasing him, she was going to keep him in drydock.

Earlier that day a hearing had been held in the personnel director's office in which the union appealed the termination of another of its members, who also happened to be a union delegate. The hearing lasted almost two hours. At the conclusion the termination was upheld, and the union concurred in this decision. But didn't that physician say that you couldn't fire anyone? Wherein lies the difference?

In the first case, a look at the employee's folder revealed no warning notices, no negative performance evaluations, and no record of unsatisfactory performance. The physician who headed the department asserted loudly and clearly that the employee was inefficient, often late, often absent, surly, and insubordinate. Yet not a line of documentation existed to support these accusations. There was no indication of counseling and no indication of any attempt to redirect the employee's poor work record to an acceptable one.

In the case of the union delegate, who had been with the institution for 3 years, the personnel folder contained several warning notices, a notice of suspension, and a final warning notice. In addition, the performance evaluation reflected specific problems that had been clearly enumerated, with dates, regarding attendance, punctuality, and attitude.

The supervisor who said "You can't fire anyone here" was pronouncing a self-fulfilling prophecy. Believing this notion, she documented nothing. She was guilty of the cardinal sin in employee discipline: offering innocuous performance evaluations to escape the unpleasantness of that "chore." Many hospital supervisors will not admit their unwillingness to take the time or effort to discipline and to face the unpleasant tasks of counseling, issuing warning notices, and confronting the employee in a hearing that could result in a suspension or discharge or to a change to a more positive pattern of behavior.

The truth of the matter is that the doctor was right. She was not able to fire anyone for a capricious or arbitrary reason or where just cause could not be established. For other than clearly overt acts of insubordination, refusal to follow a direct order, or acts that endanger or compromise good patient care, the supervisor has the responsibility of documenting his or her case. This in no way means that the supervisor is unable to act; it simply means he or she must show that the employee was fully cognizant of the problems and that a pattern of warnings was used to denote progressive disciplining.

GOOD AND JUST CAUSE[3]

A number of years ago in a widely quoted case an arbitrator enunciated tests that could be used to learn whether an employer had just and proper cause for disciplining an employee.[4] Since most collective bargaining agreements do not explain or define the term "just cause," which is often used in such contracts, the arbitrator listed serious questions that had been developed from other arbitrators' decisions over the years and could serve as criteria for determining just cause.

'Just Cause' Criteria

These questions were:

1. Did the company give to the employee forewarning or foreknowledge of the possible or probable disciplinary consequences of the employee's conduct?

   Note 1: Said forewarning or foreknowledge may properly have been given orally by management or in writing through the medium of typed or printed sheets or books of shop rules and of penalties for violation thereof.

   Note 2: There must have been actual oral or written communication of rules and penalties to the employee.

   Note 3: A finding of lack of such communication does not in all cases require a "no" answer to Question #1. This is because certain offenses such as insubordination, coming to work intoxicated, drinking intoxicating beverages on the job, or theft of the property of the company or of fellow employees are so serious that any employee in the industrial society may properly be expected to know already that such conduct is offensive and heavily punishable.

   Note 4: Absent any contractual prohibition or restriction, the company has the right unilaterally to promulgate reasonable rules and give reasonable orders, and same need not have been negotiated with the union.

2. Was the company's rule or managerial order reasonably related to (a) the orderly, efficient, and safe operation of the company's business and (b) the performance that the company might properly expect of the employee?

   Note: If an employee believes that said rule or order is unreasonable, he or she must nevertheless obey same (in which case he or she may file a grievance thereover) unless the employee sincerely feels that to obey the rule or order would seriously and immediately jeopardize his or her personal safety and/or integrity. Given a firm finding to the latter effect, the employee may properly be said to have had justification for his or her disobedience.

3. Did the company, before administering discipline to an employee, make an effort to discover whether the employee did in fact violate or disobey a rule or order of management?
   Note 1: This is the employee's "day in court" principle. An employee has the right to know with reasonable precision the offense with which he or she is being charged and to defend his or her behavior.
   Note 2: The company's investigation must normally be made before its disciplinary decision is made. If the company fails to do so, its failure may not normally be excused on the grounds that the employee will get his or her day in court through the grievance procedure after the exaction of discipline. By that time there has usually been too much hardening of position. In a very real sense the company is obligated to conduct itself like a trial court.
   Note 3: There may of course be circumstances under which management must react immediately to the employee's behavior. In such cases the normally proper action is to suspend the employee pending investigation, with the understanding that (a) the final disciplinary decision will be made after the investigation and (b) if the employee is found innocent after the investigation he or she will be restored to the job with full pay for time lost.
   Note 4: The company's investigation should include an inquiry into possible justification for the employee's alleged rule violation.
4. Was the company's investigation conducted fairly and objectively?
   Note 1: At said investigation the management official may be both "prosecutor" and "judge," but he or she may not also be a witness against the employee.
   Note 2: It is essential for some higher, detached management official to assume and conscientiously perform the judicial role, giving the commonly accepted meaning to that term in his or her attitude and conduct.
   Note 3: In some disputes between an employee and a management person there are no witnesses to an incident other than the two immediate participants. In such cases it is particularly important that the management "judge" question the management participant rigorously and thoroughly just as an actual third party would.
5. At the investigation did the "judge" obtain substantial evidence or proof that the employee was guilty as charged?

Note 1: It is not required that the evidence be conclusive or "beyond all reasonable doubt." But the evidence must be truly substantial and not flimsy.

Note 2: The management "judge" should actively search out witnesses and evidence, not just passively take what participants or "volunteer" witnesses tell him or her.

Note 3: When the testimony of opposing witnesses at the arbitration hearing is irreconcilably in conflict, an arbitrator seldom has any means for resolving the contradictions. His or her task is then to determine whether the management "judge" originally had reasonable grounds for believing the evidence presented to the "judge" by his or her own people.

6. Has the company applied its rules, orders and penalties even handedly and without discrimination to all employees?

   Note 1: A "no" answer to this question requires a finding of discrimination and warrants negation or modification of the discipline imposed.

   Note 2: If the company has been lax in enforcing its rules and orders and decides henceforth to apply them rigorously, the company may avoid a finding of discrimination by telling all employees beforehand of its intent to enforce hereafter all rules as written.

7. Was the degree of discipline administered by the company in a particular case reasonably related to (a) the seriousness of the employee's proven offense and (b) the record of the employee in his or her service with the company?

   Note 1: A trivial proven offense does not merit harsh discipline unless the employee has properly been found guilty of the same or other offenses a number of times in the past. (There is no rule as to what number of previous offenses constitutes a "good," a "fair," or a "bad" record. Reasonable judgment thereon must be used.)

   Note 2: An employee's record of previous offenses may never be used to discover whether he or she was guilty of the immediate or latest one. The only proper use of his or her record is to help determine the severity of discipline once he or she has properly been found guilty of the immediate offense.

   Note 3: Given the same proven offense for two or more employees, their respective records provide the only proper basis for "discriminating" among them in the administration of discipline for said offense. Thus, if employee A's record is significantly better than those of employees B, C, and D, the company may properly give A a lighter punishment than it gives the others for the same offense, and this does not constitute true discrimination.

Note 4: Suppose that the record of the arbitration hearing establishes firm "yes" answers to all the first six questions. Suppose further that the proven offense of the accused employee was a serious one, such as drunkenness on the job; but the employee's record had been previously unblemished over a long, continuous period of employment with the company. Should the company be held arbitrary and unreasonable if it decided to discharge an employee? The answer depends of course on all the circumstances. But, as one of the country's oldest arbitration agencies, the National Railroad Adjustment Board has pointed out repeatedly in innumerable decisions on discharge cases, leniency is the prerogative of the employer rather than of the arbitrator; and the latter is not supposed to substitute his or her judgment in this area for that of the company unless there is compelling evidence that the company abused its discretion. This is the rule, even though an arbitrator, if he or she had been the original "trial judge," might have imposed a lesser penalty. Actually the arbitrator may be said in an important sense to act as an appellate tribunal whose function is to discover whether the decision of the trial tribunal (the employer) was within the bounds of reasonableness above set forth—in general, the penalty of dismissal for a really serious first offense does not in itself warrant a finding of company unreasonableness.[5]

The burden of providing good and just cause for discipline rests on administration. If cause has been proved, a penalty imposed by the administration will not be modified by an arbitrator unless it is shown to have been clearly arbitrary, capricious, discriminatory, or excessive in relation to the offense. The key point to understand about limitation on the right to discipline is that administration may discipline up through discharge only for sufficient and appropriate reasons.

It behooves the administration to develop a sound procedure, based on due process, for the discipline of unionized employees. Even if it is not mandated by a collective bargaining agreement, due process should be available to all employees. Arbitrators will normally support a management action if progressive discipline includes first a verbal reprimand and full explanation of what is necessary to remedy the situation and then a written reprimand for a second infraction and a clear warning of the future penalties that may be imposed. A final warning and suspension may follow, and the ultimate penalty of discharge may be subsequent.

The arbitrator will also consider whether or not the employee was fully aware of the standards against which his or her behavior was measured. These standards include basic rules and regulations that outline offenses that subject employees to disciplinary action and outline the extent of such disciplinary action. Exhibit 9-1 presents a checklist of questions and standards that the supervisor can address in determining whether to take corrective action.

Disciplining has become more juristic and legalistic with the advent of a union, but that does not mean that it is impossible to discipline employees. It does mean that the administration must record actual events, offenses, and transgressions. You cannot simply wish away problem employees.

Justin, a prominent labor arbitrator, lists some noteworthy rules of corrective discipline.

1. To be meaningful, discipline must be corrective, not punitive.
2. When you discipline one, you discipline all.
3. Corrective discipline satisfies the rule of equality of treatment by enforcing equally among all employees established rules, safety practices, and responsibility on the job.
4. It is the job of the supervisor, not the shop steward, to make the worker toe the line or increase efficiency.
5. Just cause or any other comparable standard for justifying disciplinary action under the labor contract consists of three parts:
   - Did the employee breach the rule or commit the offense charged against him or her?
   - Did the employee's act or misconduct warrant corrective action or punishment?
   - Is the penalty just and appropriate to the act of offense as corrective punishment?
6. The burden of proof rests on the supervisor. He or she must justify each of the three parts that make up the standard of just cause under the labor contract.[6]

FORMS OF DISCIPLINE[7]

The Oral Reprimand

Progressive disciplining usually starts with oral reprimands or warnings. This function often is handled in a counseling session. What is the

Exhibit 9-1 Checklist for Corrective Action

What is the past record of the employee?	Was the employee disciplined previously for the same type of offense? When? Should he or she receive a more severe penalty than a first offender?
Have you all the facts?	Refer to personnel records. Get concrete facts about this specific situation; refer to rules, standards, and policies; evaluate opinions and feelings. Was there an extenuating reason for the employee's behavior? (Sickness, money trouble, etc.)
Has the employee had a fair chance to improve? When?	Has he or she been given some help, advice, or explanation? Does he or she know what is expected? Did he or she know the rules and standards at the time of the infraction?
When was the employee first given a fair warning of the seriousness of his or her behavior?	Was a written record made and filed? Who gave the warning?
What action was taken in similar cases?	Are there others in your department who experienced different treatment under similar circumstances? In other departments?
What will be the effect of your action on the group?	Are you fully justified? What will be the effect on groups outside your department?
Are you going to handle this by yourself?	Should you clear with your boss or with the personnel director? Do you need assistance or further information? How is your timing?
What other possible actions are there?	Will your action help the hospital, help improve the work output in your department, and help the employee to improve? Should he or she be warned or suspended?

Source: Checklist developed by Dr. Leslie M. Slote.

purpose of the action? It should be to nip in the bud behavior that is inappropriate to the work area. The necessary ingredients for a successful counseling encounter are complete privacy, a well-planned agenda, enough time to arrive at agreement, and a positive attitude on the part of the supervisor.

In such sessions employees should receive a complete outline of the action in question. Details should not be spared, and dates, times, and places should be communicated. The specific institution policy or rule in question should be enunciated. The specific documents (such as a union contract or a personnel policy manual) containing such rules should be examined. The employee should be given complete freedom to answer the charge, explain the behavior, and admit or deny the action.

It is obvious that an effective counseling session will develop from the point at which the employee agrees that the action occurred and was inappropriate. If such an agreement is reached, a plan to improve performance should be discussed. It also is important at this time to acknowledge the positive aspects of the employee's behavior.

After the counseling session has been completed, anecdotal notes should be prepared by the supervisor and placed in the department file. It is not appropriate at this point to forward such notes to the personnel department for inclusion in the employee's folder.

A supervisor who wishes to effect corrective disciplining should be more interested in changing behavioral patterns and attitudes than in reprimanding the employee. Lateiner, a widely recognized authority on supervisory techniques, offers some pointers to the supervisor interested in making criticism more constructive.

1. Don't reprimand a worker who is angry or excited. Wait until he or she has cooled down. Wait until you cool down, too.
2. Don't bawl out someone in front of other people. This is embarrassing and humiliating and is likely to do more harm than good.
3. Find out how the worker feels and thinks about the situation. If you want someone to do something differently, you first have to find out what he or she already knows.
4. When you criticize a person, it is much better to compare his or her performance to department standards than to the performance of another employee. A person is more likely to feel resentful or insecure if he or she is compared unfavorably to a co-worker.
5. Most important, if you are to reprimand constructively you must show a person how to improve his or her performance. You don't want to destroy an employee's self-confidence. You want to build up

> confidence by guiding the worker in the direction of a satisfactory performance.[8]

The oral reprimand or warning interview is a useful way for the supervisor to establish a sound relationship with all employees, both those who require such warnings and those who do not. Employees normally respect supervisors who apply the rules of the institution fairly. Although criticism can be a disturbing element, the need for constructive criticism can be fully appreciated by employees.

If the supervisor is to discipline firmly and wisely, it is essential that the employee relations administrator or personnel director be fully supportive in instances in which institutional policy is being protected and carried out. It is equally important that the department head or director of the institution provide clear evidence that the supervisor will be backed up at crucial moments. This does not mean that there will never be a situation where the supervisor is overruled, but such incidences should not be based on political pressures, legal technicalities, or sentimentality. The responsibility of meting out discipline is difficult enough without undercutting the first-line supervisor.

It should be made clear that the oral reprimand or warning is not appropriate or effective in the face of flagrant offenses such as insubordination, theft, fighting, or carrying firearms. Such actions call for sharper responses, often termination.

The Warning Notice

Overt flaunting of institutional rules and appropriate behavior patterns is dealt with by the first-line supervisor through a formal warning notice, suspension, or discharge if, and only after, a formal warning interview has been held (this proscription does not apply if the transgression is a major and flagrant one, such as one of those mentioned under exceptions to the oral reprimand). Some examples of negative behavior that may call for a written warning notice are:

1. insubordination or impertinence
2. unauthorized or chronic absenteeism
3. chronic lateness
4. loafing or sleeping on the job
5. misrepresentation of timecards or records
6. drinking alcoholic beverages on the job
7. dishonesty

8. fighting on the job
9. gambling

The warning notice should not come as a surprise to the employee. It is essentially the second step in the arsenal of weapons for reversing a poor behavioral pattern. It can be preceded by the oral reprimand but may directly follow a clear violation of institutional rules and regulations. In preparing the warning notice, the supervisor again is concerned with facts and not with subjective opinions.

The institution normally provides a form to be used for written warning notices. This form calls for a clear statement of the specific rule or policy that has been violated. The supervisor may have to refer to the union contract, the personnel policy manual, or a written bulletin containing the specific rule. After this reference point, the written warning notice should describe the act in question. Once again the supervisor must be specific and complete. Dates, time, and, where appropriate, witnesses should be included.

The most important part of the warning notice is a statement to indicate that immediate satisfactory improvement must be shown and maintained unless further disciplinary action is to be taken. In many cases, this immediate satisfactory improvement can be outlined in detail. For example, an employee has shown a pattern of absenteeism—say three days each month for the last six months (many of the days were Mondays, making three-day weekends possible). The supervisor indicates that the employee's pattern of Monday absences is not acceptable, that attendance will be monitored over the next two, three, or four months to gauge improvement, and that if there is no improvement the individual will be subject to suspension and possible termination.

The warning notice is presented to the employee in private; if possible, the employee should be asked to sign it, acknowledging receipt. More important than acceptance of the warning form is the employee's acknowledgment that the behavior is inappropriate and that improvement must be forthcoming. In some cases—more often than not where unions are involved—employees refuse to sign warning notice forms. This should be expected and understood, but the supervisor's responsibility does not end here. The supervisor, to emphasize the importance of the action and ensure the "legality" of the presentation, should ask another supervisor to witness the actual reading and offer of a copy of the warning notice to the employee. This is necessary only if the employee refuses to sign the form. Despite all this, it is important to remember that the supervisor's cardinal responsibility in this procedure is to attempt a restructuring of the employee's behavior; the primary responsibility or objective is not to punish the individual.

One bit of advice is necessary before exploring the final two steps in the disciplinary arsenal of weapons; suspension and termination. There is no panacea that can be offered for behavior control. In a few cases, oral reprimands or warning notices will never be enough. In still more cases, suspensions may be counterproductive. The supervisor must keep in mind that constructive disciplining is a means of achieving the end product: a change in behavior patterns.

Suspension

Suspension is not universally accepted as an effective way to correct behavior patterns. Many employees find suspension a respite from the stress of the work area. Some even enjoy being out on strike. For an employee with a chronic absentee record, a suspension certainly is not the most effective sort of punishment.

A one-day suspension can be as effective as a one-week one. The shock of the penalty usually brings employees to their senses. The length of the suspension has little effect on the probability of rehabilitation. The action can cause inordinate difficulties in scheduling and in meeting production quotas. A one- or two-day suspension is often a sufficient final warning to employees before termination. The penalty should be accompanied by a written warning notice indicating prior attempts, both formal and informal, toward rehabilitation. Most important, the suspension should indicate that it constitutes the final warning.

Termination

In sustaining a discharge where an arbitration procedure is available, the following minimal requirements must be met; in fact, they should be operative whether or not there is an arbitration procedure and whether or not there is a union.

1. Facts clearly indicating that the employee actually committed the offense must be presented. Opinion must be separated from hard documentation. Witnesses may be essential.
2. The supervisor must be able to display a consistent approach to the offense in question; there must be no playing of favorites.

3. The record should indicate a progressive disciplining ladder, except in the case of blatant and serious offenses.
4. The punishment must fit the crime.

Progressive disciplining normally must precede the discharge of an employee. The procedure of progressive disciplining as outlined includes a verbal reprimand and a full explanation of what is necessary to remedy the situation. Normally a second infraction calls for a written reprimand with a clear warning of future penalties that may be imposed. A suspension may follow with a final warning, and the ultimate penalty is discharge.

There is a further consideration in cases that involve discharge: consistency. A double standard often is found in health care institutions: one standard for the medical staff and another for the other employees. The supervisor should be aware of the possibility of employee complaints to the union and to outside agencies of disparate treatment of professionals and nonprofessionals.

Arbitrators tell us what is required to sustain a discharge. The following points were enunciated by Friedman, a prominent arbitrator, but many other arbitrators have set up similar criteria for the sustaining of discharges.

1. The employer must prove that the alleged acts occurred and were of sufficient gravity to warrant termination.
2. The employer must show that the misconduct was not condoned and that the employee was specifically warned of the consequences through progressive discipline, such as written warnings and suspension.
3. The evidence must demonstrate that the employee made no genuine effort to heed the warnings even though the consequences of continued misconduct were known.
4. The employee cannot be singled out for disparate treatment for offenses that do not subject others to similar discipline.
5. When a long-service employee is involved, there must be sound cause to believe that the events are not transitory but form a consistent and recurrent pattern that is unlikely to change in the future.

SUSTAINING DISCIPLINARY ACTION IN ARBITRATION[9]

Many disciplinary actions are appealed to outside arbitration, where a neutral third party judges the appropriateness of the action. Below are some of the factors that arbitrators consider in sustaining or overruling management's action.

Absenteeism

1. The length of time in which the employee had a poor attendance record must be noted.
2. The reason for the worker's absence must be stated.
3. The nature of the employee's job must be described.
4. The attendance records of other employees must be included.
5. The fact that the employer has (or does not have) a clear disciplinary policy on absenteeism that is known to all employees and that is applied fairly and consistently must be made clear.
6. The fact that the employee was (or was not) adequately warned that disciplinary action could result if attendance failed to improve must be documented.

Insubordination

1. The supervisor's instructions must be very clear and must be understood by the employee to be an order; the supervisor must clearly state the penalty for failure to comply.
2. Merely protesting an order is not insubordination; refusal to carry it out is.
3. The use of objectional language to supervision often is cause for discipline. Where such language is commonplace in the worker's area, it may not be grounds for discharge.

Misconduct

1. Thefts and other kinds of dishonesty are regarded as causes for discharge. Such a discharge requires convincing proof of the employee's guilt.
2. Fighting on the institution's premises is a dischargeable offense except where the employee is acting in self-defense.
3. Misconduct occurring away from the institution outside of working hours is punishable only if it affects the employment relationship in some way.

Dishonesty

1. Evidence required to support a discharge for dishonesty usually is "proof beyond a reasonable doubt."
2. Falsification of job applications, if not an oversight or a lapse of memory but rather a deliberate act with intent to defraud, is grounds for disciplining.
3. Falsifying institution records regarding work done usually justifies discharge. The employee's action must be deliberate and intended to cheat the institution. This includes punching a co-worker's timecard, improperly punching one's own timecard, falsifying expense accounts, or making false statements to obtain medical or health insurance.
4. Stealing institution property subjects the employee to discharge.

Gambling

1. Discharge normally is too severe a penalty for a first offense of gambling.
2. Discharge is appropriate where the employee is connected with an organized gambling racket.
3. The evidence connecting the employee with gambling must be substantial and convincing.

Intoxication and Alcoholism

Arbitrators usually sustain discharge for drinking or drunkenness in these situations:

1. frequent absenteeism as a result of drinking
2. drinking on the job combined with other misconduct
3. drinking on the job that results in inability to perform the work (but not generally for a first offense)
4. chronic alcoholism with no signs of rehabilitation

A decision to discharge for chronic alcoholism is especially supportable in arbitration if the employer can show that the employee was offered admission to a valid rehabilitation program, whether company run or otherwise, and that the individual either refused to go or attended and dropped out, or failed.

Sleeping and Loafing

1. Discharge for sleeping on the job, with the possible exclusion of a first offense, is sustained as long as there is an institution rule or established practice calling for such termination.
2. Discharge may be sustained in the absence of a specific rule if the sleeping involves any danger to the safety of employees, patients, or equipment.
3. The employer has a heavy burden of proving that the employee was, in fact, sleeping.

Incompetence

1. The charge of incompetence must be properly investigated or substantiated.
2. The employee must be given adequate warning and an opportunity to improve the performance.
3. Other employees with equally poor performance records must be treated in the same manner.*

REASONS FOR DISCIPLINE PROBLEMS

Too often institutions develop rules and policies that run counter to the prevailing customs operative over the years in the workplace. The American Management Associations offer us some critical reasons why disciplinary problems develop in our departments.

1. The rules and regulations are viewed by employees as meaningless. It is important to recognize that there is a great deal of difference between an employee's being told about a rule and learning the "why" behind it.
2. Violations of the rules occur when employees do not fear punishment for their violations. You need to prove by your actions that violators will be disciplined.
3. There are employees who will violate rules because they feel that they are underpaid or perhaps because they feel that management discriminates against them. Inherent in this problem is manage-

---

*Reprinted from *Grievance Guide,* 6th ed., with permission of the Bureau of National Affairs, Inc., © 1982.

ment's failure to make clear exactly what the organization's discipline policy is, why it exists, and what the consequences are when it is violated.
4. Some violations are truly unintentional and reflect a lapse in memory or caution. In this category we find most of the discipline problems as well as the bulk of the safety problems in organizations.[10]

The Bureau of National Affairs conducted a study of many successfully administered policies that revealed the following pattern.

1. Company rules are carefully explained to employees. This is especially important in the case of new employees. Indoctrination courses, employee handbooks, bulletin board notices, and many other forms of bringing rules to the attention of employees are used.
2. Accusations against employees are carefully considered to see if they are supported by facts. Witnesses are interviewed their statements are recorded, and a careful investigation made to see that both sides of the story are available and fairly presented. Circumstantial evidence is kept to a minimum in judging the facts. Personality factors and unfounded assumptions are eliminated.
3. A regular "warning" procedure is worked out and applied. Sometimes all warnings are in writing, with a copy handed to the employee and one filed in the employee's record in the personnel office. Sometimes first warnings are orally delivered, but a written record of the warning is filed away. Warnings are given for all except the most serious offenses (those which management has made clear will call for immediate discharge).
4. Some companies bring the union into the discipline case early in the procedure. Copies of warning notices go to the union. The union is given advance notice of other disciplinary actions which management intends to take. Sometimes the action is held up until the union has time to make its own investigation.
5. Before disciplinary action is taken, the employee's motive and reasons for the violation of rules are investigated. Then the penalty is adjusted to the facts—whether the employee's action was in good faith, partially justified, or totally unjustified.
6. Before disciplinary action is taken, the employee's past record is taken into consideration. A good work record and long seniority are viewed as factors in the employee's favor, particularly where a minor offense is involved or where it is a first offense. Previous offenses are not used against the employee unless he or she was reprimanded at

the time they occurred or warned that they would be used against him or her in any future disciplinary action.

7. Companies make sure that all management agents, particularly first-line supervisors, know the company's disciplinary policies and procedures and carefully observe them. This is particularly important in the case of verbal warnings or informal reprimands.
8. Discipline short of discharge is used wherever possible.*

DISCIPLINING FOR OPTIMUM RESULTS

Much of the debate over appropriate discipline concerns the spirit, extent, or degree of enforcement that brings optimum results. Pfiffner and Fels put this critical question in proper focus.

> Should discipline be strict and severe or tolerant and easy-going? The answer will not be found by locating the optimum point between strict and easy, but rather in the fundamental nature of the social organization which the supervisor must understand as part of his or her disciplining duties. If the basic mores of an organization are developed in a manner that commands the respect and conformance of its members, disciplining should offer no special problem. The rank and file member will observe the mores either automatically or because of the pressures exerted to do so by other members of the group. That is, he probably will if he has a feeling of belonging and thus recognizes that to belong requires a contribution in accordance with his means and talents. Thus, in essence, the supervisor's attempts to discipline must see discipline as a means not of immediately stopping an undesirable behavior only, but of reaching a goal of desirable citizenship.**

KEY POINTS TO EFFECTIVE DISCIPLINING

1. Your primary concern in disciplining employees is to salvage them, not to scrap them.
2. Although punishment is part of disciplinary action, it is not the primary part.

---

*Reprinted from *Grievance Guide*, 6th ed., pp. 4-5, with permission of the Bureau of National Affairs, ©1982

**Reprinted from *The Supervision of Personnel*, 3rd ed., by J.M. Pfiffner and M. Fels, pp. 111-112, with permission of Prentice-Hall, Inc., Englewood Cliffs, N.J.

3. Direct your attention, and therefore your plan of action, toward correcting improper employee actions.
4. Don't play favorites. Be consistent; the rule of equality of treatment should pervade all your disciplinary actions.
5. In the final analysis, you (the supervisor) are responsible for maintaining appropriate employee behavioral patterns and productivity.
6. Whether or not the employees in your department are unionized, just cause must be established for all disciplinary actions.
7. It may sound trite, but the punishment must fit the crime.
8. Progressive disciplining involves oral reprimands (including counseling), written warnings, and suspensions; termination is defensible where the infraction or behavior was serious (theft, fighting, or carrying firearms) or was preceded by the aforementioned steps.
9. Self-discipline develops when employees trust the supervisor and the management, feel that their job is important and appreciated, and feel that they belong.
10. Positive discipline encompasses the following sound supervisory practices.
    - Inform all employees of the rules and the penalties. The "why" of the rule is just as important as the "what."
    - Don't play the game of "Do as I say, not as I do." Set a good example. Employees look to their supervisors for fairness in application of the rules.
    - Don't leap before you look. Get all the facts. Keep uppermost in your mind the old adage that there are always at least two sides to every story.
    - Beware of incomplete facts or appearances. Judge the act within its context. Look for the least obvious motives and reasons.
    - Move quickly but not hastily. Don't let selected instances of misbehavior develop into habits.
    - Corrective discipline should be meted out in private.
    - Objectivity and fairness are two hallmarks of positive, corrective disciplinary action; consistency is a third hallmark.
    - Throughout the disciplinary process, keep your eye on the goal of the process: to correct improper behavior and to salvage the employee.
    - Use punishment as the last resort.[11]

NOTES

1. Daniel Yankelovich, address to the National Conference on Human Resources, Dallas, Texas, 25 October 1978.

2. For a complete discussion of Theory X and Theory Y management styles, see Douglas McGregor, *The Human Side of Enterprise* (New York: McGraw-Hill, 1960).

3. A portion of this section was excerpted from Norman Metzger and Joseph M. Ferentino, *The Arbitration and Grievance Process: A Guide for Health Care Supervisors* (Rockville, MD: Aspen Publishers, 1983), chap. 1 ("How to Discipline"), 3-7.

4. *Enterprise Wire Company (Blue Island, IL) v. Enterprise Union,* 46 L.A.359 (1966).

5. Marvin Hill, Jr. and Anthony V. Sinicropi, *Remedies in Arbitration* (Washington, DC: Bureau of National Affairs, 1981), 283-86.

6. Jules J. Justin, *How to Manage with a Union, Book One* (New York: Industrial Relations Workshop Seminars, 1969), 294-95; 301-302.

7. This section was excerpted from Metzger and Ferentino, *The Arbitration and Grievance Process,* chap. 1 ("How to Discipline"), 9-13.

8. Alfred R. Lateiner, *Modern Techniques of Supervision* (Stamford, CT: Lateiner Publishing, 1968); originally published in Lateiner, *The Technique of Supervision* (New London, CT: National Foreman's Institute, 1954), 28-39.

9. This section was excerpted from Metzger and Ferentino, *The Arbitration and Grievance Process,* chap. 1 ("How to Discipline"), 13-16.

10. "Discipline in the Work Place Today," in *Supervisory Sense* ed. Florence Stone (New York: AMACOM Division of American Management Associations, 1980), 10-11.

11. The author expresses special gratitude to Ms. Rita Hubert, graduate student in the Masters Program for Health Care Administration of the Rensselaer Polytechnic Institute.

Chapter 10

How to Handle Employee Complaints: An Opportunity Rather Than a Chore

> *Any procedure for resolving employee complaints must function in an orderly and timely manner. Its objective must be to attempt to resolve complaints in a way that in the long run facilitates working relationships. The most meaningful measure of any system is employees' perceptions of its overall fairness.*
>
> *Louis V. Imundo*
>
> The Effective Supervisor's Handbook
>
> *(New York: AMACOM, Div. of American Management Associations, 1980) p. 172.*

> On reading the title of this chapter the first thought that will come to some readers is "What about employees' grievances?" It is with specific purpose that the word "grievance" does not appear in the title. This is because no real distinction can be made between a complaint and a grievance. In essence, complaints and grievances are the same.[1]

This was the beginning of a chapter entitled "Resolving Employee Complaints" in *The Effective Supervisor's Handbook,* by Louis V. Imundo. Many so-called grievances are informational in nature, resulting from a lack of communication or a breakdown in communication; for example, an employee misreads a rule, a clause, or a policy. Others result from a discontent with the rule, the clause, or the policy; these are gripes. Whether they are gripes, complaints, or bona fide grievances, they must be addressed.

Arbitrator Herbert Marx wrote:

> The significance of the grievance procedure leading up to the arbitration hearing is often grossly underestimated. The major

> purpose of the grievance procedure is to resolve disputes bilaterally before they get to arbitration. Too often this principle is forgotten or disregarded and the parties use the grievance procedure simply as a means either to expedite the dispute to arbitration, or to get the one party to concede because it does not wish to undergo the risk, inconvenience and expense of arbitration.[2]

The supervisor must be appreciative of and keenly sensitive to the common misuses of the grievance procedure. The real purpose of this procedure, as Marx says, is to resolve disputes bilaterally. Many formal seminars and an equally large number of informal discussions among labor relations practitioners and labor lawyers point out the importance of the role of the supervisor in the adjudication of grievances. The handling of employee grievances affords the supervisor the greatest opportunity to win employee respect and confidence. The most important employer-employee relationship is the one that exists between the worker and his or her immediate supervisor. It is essential for supervisors to know their people, be genuinely interested in them, and recognize their needs and problems. This good relationship can not only head off many grievances before they reach the formal grievance stage but also leads to increased productivity.

The supervisor is often the day-to-day interpreter of institutional policy, rules, and regulations as well as the administrator of the union contract. If there is a Pandora's box in the day-to-day employer-employee relationship, it is the area of grievances. An unattended accumulation of minor irritations may inflate and finally explode in the supervisor's face. A little bit of attention at the beginning will go further than a great deal of harried and pressured attention at the end. As a matter of fact, most complaints can be satisfactorily resolved by the supervisor before they become formal grievances.

Harrison offers us a clear rationale for the grievance procedure.

> One hopes that in the course of the grievance procedure the parties will reach an agreement that disposes of the grievance. To that purpose the grievance procedure allows for review of a dispute by those union and company representatives who should be able to judge a case more objectively than the supervisor and employee(s) immediately involved. Furthermore, the procedure allows both parties time to obtain the facts needed to fully understand the case. Both parties hope that the increased objectivity and information will combine to produce a resolution of the

> dispute. Even if they do not, they should make clear to the parties what their differences are; what exactly each is intending; and upon what evidence their respective cases are based. In short, before going to arbitration the parties should have thoroughly discussed their differences and should clearly understand one another's intentions. There should be no surprises at the arbitration hearing.[3]

To modify one aspect of Harrison's statement: if the supervisor is to discharge his or her responsibilities as a leader and representative of the employees in his or her department, then he or she must maintain an objectivity beyond the emotional issues involved. The grievance procedure, and especially the supervisor's role at the first step, should not be a rubber stamp of inappropriate actions taken by management. It should be a careful review that directs the supervisor's attention to the adjudication of the grievance on the basis of facts and justice.

A grievance may have some basis in fact, or it may be fabricated or exaggerated beyond reality. A grievance may not truly be a grievance as defined in a union contract or under institutional policy. More often than not, it may be a gripe or just information seeking on the part of the employee. In any case it must be dealt with and resolved.

MINIMIZING GRIEVANCES

Although there is no way to eliminate grievances completely, there are common-sense guidelines that will reduce the number and the cost of grievances.

1. Be alert for common causes of irritation within your department. Minimize grievances, although it is obvious that there is no way to eliminate grievances completely. Nevertheless, a supervisor who is alert to the common causes of complaints and dissatisfactions within a department, and who attempts to correct minor irritations promptly before they explode into major problems, can help eliminate unnecessary grievances. The effective supervisor knows the contract and company personnel policies thoroughly and does not knowingly violate the provisions of either document. This, of course, requires that institutions set up training programs directed at reviewing such policies.

2. Keep promises. Do not make commitments you cannot keep. Many grievances involve nonfulfillment of commitments made by supervisors. Before promises are made to employees, supervisors should check whether it is possible to make good on them; indeed, promises that are made should not be forgotten.
3. Let your employees know how they are getting along. Don't wait for the formal performance review to keep an employee informed of progress or problems. This will minimize the number of grievances that develop when employees are warned about poor performance after having received positive performance reviews earlier in the year.
4. If an employee doesn't measure up, let that employee know. Find out why there is a problem and provide direction and coaching. An employee who does not measure up should be counseled regarding the need to meet standards.
5. Encourage constructive suggestions; act on these suggestions where feasible and give proper recognition to the originators. Worker participation in policy changes will go a long way toward minimizing grievances that may develop as a result.
6. Another key area of dissatisfaction arises from perceived or actual favoritism in working conditions or employee benefits. Assign and schedule work; avoid favoritism.
7. Be sure that your employees understand the meaning of and reasons for your orders and instructions. Use language that is meaningful from their point of view.
8. Be consistent in your words and actions unless there are important reasons for deviation. Where deviation is justified, clearly communicate those reasons to the employees. Explain changes in or deviations from policy, procedure, or established practice.
9. Act promptly on reasonable requests from your employees. Don't keep employees waiting for answers to their questions. Nothing is more destructive than a grievance allowed to grow because of a delayed response on the part of the supervisor. Remember that you may have to say "no" but that a constructive and sympathetic "no" may do less damage than a harsh "yes."
10. If corrective action must be taken, take it promptly, but do not discipline an employee in public.

SOURCES OF GRIEVANCES[4]

One large corporation, many years ago, insisted that its personnel forms not contain the word "pregnant" when an employee requested a leave of absence for child-bearing purposes. It insisted on using the word "gravid," which dictionaries define as "pregnant." That word did not change the employee's condition. Pregnant or gravid, the employee was with child. Similarly, grievance procedure or no grievance procedure, institutions have employees with problems that must be resolved.

There are hospital administrators, especially in nonunion environments, who are opposed to formal grievance procedures. They contend that grievance procedures produce grievances. Here again is the ostrich approach to employee relations. Employees must have an avenue of appeal from first-line supervisors' decisions. A large majority of grievances result from a decision made or communicated by the first-line supervisor. Therefore, if a theory of due process is to prevail, it becomes necessary to permit an employee who contests an immediate supervisor's decision to have an avenue of recourse beyond the ruling.

Arbitrators say that they will consider, as an integral part of their decision, whether or not the institution conducted a fair and objective investigation. Such a procedure is inherent in a formal grievance mechanism. As Marx said, the significance of the grievance procedure that leads up to the arbitration hearing is often greatly underestimated.

Some institutions prefer an informal rather than a formal grievance procedure. This approach rarely is effective. A low-level employee will find it difficult to express frustrations, fears, and needs to a person in a much higher position who appears to be isolated from the everyday problems of the rank-and-file worker. Most high-level executives find the grievance procedure activity to be an imposition on their busy schedules. The process itself is forbidding. The employee must make an appointment, be announced by a receptionist who often is protective of the executive's time, and then enter an office that can be large, formal, and unfamiliar. The grievant then must face an executive whom he or she may not have spoken to in a year and may not in the year ahead. At this point, the grievant is expected to talk and argue freely. This is just not feasible. As Michael J. Quill, the late and often pungent union leader, used to put it sarcastically: "It just don't seem sane."

The central purposes of the grievance procedure are to dispose of the grievance fairly and equitably and, where possible, to reach an agreement. For these to be accomplished, facts must be obtained and evaluated objectively; fact-finding is at the heart of the grievance procedure. Such a process requires objectivity beyond the emotional issues involved. My own experience has led me to conclude that effective grievance handling, resulting in fair and equitable resolution of employee disputes, requires:

1. energetic pursuit of all the facts
2. omission from the hearing procedures of preconceived ideas about the validity of the grievance
3. a desire to dispose of the grievance by protecting the rights of both the institution and the employee
4. a willingness to admit that management is wrong, if that is the case

THE SUPERVISOR AND THE GRIEVANCE PROCEDURE[5]

The supervisor must know all the employees in the department and be genuinely interested in them to recognize their needs and problems. This can eliminate many complaints before they reach the grievance stage as well as serve as a means of increasing productivity and efficiency.

It is the supervisor's responsibility to know the details of the collective bargaining contract as well as personnel policies and how to apply them. Although it is clear that many employees' grievances cannot be considered as bona fide, inasmuch as they are not covered by personnel policy or the union contract, it is important that they be heard.

Taking a legalistic approach to the procedure and summarily dismissing a grievance as only a "gripe" will be counterproductive; hard feelings will ensue, and many matters that are properly subjects of the grievance procedure and otherwise might not be grieved will be used to exert pressure on management. A supervisor's listening to a complaint, even though it is a petty gripe, can be enough in itself; the mere pouring out of the problem (catharsis) may well be enough to satisfy the employee that someone is interested. It is not suggested that every petty gripe be given undue importance; however, the employee should not be brushed off without having the complaint fully heard.

The supervisor should listen attentively, get the complete facts, and look for the underlying attitudes and feelings. The aggrieved employee should be permitted the time and the privacy to seek explanations and satisfaction. Very often complaints reflect dissatisfaction in areas other than those expressed. The hidden agenda may be far more important than the obvious subject of the grievance. Therefore, it is essential for a supervisor to find out what is really bothering the employee.

A most helpful suggestion for facilitating this process is to rephrase the employee's statements in your own words. This serves several purposes.

1. The employee can correct any misunderstanding on the supervisor's part.
2. The employee has the opportunity to bring the complaint into sharper perspective.
3. The supervisor and the employee will be certain to understand the situation thoroughly.
4. The employee is assured that the supervisor is "on the same wavelength" and is empathetic enough to try to understand the problem from the worker's point of view.

PRINCIPLES OF GRIEVANCE ARBITRATION[6]

The basic principles of grievance adjustment have been enunciated in many ways by many experts, but rarely is there disagreement as to the core ingredients.

1. Inherent in successful grievance adjustment is a commitment to adjusting the employee's complaint promptly and on the basis of its merits.
2. Since the majority of grievances derive from a decision by a first-line supervisor, there must be a direct avenue of appeal beyond that ruling, that is, a second or third step in that procedure.
3. A grievance procedure that has as its terminal step a review inside the institution is not as effective as one that provides for outside review (arbitration) by an impartial third party.
4. There should be a strong desire to resolve dissatisfaction and conflicts before they become real problems.
5. Supervisors should empathize with their employees, try to understand their problems, and be able and willing to listen in a nonjudgmental fashion.
6. Supervisors should balance their personal commitment to the interests of the institution with a sense of fair play on behalf of the employees. Supervisors represent the employees to the administration and the administration to the employees.
7. Employees deserve a complete and empathetic hearing of all grievances.
8. The most important job in the handling of grievances is getting the facts. Therefore, supervisors must listen attentively, encourage full discussion, and defer judgment.
9. Supervisors must look for the hidden agenda, look beyond the selected incident, and judge the grievance in context.

10. Hasty decisions often backfire. On the other hand, the employee deserves a speedy reply.
11. The supervisor should try to separate fact from opinion or impressions while investigating a grievance, consult others when appropriate, and, most important, check with the personnel office.
12. The supervisor, after coming to a decision, should communicate it to the employee promptly, giving the reason for the ruling and informing the person of the right to appeal an adverse outcome.
13. Decisions must be made and then sold to the employee. The decision is less effective if the individual does not understand the rationale.
14. Common sense is an essential ingredient in arriving at a decision.
15. Written records are most important. They serve as a review for the supervisor to ensure consistency.

Hearing the Grievance

Hearing the complaint requires attentive listening: get the complete facts and the underlying attitudes and feelings. Let the employee talk without interruption. Then ask questions until you are satisfied that you understand the specifics of the grievance and the true agenda. Do not become predisposed or argumentative in response to the employee's answers. Very often complaints reflect dissatisfaction in areas other than those under discussion. It is essential that you find out what is really bothering the employee—the hidden agenda. An excellent approach is to rephrase the employee's statement in your own words. This "reflection" completes a feedback loop, which permits you and the grievant to be in total agreement regarding the problem. If you are to address employee dissatisfaction you must "hear" what the employee is saying; you must be tuned in to his or her wavelength.

Further explanation or discussion should be reserved until after the facts have been checked, applicable policies and union contract provisions reviewed, and past practices, grievances, and commitments analyzed. Don't promise anything at this time other than a careful investigation. Specify a time within which an answer will be forthcoming. Don't mislead the employee by promising to do something about a complaint unless you are sure that remedial action is in order.

There may be instances where a quick response is indicated. If you are absolutely certain of the facts, an immediate reply is in order. In most instances, however, a hasty decision can be disastrous. If you are not sure of the facts or of the appropriate policy provision or contract interpretation, or if you are doubtful that the emotional climate is conducive to resolution, delay your response.

Getting the Facts

We now come to one of your most important responsibilities in administering the grievance procedure: getting the facts. If you are to discharge your grievance-handling responsibilities properly, your first task on receiving the grievance and hearing the complaint is to investigate, not to evaluate. Very few grievances can be adjudicated on the spot. If an employee feels that the decision on his or her specific grievance is too quickly made or is made in advance, the grievance procedure will fail as a mechanism for gaining employee commitment and reducing employee unrest. It is your responsibility to investigate thoroughly all the facts and alleged occurrences brought to your attention at the hearing or through the formal grievance form. Emotional arguments must be filtered out, and a study of the facts should be the key to making a sound decision.

A complete investigation includes interviewing other employees who may have been involved, reviewing relevant records, and, in general, stepping back from the problem to gain objectivity. New facts and additional viewpoints are almost always uncovered in this manner. Your purpose is to interpret and administer institutional policy and, if applicable, the collective bargaining agreement, not to create policy or new clauses of the contract or of the personnel manual by making special rulings or decisions that are inconsistent with those documents or with precedent. Often records will give information about the grievant's past performance and can be helpful in understanding the present case by reviewing prior discipline, individual attendance and punctuality records, written performance evaluations, and other documents.

In your investigation, look for information concerning previous settlements of similar grievances and relevant policy or contract interpretations. You may call on other supervisors or the personnel manager. Precedent becomes very important. A hasty decision may provide a precedent with far-reaching impact. Many a supervisor has found that a hasty or careless decision for a relatively minor occurrence becomes important later in a different situation with more serious consequences. It is, therefore, essential that you investigate before you act. One important caveat: be sure that you have not been misled by surface similarities between the grievance you are handling and the grievances that have been previously settled. Two grievances frequently look alike when you first review them, but after close study of the facts they may be diverse and, therefore, the decision may need to be different. Very often the grievance on its surface may vary sharply from its underlying causes. If you can discover the underlying causes of grievances, rather than focusing on their surface appearances, you can set about solving real labor relations problems. The way to do this is to develop a system for grievance analysis.

Decision-Making

After analyzing all the facts uncovered by a thorough investigation, it is time to develop a solution to the problem and an answer to the grievance. It is a good idea to discuss your proposed solution with others. Checking out your hunch, your conclusion, or your suggested options with others who are in a position to assess their probable impact is a wise idea. Ask your administrator, the personnel manager, or other supervisors how this type of problem has been handled in the past. Consultation is a sign of caution, not indecision. You will not be criticized for reviewing your options with others if you have assembled the facts carefully and approached the grievance objectively.

At this point your answer must be recorded in written form. Wherever possible, completely explain the reasons behind your decision. It is important that you deal with the specific complaint and not go beyond that complaint. Frame your answer carefully. If it is difficult to formulate reasons, then the decision might be open to question. Ensure that the answer deals with the specific complaint. Avoid commitments to future actions unless such commitments have been thoroughly reviewed. Unless this is reviewed beforehand, you may commit the institution to a binding precedent on an issue much broader than the one involved in the specific case.

Communicating to the Employee

Supervisors who admit their mistakes are more respected than those who cover up mistakes. If a grievance has merit and an error has been made, admit this to the employee and indicate your intention to take immediate corrective action. Make certain that you take such corrective action.

If the complaint has no merit and the grievance is to be denied, a full explanation should be communicated to the employee. Attempt to gain the employee's understanding and acceptance of your decision. If the employee remains dissatisfied, don't get impatient and irritated. Appeals are normally provided for in institutional grievance procedures, and the procedure for such an appeal should be explained to the employee.

Supervisors may have the most trouble with this part of the grievance procedure. It is probably the best opportunity to obtain understanding from the employee of how you handled his or her problem. As previously noted, a sympathetic "no" often goes a much longer way than a harsh "yes." If you have done your homework in getting the facts and in checking out all the details, there is no reason why you should be concerned about communicating your decision to the employee.

An excellent review of 20 supervisory principles in complaint and grievance handling is included in Appendix 10-A.

Preparing a Written Record

No matter whether the grievance is denied, granted, or settled by compromise, the supervisor must prepare a complete statement of all that occurred—the grievance, the facts, the investigation, the interpretation, and the decision. Normally grievances are submitted on grievance forms, which indicate the "disposition." If the grievance is denied, the written record will be useful in hearing the appeal. If the grievance is granted in whole or in part, it constitutes a precedent, and the resolution of future cases may hinge on the details of the present case. No effective employee relations program can depend on memory and hearsay. The passage of time distorts the recollection of what occurred.

Once the written record contained on the grievance form is completed, it should be presented to the employee, and a copy should be kept in the departmental files. Every so often a supervisor who has keen interest in maintaining consistency and a fair and firm record in handling grievances will review his or her departmental grievance file.

GRIEVANCE ANALYSIS

An important adjunct of your responsibility in the grievance procedure is developing a system for grievance analysis. Take an objective look at the entire grievance and then break it down into its parts as follows.

1. *Study the grievance in a general way.* Is it related to other grievances that have recently been filed? Is it admissible to the grievance procedure under the terms of the contract and under provisions in the

personnel policy manual, or might it be described as an expression of discontent or frustration on the part of the worker?

2. *Analyze the specific parts of the grievance.* What actual conditions, job-related or not, are the source of the worker's complaint? Are the conditions brought up in the complaint the causes or merely the targets at which he or she aims the arrows of discontent? What is the true agenda of the grievance?
3. *Study the employee.* What are his or her motivations, attitudes, and relations with other workers? Is he or she a habitual complainer? Is there a political undercurrent that directs the employee toward a particular stand?
4. *Look for any off-the-job conditions that might affect the employee's on-the-job behavior.* Is there some reason, aside from the stated reasons in the grievance itself, why the grievant might be unhappy?

Only after a complete, thorough, and objective search and review of the facts can the answer be prepared.

WAYS TO IMPROVE HUMAN RELATIONS WHEN HANDLING GRIEVANCES[7]

1. *Be available.* Supervisors should realize that their people are individuals and should fit their methods to them. Supervisors can cool off the hothead with patience; sense when something is troubling the quiet worker who keeps anger bottled up until it explodes; and calm sensitive employees who may think that they are being slighted. Supervisors can't solve the problems of strangers, and unless they are approachable they will have strangers working for them.
2. *Be relaxed.* When employees bring in gripes, real or fancied, supervisors should let them sound off. If they know that their supervisors are listening and will give them a fair hearing, the complaints won't look so big.
3. *Get the facts.* Supervisors must get the story, ask questions and straighten out any inconsistencies, and be objective and sympathetic.
4. *Investigate carefully.* It is important never to accept hearsay. Supervisors must find out for themselves the answers to such questions as who, what, when, where, and why. They must check how the union contract or institutional personnel policy covers the alleged offense and review the files for precedents.

5. *Be tactful.* Many employees will start to tell a supervisor about unfair treatment, only to realize halfway through the story that they don't have a real complaint. If supervisors help such employees "save face," they make a friend. A worker never should leave the grievance interview humiliated and embarrassed.
6. *Act with deliberation.* Snap judgment leads to impulsive action, so that supervisors must take time to get the facts. What caused the grievance? Where did it happen? Has there been favoritism, unintentional or deliberate? Was this grievance related to others?
7. *Get the answer.* It may be impossible to address the grievance immediately, but employees must not be given the runaround. If supervisors cannot get the facts needed to settle the case, they should say so. An employee who knows that the supervisors are working on the problem is likely to be more reasonable.
8. *Consider the consequences of the decision.* It is essential to know the effect that the settlement will have, not only on the individual but on the group.
9. *Admit mistakes.* All supervisors are human and make mistakes; if decisions occasionally are reversed by superiors, admit the error. Supervisors must not bear a grudge against the employee who was proved right at their expense.
10. *Sell the decision.* When an employee's grievance is denied, it is necessary to explain why. A blunt "no" causes resentment. Supervisors must not pass the buck by blaming higher management for the denial.

SOME RESEARCH

First-line supervisors in ten unionized plants were studied by Jennings* to determine their attitudes toward the grievance procedure. Jennings was looking at (1) the significance of grievance handling as a supervisory responsibility; (2) the foremen's responsibilities and activities in grievance handling; and (3) actions taken by other line and staff management officials in the grievance process. His results were as follows.

1. Supervisors perceived that top management regarded grievance handling responsibilities as an important aspect of the supervisor's job.

---

*Reproduced from the May 1974 issue of the *Labor Law Journal,* published and copyrighted 1974 by Commerce Clearing House, Inc., 4025 W. Peterson Avenue, Chicago, IL 60646.

2. Supervisors did not consider the resolution of grievances extremely important.
3. When supervisors spent a great deal of effort resolving grievances, they did not feel that they were given much credit for this activity.
4. A majority of the supervisors did not believe that they had the primary responsibility for the grievance procedure.
5. A majority believed that their grievance decisions were usually upheld by higher-level management.
6. A majority of foremen usually consulted the industrial relations representative before responding to a grievance.[8]

What can we learn from Jennings' study? It appears that supervisors are not ranking grievance handling high enough in the total range of supervisory responsibilities. This may well have developed because upper management, although realizing the importance of this aspect of a supervisor's job, has not extended appreciation or recognition for that role. It seems essential that supervisors be given appropriate credit for minimizing or resolving grievances. Most arbitration cases (arbitration is usually the last step in a grievance procedure, wherein a third party not connected with the institution or the union judges the merits of the grievance and produces a binding decision) are won or lost on the basis of the supervisor's testimony. It is also obvious from Jennings' findings that communication with staff experts in industrial relations is essential to producing consistent and defensible decisions.

A study by Turner and Robinson examined the effect of grievance resolution on union-management relationships. Specifically, these investigators examined the hypothesis that the greater the number of grievances resolved at the lower steps of the grievance procedure, the greater the likelihood of a harmonious union-management relationship. Their findings supported the hypothesis.[9]

To summarize, research indicated that upper management depends significantly on the first-line supervisor to resolve grievances. Yet supervisors seem not to give a high priority to this important responsibility. This would lead us to believe that supervisors do not fully realize that their role is fundamental in minimizing grievances and preventing a grievance from becoming a major dispute. Research data also indicate that the resolution of grievances in the lower steps of the grievance procedure leads to more harmonious labor-management relationships. The first-line supervisor is key to that improvement.

SUPERVISOR ATTITUDE

Pegnetter and Levey refer to improper supervisory reaction to grievances submitted by rank-and-file employees. They list the following.

- Some supervisors feel that their employees' selection of a union is a personal affront so that they overreact and take a hard-line approach to dealing with grievances and the union representative. A high grievance rate then develops.
- Other supervisors may sympathize with employees or ignore contract administration. The result is no grievances because the supervisors are giving in to employee complaints or continuing to handle them in their own way.[10]

The submission of a grievance by an employee should not be considered a threat to the leadership of the first-line supervisor but rather an opportunity to deal consistently and fairly with employees. It should be clear that the system for dealing with problems that arise on a day-to-day basis, either in a unionized environment or a nonunionized environment, is the grievance procedure. Pegnetter and Levey have described the grievance procedure as a trade-off in collective bargaining for both labor and management.[11] It has almost universal application as a method for the peaceful resolution of disputes between employees and management.

There are important gains that accrue for both health care management and employees under a formal grievance procedure. The employees obviously gain a sense of fair treatment. They have protected freedom to bring forward any claims that management has mishandled their rights under the contracts, and they are represented by union officers who are available to help them understand the procedures and rights available. The gains for management are two-fold. The grievance procedures provide a method for solving employee problems, without resorting to confrontational methods such as slowdowns, work stoppages, and strikes. In addition, employees who feel that they will have a fair hearing—and one that is expeditious—will be less likely to become alienated and more likely to be productive.

TIPS FOR HANDLING GRIEVANCES EFFECTIVELY

The principal requirements for handling grievances effectively are:

1. a strong desire to make the personnel policy manual and/or labor

contract work, to resolve dissatisfactions and conflicts, and to supervise more effectively
2. a strong effort on the part of first-line supervisors to settle grievances at the very first step in the grievance procedure
3. a sound working knowledge of the personnel policy manual and the labor contract, including new interpretations and precedents
4. a consistent approach to carrying out provisions of the personnel policy manual and/or labor contract

Since you as the supervisor play the key role in the handling of grievances, the following advice will enable you to play that role effectively.

1. The people who work for you are just that, people. Treat them as individuals.
2. It is essential that you maintain and preserve the dignity of the employee. This may be difficult when dealing with grievances, but it is at the heart of a sound supervisor-employee relationship.
3. Remember that employees want to be appreciated; they want to know that you recognize their meritorious performance. Give credit where credit is due. This will minimize many grievances that spring from a lack of recognition.
4. Look to your employees for suggestions and advice. Give them the feeling that they are "in on things." Many grievances arise because the employees are not prepared for change.
5. "A stitch in time saves nine." This old adage is most appropriate in effective grievance handling. Look around and try to anticipate areas and actions that may cause irritation. By anticipating problems you will minimize them.
6. Employees who are properly trained are less likely to have grievances. Employees who know what they are doing and, therefore, do it well are less frustrated. This is of particular relevance when dealing with the new employee.
7. Unclear, unexplained orders or instructions can lead to grievances. Make certain that you communicate clearly and back up orders and instructions with a "why."
8. When you must administer discipline, be objective, equitable, and consistent. The majority of grievances stem from real or perceived inequality of treatment.
9. Don't belittle employees or underestimate them. If they have a grievance, it does not really matter whether it falls under the personnel policy manual or the labor contract. It is real to the employee, and so you must deal with it.

CONCLUSION[12]

Pegnetter and Levey report that the grievance procedure frequently ends in binding arbitration and thus represents a trade-off in collective bargaining for both labor and management. The union gives up the right to strike over grievance disputes during the life of the contract. In return, it gets a grievance procedure with a terminal step providing for outside arbitration that is not under the unilateral control of the management. Management gives up that unilateral right to impose its interpretation of the contract on the union and gets, in turn, the union's commitment and obligation to submit disputes to the grievance and arbitration procedure.[13]

The main elements in achieving a sound grievance procedure, according to Pegnetter and Levey, are:

1. to develop a management team approach to contract administration
2. to ensure involvement in understanding the contract terms at all levels of management
3. to train supervisors in proper methods in investigating and handling grievances
4. to establish a program for the evaluation of the management team's performance in handling grievances
5. to organize a system for monitoring the grievance and contract administration activities under the labor agreement[14]

The U.S. Supreme Court provides a clear indication of the importance of the grievance procedure.

> The grievance machinery under a collective bargaining agreement is at the very heart of the system of industrial self-government. Arbitration is the means of solving the unforeseeable by molding a system of private law for all problems which may arise and to provide for their solution in a way which will generally accord with the variant needs and desires of the parties. . . . The grievance procedure is, in other words, part of the continuous collective bargaining process.[15]

KEY POINTS TO EFFECTIVE HANDLING OF GRIEVANCES

1. Employees deserve a complete and empathetic hearing of all grievances that they present.

2. The most important job in the handling of grievances is getting the facts. Therefore, listen attentively, encourage a full discussion, and defer judgment.
3. Look for the hidden agenda. Look beyond the selected incident and judge the grievance in context.
4. Hasty decisions often backfire. On the other hand, the employee deserves a speedy reply. To determine the proper disposition of a grievance, ask yourself the following questions.
   - What actually happened?
   - Where did it happen?
   - What should have happened?
   - When did it happen?
   - Who was involved?
   - Were there any witnesses?
   - Why did the problem develop?[16]
5. While you are investigating the grievance, try to separate fact from opinion or impressions. Consult others when appropriate. Most important, check with your personnel people.
6. After you have come to your decision, promptly communicate that decision to the employee. Remember that a sympathetic "no" is far more effective than a harsh "yes." Therefore, give the reason for the decision and inform the employee of his or her right to appeal.
7. Remember that you have to sell your decision. The decision is yours, so don't pass the buck by placing the blame on your supervisors.
8. There is no substitute for common sense in arriving at a decision.
9. Written records are most important; they serve as a review for the supervisor to ensure consistency.
10. Follow up is essential. Even if the employee does not appeal your decision, you should check back to see whether the decision "took" or was upheld. There is no better way to win employee respect than to give due recognition to employee problems. A little bit of follow up goes a long way.

NOTES

1. Louis V. Imundo, *The Effective Supervisor's Handbook* (New York: AMACOM Division of American Management Associations, 1980), 120.

2. Herbert L. Marx, Jr., "Arbitration From the Arbitrator's View," in *Handbook of Health Care Human Resources Management,* ed. Norman Metzger (Rockville, MD: Aspen Publishers, 1981), 830.

3. Allan J. Harrison, *Preparing and Presenting Your Arbitration Case* (Washington, DC: Bureau of National Affairs, 1979), 4.

4. This section was excerpted, in part, from Norman Metzger and Joseph M. Ferentino, *The Arbitration and Grievance Process* (Rockville, MD: Aspen Publishers, 1983), chap. 2, 19–21.

5. This section was excerpted, in part, from Metzger and Ferentino, *The Arbitration and Grievance Process,* chap. 2, 21–22.

6. This section was excerpted from Metzger and Ferentino, *The Arbitration and Grievance Process,* chap. 2, 23–24.

7. This section was excerpted from Metzger and Ferentino, *The Arbitration and Grievance Process,* chap. 2, 25–26.

8. Ken Jennings, "Foremen's View of Their Involvement with Other Management Officials in the Grievance Process," *Labor Law Journal* 25, no. 25 (May 1974): 305–16.

9. James T. Turner and James W. Robinson, "A Pilot Study of the Validity of Grievance Settlement Rates as a Predictor of Union-Management Relations," *Journal of Industrial Relations* 14, no. 3 (September 1972): 314–22.

10. Richard Pegnetter and Samuel Levey, "Grievance Procedures in Health Organizations," in *Handbook of Health Care Human Resources Management,* ed. Norman Metzger, (Rockville, MD: Aspen Publishers, 1981), 783–84.

11. Ibid., 771.

12. This section was excerpted from Metzger and Ferentino, *The Arbitration and Grievance Process,* chap. 2, 28.

13. Pegnetter and Levey, "Grievance Procedures," 771.

14. Ibid., 784.

15. *United Steelworkers of America v. Warrior and Gulf Navigation Co.,* 363 U.S. 574, 581 (1960).

16. J. Brad Chapman, "Constructive Grievance Handling," in *Supervisory Management: Tools and Techniques,* ed. Gene Newport (New York: West Publishing Company, 1976), 268.

Appendix 10-A

Twenty Supervisory Principles in Complaint and Grievance Handling*

PRINCIPLE 1: WHAT IS A GRIEVANCE?

Any person in a position to deal with grievances must understand clearly just what they are. The following points will help clarify what constitutes a grievance.

1. Anything about the job that irritates an employee or tends to make working conditions unsatisfactory may be a grievance.
2. A grievance may exist even though no verbal or written complaint is presented. Such silent or unuttered grievances may be as destructive of good will as those that are aired.
3. Even though the complaint may be imaginary or based on lack of knowledge of the facts, it is a grievance nonetheless until properly cleared up.
4. A worker who merely thinks a grievance exists may be just as discontented as the worker who has a just complaint, and the same careful handling is necessary.
5. A grievance may be trivial or important, affecting an individual or a group, caused by fellow workers or by management, financial or nonfinancial, imaginary or real—but it is a grievance in any case and requires fair, open-minded, patient, and considerate treatment.

PRINCIPLE 2: KEEP YOUR DOOR OPEN

Any person in a position to receive complaints and handle grievances must keep the door open; that is, he or she must always exhibit a willingness to hear and consider complaints.

---

*Adapted from *The Arbitration and Grievance Process: A Guide for Health Care Supervisors* by N. Metzger and J.M. Ferentino, pp. 235–245, Aspen Publishers, Inc., ©1983.

1. Nothing aggravates a grievance more than the feeling that a superior is hostile to the idea of listening to complaints.
2. Unless a worker has a safety valve (knows where to go to express a grievance fully), any complaint that he or she holds will be magnified out of all proportion.
3. Make it known by word and action that you welcome the presentation of a complaint rather than have one of your people nurse a grievance in disgruntled silence.
4. Encourage workers, by your treatment of them, to make their complaints to you, who may be able to do something about them, rather than to fellow workers, who probably can do nothing to correct them.
5. It is not enough to say that you welcome frank and honest grievances; you must prove by the interest you show in correcting complaints that you are sincere in your open-door policy.

PRINCIPLE 3: PUT THE WORKER AT EASE

When one of your people comes to you with a grievance, do everything you can to make it possible for that individual to state a case.

1. Do not let the worker with a grievance see a chip on your shoulder. Getting excited because the employee may be angry only tends to arouse the person more and makes the situation more difficult.
2. Put the grievant at ease immediately by taking a friendly attitude that rids the situation of any feeling of hostility.
3. Do, say, or show nothing in any way that indicates that you resent the worker's approach or feel that the employee is "butting into" your affairs.
4. Let the worker know that you appreciate this straightforwardness in bringing the grievance to you rather than bottling it up or stirring up trouble by grumbling to others about it.
5. Put the worker at ease with assurances that he or she has a perfect right to express problems frankly to you by making it clear that you are ready and willing to take all the time necessary to discuss the complaint and by manifesting a readiness to give open-minded consideration to what the grievant has to say.

PRINCIPLE 4: LISTEN WITH SINCERE INTEREST

The sincerity with which you listen to a grievance and the interest you show in what the worker has to say are of utmost importance in achieving a meeting of the minds.

1. Don't merely say to a worker "Go ahead and tell your story—I'm listening." Your attitude and words must reflect a sincere interest in the story.
2. Don't try to rush the worker to get it over with, because that will indicate that you are not interested.
3. Listen without interrupting except to indicate by questions that you are sincerely interested in getting the worker's whole viewpoint.
4. Evidence of a lack of interest in the complaint will convince the employee that you won't give the case full consideration.
5. Even though a grievance may seem trivial, its importance to the worker is such that no competent supervisor who listens to it can afford to show anything less than a deep and sincere interest in all the facts, assertions, and opinions involved.

PRINCIPLE 5: DISCUSS, DON'T ARGUE

In dealing with a worker with a complaint, the supervisor must keep the situation on a discussion basis. No one wins in an argument. Calm discussion is best because:

1. An argument only tends to convince each party that it is right and the other side is wrong.
2. An argument raises emotional temperatures until each participant is more interested in winning than in getting at the true facts and settling the differences on the basis of reason.
3. The grievant in an argument fights more stubbornly because of a feeling of being the underdog.
4. Allowing yourself to be drawn into an argument causes loss of poise, dignity, and self-respect and is likely to put the grievance on a personal basis rather than on the basis of facts.
5. Calm discussion permits settlement by reason rather than by emotion, threat, or resort to show of authority. No settlement on such grounds is likely to be lasting or mutually satisfactory.

PRINCIPLE 6: GET THE STORY STRAIGHT

Intelligent handling of a grievance is impossible until the supervisor gets the story absolutely straight.

1. Ask the worker to state the complaint in clear and complete detail, from beginning to end.
2. By a series of questions, get the employee to explain the case fully a second time.
3. Having the story repeated has the effect of lowering the employee's temperature because each time the person gets it off his or her chest the grievance tends to come down closer to its true and reasonable proportions. Discrepancies, if any, show up. The supervisor obtains a clearer impression of the facts.
4. Patient use of ample time to get the story straight gives the supervisor an opportunity to do some clear thinking. The supervisor then is in a position to deal justly with the grievance.

PRINCIPLE 7: GET ALL THE FACTS

In adjusting a grievance fairly and intelligently, all the facts must be mutually understood by both parties. Decisions based on half-facts cannot be mutually satisfactory.

1. Unless all the facts come out, the supervisor may become the victim of a bluffer.
2. To get all the facts, consult not only the grievant but all others whose observation, experience, and knowledge of the situation may contribute to a thorough understanding.
3. When it is evident that the supervisor is seeking all the facts, any temptation for the grievant to misrepresent the true situation will be removed.
4. In seeking all the facts, proceed tactfully with the stated purpose of arriving at a fair decision rather than with an attitude of suspicion and apparent disbelief in the grievant's statements.
5. Although promptness in handling a grievance is important, an attempted quick settlement should not interfere with taking sufficient time to get all the facts. Start action on and consideration of the grievance promptly, but take the time to get all the information required for an intelligent decision.

PRINCIPLE 8: CONSIDER THE WORKER'S VIEWPOINT

A thorough application and understanding of the worker's viewpoint is essential.

1. When presented with a grievance, consider, first, all the possible reasons why the worker might feel aggrieved and, second, all possible reasons why that viewpoint might be a mistaken one.
2. If a supervisor starts to think of defenses against a complaint before listening and completely understanding the worker's viewpoint, it will be practically impossible to understand the grievance thoroughly.
3. While listening to a grievance, keep asking yourself "How would I feel about this situation if I were in that worker's shoes?"
4. A sincere interest in getting the worker's viewpoint will convince the person of your desire to be fair, which is the first essential in any equitable and harmonious settlement of a difference between people.
5. Be honest with yourself and with the worker by giving proper weight to the other's viewpoint and the reasons why the person feels that way.

PRINCIPLE 9: SAVE THE FACE OF THE COMPLAINER

Tactfully find a way for a complainer to save face. This applies particularly in situations in which the employee has based a grievance on misinformation or imaginary causes or has overstated the demands.

1. No person who has brought up a grievance likes to back down, admit to being wrong, or go off half-cocked. Neither does a worker like to appear to be stupid for having brought up the complaint.
2. To help the complainer save face and willingly accept a reasonable adjustment, make it as easy as possible for the worker to retract or decrease the demand.
3. Make it easy for the complainer by some statement such as "Of course, I can see how you would get that viewpoint, based on the facts at your disposal" or "I probably would feel the same way if I only had part of the information."
4. Make it a point to discuss grievances in private so that there is no temptation for the complainer stubbornly to maintain an unreasonable position rather than back down in the presence of others.

PRINCIPLE 10: AVOID SNAP JUDGMENTS

Snap judgment in dealing with a grievant involves the dangers of making a mistake and of creating the impression that your mind is made up before you've heard the evidence. Avoid snap judgments for the following reasons.

1. Snap judgments are unfair to both supervisor and complainer because it is too easy to make an error, and a mistake will result in damage to you both.
2. Snap judgments are too-obvious evidence of a closed mind or of a careless, indifferent attitude toward the worker's problem.
3. Even though the decision based on snap judgment may happen to be correct, the aggrieved worker will feel that the complaint did not receive full consideration.
4. A decision favorable to the complainer, if based on a snap judgment, may boomerang or set a precedent that can cause far more trouble, embarrassment, and bad feeling in the future.
5. Mistakes resulting from snap judgment undermine a supervisor's prestige and reputation for fair dealing.

PRINCIPLE 11: WEIGH THE CONSEQUENCES OF SETTLEMENT

In settling a grievance, forethought must be given to the possible consequences of the action.

1. Even though the decision may be correct, it may generate opposition and antagonism that may cancel out the advantages of the settlement.
2. Conditions may justify settlement on compromise terms rather than on a strictly correct basis because the latter may lead to unfavorable consequences later.
3. Weigh the benefits of a settlement that the employer receives against what you may have to yield in order to reach that agreement.
4. The settlement you propose may be logical, but you must analyze whether it is psychological—that is, how will it strike the worker's feelings, self-interests, or prejudices?
5. Always consider how a settlement may affect the future cooperative working relationship with the aggrieved employee and the future attitude of other workers.

PRINCIPLE 12: BE WILLING TO ADMIT MISTAKES

Some of the greatest errors in the handling of grievances are made because persons listening to and adjusting complaints are unwilling to admit their own mistakes.

1. Frankly admitting a mistake can never injure your prestige as much as covering up an error or refusing to admit that you made one.
2. Even though an employee with a grievance that resulted from a mistake you made may not call your attention to the error very tactfully, don't try to defend your actions or decisions simply because you won't admit to having been wrong.
3. The supervisor's readiness to admit a mistake encourages the grievant to do so, too. Nobody likes a person who is never wrong.
4. A grievant will deeply resent your covering up a mistake and is sure to consider it an injustice.
5. A supervisor's refusal to admit a mistake usually leads an aggrieved worker to increase the demands, even to the point of unreasonableness, because he or she is embittered by the obvious unfairness of a superior who is not big enough to be honest.

PRINCIPLE 13: TAKE PROMPT ACTION

The promptness with which a grievance is acted on is an important factor in determining worker satisfaction or dissatisfaction.

1. A delay in giving a favorable decision will give the worker the impression that the action was taken grudgingly or unwillingly, which will cause him or her to feel less appreciation for the supportive step.
2. Other matters of seemingly greater importance may push a grievance to the back burner, but nothing is more important to a worker than prompt action on a complaint.
3. Delays indicate a lack of interest in the worker's problem and breed a feeling of resentment.
4. Avoid any temptation to delay deciding on a grievance. Take no more time than is actually necessary to get all the facts and to verify them.
5. For the employer to get maximum benefit from settling a grievance, the decision must be made promptly and with justice for all concerned.

PRINCIPLE 14: DON'T PASS THE BUCK

Buck passing in handling grievances creates more embarrassing problems than it cures.

1. To pass the buck when presented with a grievance will create the feeling that you are giving the worker the runaround.
2. Your making the excuse that "It's over my head" or "I haven't got the authority" only increases the worker's feeling of futility and desperation.
3. To pass the buck by saying "I'd do it but it's against hospital policy" creates the impression that you agree with the worker (whether you do or don't) and gives the person a feeling of being right (whether or not that is correct).
4. If you don't have the authority to settle the grievance, don't pass the buck or put the worker to further inconvenience. State frankly that you lack the authority but that you will get a decision from the person who does.

PRINCIPLE 15: HOW TO SAY "NO"

Not all who come with grievances are justified in their complaints or their requests. To some the answer must be "no," but there is a right way and a wrong way to say "no."

1. Don't be afraid to say "no" if that is the right answer. To pussyfoot or straddle the fence only makes more trouble in the end.
2. Don't pass the buck by telling a grievant that you personally would like to say "yes" but that your superior doesn't see it that way.
3. By your attitude, make the person with a grievance realize that if the request were justifiable and properly grantable you would be more pleased to say "yes" than "no."
4. Don't say "no" abruptly without clear evidence that you are giving the request thoughtful, fair, and complete consideration.
5. If you do have to say "no," present all the reasons for your answer in a patient, considerate, and sympathetic manner.

PRINCIPLE 16: ACTING ON IMAGINARY GRIEVANCES

Grievances based on imaginary causes can be just as irritating to workers as those attributable to real and justifiable reasons.

1. Even though you know that the complaint is groundless, handle it with the same consideration and sincerity as you would a real grievance.

2. In dealing with an imaginary grievance, make every effort to establish a clear understanding of the real facts.
3. Consider the fact that the imaginary grievance is based on conditions that the worker believes do exist, and don't jump to the conclusion that the person is "all wet."
4. Be willing to let the discussion ramble. Don't try to pin it down to the narrow limits of the question at issue. This will give the aggrieved an opportunity to adjust emotionally to the necessity of accepting a negative decision.
5. Be sure to leave the way open for further discussion in case the worker claims later to have found further evidence to substantiate the complaint.

PRINCIPLE 17: DON'T LET IT HAPPEN TWICE

If a word to the wise is sufficient, the same grievance should not be permitted to arise twice. Repetition should be prevented because:

1. Allowing the same aggravating conditions to recur causes the worker to lose respect for the supervisor's ability to run the job and makes the boss appear weak and inefficient.
2. Repetition of the same grievance greatly increases the worker's indignation.
3. A recurrence indicates a careless, indifferent attitude toward a worker's welfare and a lack of honesty and sincerity, particularly after settling the first instance.
4. The worker may understand that there may be some excuse for a new grievance but may rightfully feel that there is no reason for a repetition of an old one.

PRINCIPLE 18: USE AUTHORITY JUDICIOUSLY

The supervisor is in a position of authority over the person with a grievance and should use this power judiciously.

1. Set out at once to remove, as far as possible, any feeling that your authority will be used to force a settlement.
2. Establish negotiations on a discussion basis, in which facts rather than the supervisor's authority will determine the decision.

3. Even though you have the authority to issue a ruling without discussion, remember that an arbitrary decision may be received rebelliously whereas the same settlement reached through free discussion may be accepted favorably.
4. Don't use your authority in such a way as to repress free expression by grievants. Talk right across the board in a democratic way, avoiding any feeling of difference in rank.
5. Authority, when wielded as a club, begets disrespect, antagonism, and opposition; used judiciously and temperately, it heightens respect and cooperation.

PRINCIPLE 19: DON'T LET SMALL GRIEVANCES GROW

The time to adjust grievances most effectively is when they still are small.

1. Never put off until tomorrow the adjusting of a small grievance that could be settled today, because by tomorrow it may be too big for you to handle effectively.
2. Labor troubles almost invariably have their beginnings in small grievances that are fed and fattened by indifference and neglect by the supervisors and department heads who are in direct charge of the employees and their working conditions.

PRINCIPLE 20: LEARNING FROM GRIEVANCES

Every grievance handled should be regarded as a lesson from which something worthwhile can be learned.

1. Handling a grievance gives you an opportunity to size up the worker—to judge character, attitude, loyalty, honesty, fairness, and prejudices—and to learn how best to handle that person in the future.
2. Experience in dealing with one grievance can suggest where to look for other possible complaints and how to remove their causes before they arise.
3. If a worker takes a grievance over your head without first discussing it with you, keep cool and ask yourself what there is about your own personality and methods that discouraged the employee from coming to you initially.

4. If the employee does not receive your settlement favorably, study your own tactics to see whether you have said or done anything to prejudice the individual against the terms of the decision. In that way you can learn to make corrections in your methods for future situations.
5. Watch the effect of every move you make so that you can learn how to deal effectively with people and understand what methods and attitudes win them to your point of view.

Chapter 11

How to Act or React to a Union Organizing Drive: What You Can Do

> *Any management that gets a union deserves it—and they get the kind they deserve. No labor union has ever captured a group of employees without the full cooperation and encouragement of managers who create the need for unionization.*
>
> *Charles L. Hughes*
> Making Unions Unnecessary
> *(New York: Executive Enterprises Publication Co., Inc. 1976) p. 1*

> The decision to join [a union] is by no means strictly a rational decision. It is probably more like a religious conversion than like deciding to buy a pair of shoes. The worker does not coolly estimate whether the results he will get from the union will be worth the dues he pays. He is confronted with an emotional appeal and urged to take part in a social and political crusade, and he finally decides to accept the gospel. Moreover the decision to join is usually not an individualistic decision. The first few workers [in a hospital] who join the union have to make up their own minds, and the decision may require initiative and courage. After a nucleus has been secured, however, the growth of the union develops into a mass movement. Most of the workers join because others have done so, and holdouts are gradually brought into line by the pressure of social ostracism [in the hospital].[1]

More employees vote for or against their immediate supervisor than vote for or against the top administration, the board of trustees, or consultants. What managers do, have done, do not do, and have not done has a direct effect on employees' attitudes toward unionization. The day-to-day level of intercourse between the first-line supervisor and employees often reflects the institution's commitment to its employees. Such a commitment, or lack thereof, has a critical impact on the union organizing campaign. Unions rarely organize employees; rather, it is the administration's poor employee relations record (uppermost in that grouping is the first-line supervisor) that drives employees into a union.

The myth of union organizers as outside rabble-rousers should be discarded if intelligent consideration of maintaining nonunion status is desired. Unions seldom seek out discontented workers. It is the reverse that is true: dissatisfied workers look outside their institutions for a vehicle that they believe will change the conditions from which their dissatisfaction has sprung. Management failure is the root cause of the majority of successful union campaigns. This failure springs from a lack of attention paid to the conditions that cause employee unrest. These include a lack of understanding of employee needs—the need for recognition, for belonging, for knowing what's going on, for redress, for competitive salaries and fringe benefits, and for due process—or a restricted mechanism for addressing employee's complaints. Add to this a lack of clear and usable communication lines, sound personnel policies, and appropriate and acceptable working conditions, and the pot begins to boil. The final ingredient for ensuring the loss of an institution's union-free status is the presence of arrogant, insensitive, overworked, and harried supervisors (see Figure 11–1).

It is patently clear that institutions that provide all the benefits and conditions of a "union shop"—with all the protection inherent in the union contract, such as seniority provisions, grievance and arbitration mechanisms, and promotional opportunities—will not become unionized. It is the absence of these conditions, plus the presence of insensitive management, that drives employees into unions.

WHY PEOPLE JOIN UNIONS

There is nothing mystical about the reasons that unions are successful in certain institutions and not in others. There is a marked relationship between worker morale and how much employees feel that their bosses have interest in discussing work problems with the work groups. To the worker you are the boss and the institution. When a supervisor or manager treats her or his subordinates as human beings, there is greater group loyalty and pride. Employees with group loyalty and pride do not look to unions to fill their needs. When you manage by seeing problems through

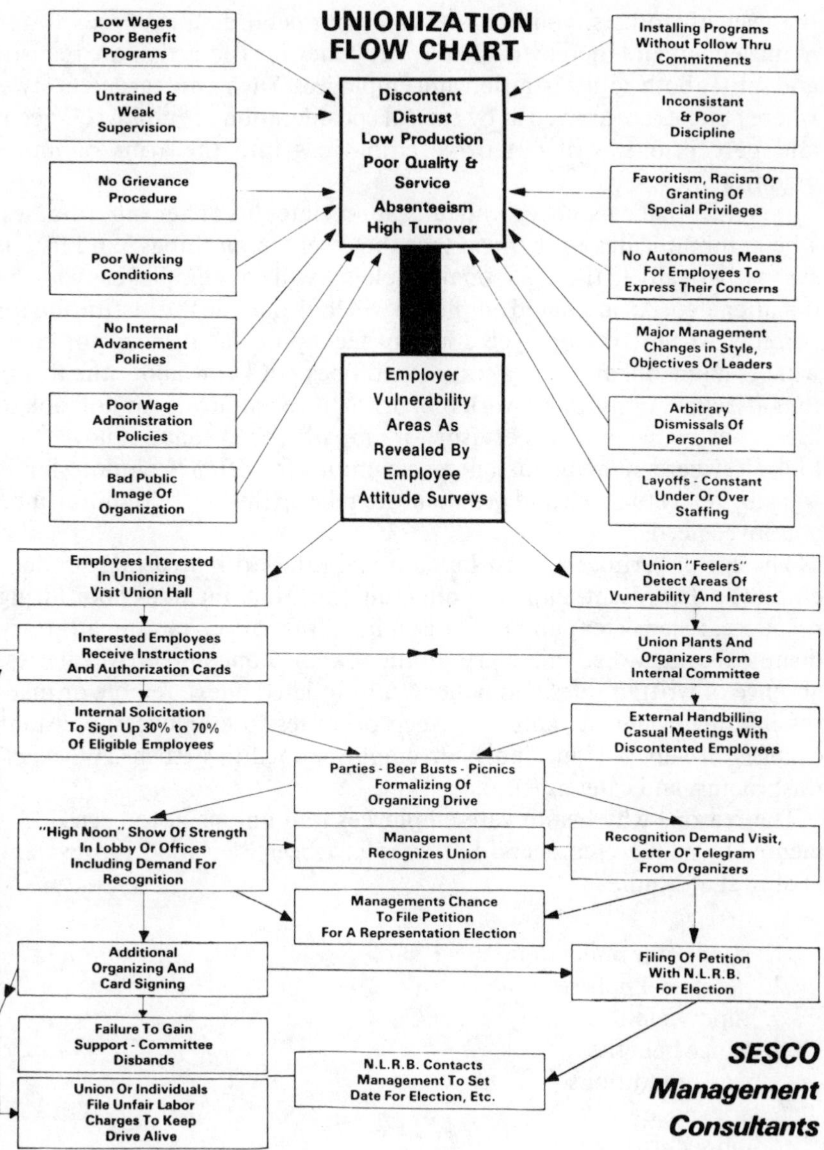

Figure 11-1 Unionization Flow Chart
Source: Reprinted with permission of SESCO Management Consulting Services, Bristol, Tennessee.

the eyes of workers, you can translate your subordinates' needs to top management and thereby help arrive at policy decisions that are realistic and satisfy both administration and employees. Such a management style, where policies are arrived at by careful consideration of employees' needs and perceptions, will not drive employees into the arms of union organizers.

It is clear that a manager who fully appreciates his or her subordinates, who communicates to them so that they feel "in on things" and listens sympathetically to their personal problems, will have employees who are not alienated. An alienated employee will look outside the institution for comfort. When an employee does not feel appreciated, does not know what is going on, and, most important, does not know about the things that affect her or his daily work life, or when an employee cannot look to his or her manager or supervisor for empathy, then that employee will look elsewhere, in many instances to a union. Too often the union stands waiting, ready to listen and promising to take up the battle for unfulfilled employee needs.

The list of "crimes against humanity" in the work area that produce employee discontent, and very often unionization, includes poor hiring practices, inconsistent and poor discipline, frustration, racism, arbitrary dismissals, poor wage and salary administration, noncompetitive salaries, absence of written rules and policies (or outdated ones), remote or inaccessible management, failure to keep promises to employees, constant changes in supervision, and poor employee facilities (such as lockers, washrooms, and cafeterias).

The reasons why health care employees join unions have been documented by many researchers. Ten areas have been identified as prevalent in almost all studies.

1. poor communication
2. personnel policies
3. supervision
4. fringe benefits
5. work conditions
6. grievances
7. job security
8. human dignity
9. shift differentials
10. wages[2]

Joiner tells us "one reason workers frequently mention for joining unions is that management does not treat them fairly, decently or honestly.

Employees view management as fair, decent and honest if it recognizes the needs of individuals and treats them with dignity."[3] Again, your attention must be directed toward the major dissatisfiers in the worker area: company policies, administration, supervision, salary, interpersonal relations, and working conditions. These must be compared to the major satisfiers: what the employee does, recognition, responsibility, advancement, and achievement. By improving managerial practices and by proper utilization of both people and technology, the manager or the supervisor can increase the satisfaction and productivity of employees. Satisfied and fulfilled employees are not receptive to union organizers.

THE UNION ORGANIZER

The typical union organizer has a natural affinity for people, is a good listener, and knows how and at what level to communicate. Chaney and Beech point out some interesting facts about the union organizer and sketch this profile.

1. He or she has a natural capacity to like people. A union organizer is a warm, gentle, outgoing person who communicates well and relates effectively to all types of people.
2. He or she has the ability to adapt to the immediate surroundings and warms up to people very quickly.
3. He or she is patient with people. The union organizer realizes that nonunion employees are not immediately sold on organization. Therefore, the organizer makes an ongoing effort to sign up or convince all employees of the values of unionism and collective action.
4. Many labor relations experts have depicted organizers as a combination missionary, salesperson, and psychologist.[4]

Godoff, who was an especially effective organizer and trainer of organizers, once talked about how he developed a staff that knows how to approach people. His people no longer talk simply about wages and benefits; they establish a rapport with the workers on a much higher level. They know when to raise the key issue of employee rights. They show workers how to establish their rights, how to meet with management as equals, how to protect themselves as individuals, and how to win identity within the hospital as important human beings. He added that the organizer who merely tells the worker "You earn twenty cents less than workers at X hospital and, therefore, you should organize" is out of the picture.

Management is more sophisticated; they know more about the union than they did before and their approach is different. He believed that his organizers kept up with this change.

In an interview, Godoff had this to say about union organizing:

> I think that you will probably get reports from the management in the areas where we work that we don't operate the way we did years ago. You are not going to see circulars floating around and a lot of excitement in the very early stages. Some of our best organizers really work for a period of weeks or months to build an organizing committee, and that means that not a single person has yet signed the card or has made any commitment in terms of paper or materials—simply developing a *very close relationship with people* on the following ratio. If it is a hospital, let's say with a thousand workers, then we will aim for a minimum of a sixty-man or -woman organizing committee with whom we are going to meet periodically, raise issues, raise questions, get all the vital information about the hospital—the number of people in the units, the division of the departments, how many in each department, the ethnic division, the character of the supervision, who is the son of a bitch among the supervisors that we can hit the hardest—and then to orient them on a question of rights, rights, rights, and rights. We say management can give you wage increases, management can give you benefits, management can do a lot of things, but one thing they are not going to give you is rights. When that becomes something that workers feel—it may be very abstract, it may be very vague—but when they feel rights, they will tell you: I haven't got rights; I want rights. And each one imagines it in his own way, but that becomes the greatest strength that the union can muster in any situation.[5]

Now let us look at what one union sets down as a guide for union organizers. Nicholas Zonarich, organizational director of the Industrial Union Department, AFL-CIO, states:

> The organizer has two immediate objectives when he makes his first contacts with the workers at the plant. He is looking for leadership for his campaign and information about the specific problems and complaints of the employees.
>
> There is no blueprint for meeting individual workers and gaining their confidence—conversations can be started in restaurants and bars, through "leads" passed on by other union

> members, and by acquaintances made through social affairs. If there is any rule at all, it is that contacts are *not* made by suddenly appearing at a plant gate with a leaflet urging employees to sign a union authorization card and mail it to a post office box.
>
> Most organizers are interested primarily in meeting the type of employee who is respected by his fellow-workers and who has influence inside the plant. Getting to know a few of these employees is more important—at this stage—than meeting the maximum number of workers.
>
> Once a potential plant leader has been contacted, it is important to win his confidence and trust. Time spent in developing this leader, answering his questions about the union, and explaining the benefits of collective bargaining will be well worthwhile after the organizing campaign gets underway and this leader becomes a union spokesman inside the plant.
>
> Articulate and respected leaders inside the plant are vital to any campaign, but the representative must use his own judgment in selecting the right people. He must be sure that they are not known as chronic "gripers" or "soreheads" and that they are not motivated simply by a desire for revenge or a driving personal ambition.
>
> In the "perfect" campaign, the organizer will find a leader for every group in the plant—a woman for the female workers, leaders within minority, racial, and national groupings, and spokesmen for the various departments and shifts. Since the "perfect" situation rarely exists, the staff man must develop a leadership group as representative as possible.[6]

Both Godoff and Zonarich make some interesting points. Godoff said that they look at "the character of the supervision, who is the son of a bitch among the supervisors that we can hit the hardest. . . ." Zonarich points out that the organizer must be sure that the leaders "are not known as chronic 'gripers' or 'soreheads' and that they are not motivated simply by a desire for revenge or a driving personal ambition." The union is looking for bona fide constituents to use in the organizing drive. They will latch on to the petty gripes and perceived injustices, but they are also looking closely for supervisors who are an easy mark—those who are not employee-centered and who have not built up group loyalty.

It is interesting to note the relationship between why employees join unions and what the union organizers look for. What follows is how the union organizer puts you and your practices under a microscope.

YOUR EMPLOYEES ARE RATING YOU

There is no question that the first-line supervisor is the person most dramatically affected by the organization of employees. The institution itself may be exposed over the years to restrictions on management rights, increased wages, and increased fringe benefits, but in the final analysis the real impact of unionization is felt at the day-to-day level of supervisor-employee intercourse.

The first-line supervisor must understand the key role that he or she plays during the union organizational drive. The union is keenly interested in and often extremely aware of the day-to-day supervisor-employee relationship, especially the issues of fairness and consistency. If the employees believe that they are not being treated fairly by their supervisor, they will be more interested in the union's carefully presented approach in the area of employee rights. If the supervisor has played favorites—has handled similar cases in different ways for different employees—then that supervisor and that institution are more vulnerable to the organizers' demand for collective power to enforce consistency and fairness. Employees look carefully at their supervisor's behavior in similar situations, looking for consistency more often than they look for the actual punishment. As we have learned earlier, a sympathetic "no" may be more effective than a harsh "yes." Similarly, a sympathetic "no" in one situation will be compared to the "yes" of an earlier situation for the test of consistency. If your decision has been different in what may appear to be similar cases, it is important that you make the difference acceptable by sharing with employees the underlying facts of both situations. But beware: if the underlying facts are similar and you still have reached a different decision, you must explain your reasons.

When groups of employees are faced with the choice of voting for or against the union, they often think in terms of their relationship with their supervisors. Critical to that relationship is a supervisor's integrity. How you are perceived by your employees when they are in the voting booth is often a reflection of your actions over the years. Have you truly represented the workers to the management and the management to the workers?

Several suggestions that can produce group loyalty and high productivity (and, most important, can reflect favorably on your integrity) should be reviewed at this time.

1. Keep employees informed about developments.
2. Recommend pay increases where they are indicated.
3. Keep your people posted on how well they are doing.

4. Take the time to listen, empathetically, to employee complaints and grievances.
5. Permit employees to discuss work problems with you.
6. Recommend employees for promotional opportunities.
7. Don't take all the credit; share the product of your department's labor with all participating and productive members of the team.
8. Display consistent and dependable behavior.
9. Discipline in private.
10. Help employees improve and broaden their skills.
11. Treat all members of your department as equals.

Labor unions capitalize on management mistakes. The need for unionization is created by the management rather than the union. If the management (including first-line supervisors) does not understand or care about employee needs, the union wins the election. It is evident that institutions and supervisors have become increasingly sophisticated and aware of what drives employees into unions.

UNION SUSCEPTIBILITY CHECKLIST

Jackson offers us an important exercise in determining how vulnerable your institution is to unionization. The following checklist serves as a model from which union-free officials may tailor their own. It should be utilized by answering the questions either "yes" or "no." Take the value allotted to each question for a "yes" answer and a zero for a "no" answer. Then add all points to arrive at a total. The point total should then be used with the chart that follows the questions to determine the extent of vulnerability.

1. Is the entire management team committed to remaining union-free in terms of time, effort, and energy? (Value: 5 points)
2. Is the management team free of "heavy-handed" managers or supervisors who abuse supervisory powers and intentionally oppress employees; "buck-passer" managers or supervisors; "forked-tongue" managers or supervisors; "foul-language" managers or supervisors; "lover boy" managers or supervisors; "game-player" managers or supervisors who purposely mislead employees into believing that they will receive some special benefits by bidding for favors; or, finally, "don't give a damn" managers or supervisors? (Value: 10 points)

3. Is the employee complement devoid of "problem" employees, such as "marginal" employees, "rebellious and defiant" employees, "permanently disenchanted" employees, or "arrogantly independent" employees? (Value: 10 points)
4. Does the facility have written and distributed policies and rules of conduct that are equitable and consistently enforced? (Value: 5 points)
5. Does the organization have at least five functioning communications programs that enhance vertical communication as well as employee recognition? (Value: 5 points)
6. Has the employer adequately settled any questionable discharge or disciplinary matters that raised suspicions among employees as to the valid cause for the action? (Value: 4 points)
7. Does the employer have an open-door policy that is working, or some other grievance procedure that has been well received by the employees? (Value: 6 points)
8. Is the working environment as comfortable and pleasant as possible in relation to the nature of the work? (Value: 5 points)
9. Does the facility provide job continuity free from periodic layoffs, shutdowns, and the like? (Value: 4 points)
10. Is there a fair and equitable promotion procedure? (Value: 4 points)
11. Is seniority honored (and publicized) when other qualifications are met relative to job bid, layoff, recall, transfer, and so forth? (Value: 6 points)
12. Does the employer provide proper and adequate training? (Value: 3 points)
13. Does the organization have a good reputation and "track record" in safety matters? (Value: 3 points)
14. Has the employer assimilated into the management team the bulk of the rank-and-file "leaders"? (Value: 4 points)
15. Does the facility adhere strictly to nondiscriminatory programs and policies? (Value: 4 points)
16. Does the employer have a personnel or employee relations department that has mastered the concept of "eliminating problems internally"? (Value: 4 points)
17. Does the organization eliminate (terminate) "problem" employees and supervisors who will not comply with the "standards" imposed? (Value: 4 points)
18. Does the employer pay comparable wages to those of competitive organizations in the same area—both union and nonunion? (Value: 6 points)

19. Is the compensation system a fair and equitable one? (Value: 4 points)
20. Does the employer furnish fringe benefits comparable to those of competitive organizations in the area? (Value: 4 points)

	How do you rate?
95 or more	*Minimal susceptibility*
80–94	*No impending crisis, but approaching dangerous levels*
70–79	*Substantial susceptibility*
0–69	*Extraordinary susceptibility**

WHAT YOU CAN AND CANNOT DO DURING A UNION-ORGANIZING DRIVE

A committee of the American Bar Association and a committee of publishers and associations included in a declaration of principles that writers who deal with any subject that has or may have legal overtones shall declare that they are not engaged in rendering legal service. This chapter does not intend to render legal advice in the complex area of union organization. If legal service or other expert assistance is required, the services of a competent professional should be sought. There is no question that, when a union approaches an institution, that institution should have sound labor relations and, if necessary, legal advice. But in the final analysis a simple dose of common sense would suffice.

As the first-line supervisor, you will be on the firing line in such a situation. You will have to know what is and is not permissible as far as the National Labor Relations Act is concerned. Given the pressures of the moment and of the supervisor-employee relationships that have developed over the years in your department, however, it may seem strange to deal with legalities at such a time.

Let us refer then to the overall common-sense approach that has been complicated by legal interpretations. There are three basic proscriptions when dealing with employees during a union-organizing campaign.

---

*From the book, *When Labor Trouble Strikes: An Action Handbook* by Gordon E. Jackson, ©1981. Used by permission of the publisher, Prentice-Hall, Inc., Englewood Cliffs, N.J.

1. Don't threaten them (in fact, don't threaten them at other times as well).
2. Don't promise them any reward for staying out of the union.
3. Don't interrogate them, especially about their preferences. Never ask "Are you for the union or are you against the union?"

When and if the union approaches employees in your institution, there will be a great deal of pressure on supervisors to deliver a vote for management. Ideally, there will be a complete and open discussion of the pros and cons of unionization led by the top management of your institution and directed toward supervisors at every level. You will be tempted to put pressure on the employees to vote against the union. The National Labor Relations Board has set up general guidelines for managerial behavior during a union-organizing drive. You may not threaten employees with the loss of their jobs or reduction in their wages, and you may not use threatening or intimidating language. Of course, even common sense directs you not to threaten employees in the exercise of their right to support a union.

Although you cannot personally urge an employee to convince other workers to oppose the union, you may tell employees that when a union enters an institution, problems must be directed to the shop steward, eliminating the one-to-one discussion between employee and supervisor. You can share with employees the disadvantages of belonging to a union, such as paying dues and initiation fees, the possibility of loss of income due to strikes, and the necessity for picket line duty. Without using threatening language, you may tell employees that the administration does not want a union and that the institution does not need a union.

You cannot promise increased wages, promotions, or benefits if employees reject the union. You can tell the employees that a union will out-promise an employer but that, in the final analysis, the union cannot guarantee anything. It must bargain with the employer and, to attain benefit levels, must reach agreement with the employer. You may remind the employees of their present benefits and compare these benefits to those in unionized institutions.

Supervisors may not ask employees their personal opinions about the union or what they believe to be the feelings of other employees. You cannot call employees away from their work areas into your office to urge them to vote against the union. You cannot systematically visit the homes of employees to urge them to vote against the union.

As a supervisor, you can tell employees that they do not have to sign union authorization cards and, indeed, do not have to speak to union organizers in their homes if they do not so desire. You can speak to employees individually or in groups at the employees' work stations, in the employee cafeteria, or in other areas where employees are accustomed to being. Remember that it is illegal to ask employees what they think about a union, how they intend to vote, or if they have signed cards or attended union meetings. It is permissible, however, to tell employees why a union is not necessary in your institution. You may continue to operate normally and continue to discipline and discharge as the situation requires, but not for the sole reason that the employee is involved in union activities (although employees are expected to work at their assignments during working hours).

PERMISSIBLE AND IMPERMISSIBLE CAMPAIGNING

We will once again review what is and is not permissible regarding management action during a union-organizing campaign. Various decisions of the National Labor Relations Board in this area have established legal distinctions that govern the rights of management to speak freely when combating a union-organizing drive. The following checklist is not all inclusive but is presented to encourage your institution to take a stand during such a period. It cannot be said too often that taking a neutral position or taking no position at all during a union-organizing campaign is tantamount to agreeing to the organization of your employees. If the hospital is against recognizing a union, it can and should take the following actions.

1. Explain the meaning of union recognition and the procedure to be followed.
2. Encourage each member of the bargaining unit (those employees who will be permitted to vote in a union election) to cast their ballot in the election.
3. Communicate to employees that they are free to vote for or against the union, despite the fact that they have signed a union authorization card.
4. Communicate to all employees why the administration is against recognizing a union.
5. Review the compensation and benefits program, pointing out the record of the administration in the past.
6. Point out to employees statements made by the union that the administration believes to be untrue, and communicate the administration's own position on each of these statements.
7. If there is a general no-solicitation rule, prevent solicitation of membership by the union during working hours.

8. Continue to enforce all rules and regulations in effect before the union's request for recognition.
9. Send letters to employees' homes stating the administration's position, record, and knowledge of the union's position in other hospitals.
10. Discuss the possibility of strikes when unions enter hospitals; discuss the ramifications of such a strike.
11. Discuss the impact of union dues and in general the cost of belonging to a union. Point out to the employees that the union can promise the employees anything but that it can deliver on promises only with the agreement of the institution.
12. Discuss with employees, individually at their work areas, the position of the institution.
13. In response to the union's promises during the pre-election period, point out to employees that if the hospital were to meet these demands it might be forced to lay off workers (this statement can be made as long as the administration points out that it would be an involuntary action and a consequence of a union's demands).

Of course, the hospital cannot and should not engage in the following activities during the union-organizing drive.

1. Do not promise benefits and threaten reprisals if employees vote for or against the union or have supervisors attend meetings or spy on employees to determine whether or not they are participating in union activities.
2. Do not grant wage increases or special concessions during the pre-election period unless the timing coincides with well-established prior practices.
3. Do not prevent employees from wearing union buttons, except in cases where the buttons are provocative or extremely large.
4. Do not bar employee union representatives from soliciting employee membership during nonworking hours when the solicitation does not interfere with the work of others or with patient care.
5. Do not summon an employee into an office for private discussion of the union and the upcoming elections (this does not preclude an employee from coming in voluntarily to discuss these things).
6. Do not question employees about union matters and meetings.
7. Do not ask employees how they intend to vote.
8. Do not threaten layoffs because of unionization or state that you will never deal with a union even if it is certified.
9. Do not hold meetings with employees within the 24-hour period immediately preceding the election.[7]

There is much that the employer can say and do during the union-organizing campaign. As discussed above, in a health care facility no-solicitation and no-distribution rules can be enforced if properly constructed and properly administered without discrimination per se against the union and in the interest of maintaining patient care. As we shall see, it is essential that as many qualified members of the employee body (those who are included in the bargaining unit) as possible vote at a time of an election. It has been shown that employees who are eligible to vote but do not vote in the union election would probably vote against the union; on the other hand, employees who favor unions will come out to vote. Therefore, as a supervisor you should encourage all employees in your department who are eligible to vote to do so.

It is essential to differentiate between communications that are threatening or carry promises of reward and those designed to bring management's position honestly and forthrightly to all eligible employees. As to the question of free speech, the National Labor Relations Board judges each case on its own merits. The essential element is the "total context," which will determine whether the communication was coercive or threatening or contained promises. Employees should be told that signing a union authorization card is not equivalent to a vote for the union; the voting will be by secret ballot, and an employee can make a final decision at that time, notwithstanding the fact that he or she has signed a union authorization card. In an election conducted by a National Labor Relations Board, the marking of ballots is decisive, not the presentation of signed authorization cards.

I repeat an important point made earlier, that I do not contend to render legal service in reviewing this critical and complex area of union organization. If legal service or other expert assistance is deemed necessary by your institution, the services of a competent professional should be sought.

SOLICITATION AND DISTRIBUTION OF CAMPAIGN MATERIAL

Many supervisors find themselves perplexed and anxious to take immediate action when employees in their departments come to work wearing buttons that urge employees to vote for a specific union. There is also concern when employees start to distribute campaign material and, finally, when employees are asked to sign union authorization cards.

The National Labor Relations Board issued guidelines for handling no-solicitation and no-distribution rules in health care facilities on 5 October 1979. In general, the Board's approach to this difficult area is guided by whether the employer's rule is for the purpose of efficiency or safety and is nondiscriminatory in nature—that is, is not directed solely against the union's organizing campaign (your institution's labor attorney will be able to advise you on solicitation and distribution). The following is an outline of the Board's guidelines.

1. *Patient rooms, operating rooms, treatment rooms:* A ban on solicitation in these areas continues to be treated as presumptively valid. There are still cases where your institution would have the burden of showing that solicitation would have a dilatory effect on procedures critical to patient care.
2. *Corridor and patient sitting rooms:* "Patient care areas" would be redefined to include corridors adjacent to any patient rooms, operating rooms, and treating rooms as well as sitting rooms on patient floors that are accessible to and used by patients. A ban on solicitation in these areas would be presumptively valid. To support its claim to the validity of permitting solicitation in such areas, a union would have to show that the presence of patients or critical medical personnel in such areas is so minimal, or that the physical layout of the area at issue is such, that it is unlikely that solicitation therein would either adversely affect the patients or disrupt patient care.
3. *Elevators and stairways:* If an elevator or stairway is used frequently to transport patients, a ban on solicitation would be presumptively valid.
4. *Nurses' stations:* Detailed evidence regarding the physical layout and use of nurses' stations would be extremely important in determining whether these areas fall within the patient care category. The union would look into such factors as the extent to which patient treatment is given in the nurses' stations; the proximity of the stations to patient rooms or sitting rooms; the physical separation of the stations surrounding patient care areas; whether there are interior partitions that separate working from nonworking areas within the station; whether employees take their breaks in the stations; and whether other types of nonwork-related activities are permitted there.
5. *Public access areas:* Areas in which employees may mingle with patients as well as visitors and the general public (such as cafeterias, vending machine areas, pharmacies and gift shops, lobbies, entranceways, and exterior grounds and walkways) will continue to be places in which solicitation is presumed to be protected.
6. *Working areas to which only employees have general access:* These areas include the kitchen, laundry, supply rooms, housekeeping, and

accounting and medical records rooms. A ban on solicitation between nonworking employees would continue to be unlawful unless the employer could prove that solicitation in these areas would disrupt critical patient care.

7. *Nonworking areas to which only employees have access:* In such areas as employee locker rooms, lounges, restrooms, and parking lots, there are few defenses available to the institution for a policy that limits employee union solicitation and distribution activity.

The area of solicitation and distribution is quite complex. It is essential that hospital administration retain labor counsel to give expert advice in setting up policies and actions regarding this area.

THE BARGAINING UNIT

The bargaining unit is defined as employees who will vote in an election to determine whether or not they wish to be represented by a union. Appropriate bargaining units are determined by the National Labor Relations Board. The health care industry had special problems that were addressed in the deliberations of the congressional committees considering the inclusion of the health care industry in 1974. One of the considerations of the committee was stated in the congressional report:

> . . . Due consideration should be given by the National Labor Relations Board to prevent the proliferation of bargaining units in the health care industry (S. 3203, Calendar #738, Senate Report #93-766, April 2, 1974).

Congress recognized the difficult burden that would be thrust on health care institutions if various employee groups could form into separate bargaining units, thereby forcing the hospital to negotiate contracts with dozens of unions. The issue of an appropriate bargaining unit is a complex one, but in general you may be dealing with units of service and maintenance employees, registered nurses, guards, technical employees, business office clericals, MDs, and other professionals.

One thing is clear: you, as a supervisor, are excluded from the provisions of the act. Therefore, the administration need not recognize a bargaining unit of supervisors; the Board may not certify a labor organization seeking to represent supervisors.

Once the bargaining unit is determined, the Board will ascertain whether there is an appropriate show of interest. This show of interest is displayed by the union presenting union authorization cards for at least 30 percent of the bargaining unit employees. Remember, however, that although this figure will enable the union to obtain an election under National Labor Relations Board auspices the union needs much more support than 30 percent to win the election.

THE ELECTION PROCESS

If the union is successful in obtaining authorization cards from at least 30 percent of the bargaining unit employees in your institution, they can seek an election under the National Labor Relations Board auspices. The critical point, which should be reiterated, is that an employee who signs an authorization card still can vote against the union. If the union does file a petition with the National Labor Relations Board for an election, the process enters its most intense phase.

Let us review what occurs when the union petitions for the election. The National Labor Relations Board will set an election date and determine the time and place for an election. This, in most cases, will occur as soon as possible on hospital premises. This is the most critical time of the organizing campaign. It is during these days, between the time the election date is announced and the actual election, that the union's campaign goes into high gear.

Union promises will include the following.

1. The union will obtain significant increases in wages.
2. The union will obtain significant increases in benefits.
3. The union will guarantee job security.
4. The union will provide dignity in the workplace.
5. The union will provide "real" due process.

It is essential that management respond to union promises not by offering their own promises but by offering the reality: the unions can promise anything, but as to delivery, everything must be negotiated with management; management is the final deliverer. It is also important that employees understand what the record of the management has been in the past and what the record of the union has been in the past.

The election is not a complicated procedure. Present at the polling area is a National Labor Relations Board representative who is directly responsible for conducting the election. In addition, both the union and the hospital provide observers. The hospital's observer cannot be a supervisor.

Within seven days after the Board's regional director has approved an election, the Board is provided with a list of all eligible employees. This list contains the names and addresses of all unit employees. Generally, employees are eligible to vote if they are on the employer's payroll for the period immediately preceding the date on which the election is held. In addition, employees who are engaged in an economic strike and have been permanently replaced are still eligible to vote if the election is held within 12 months of the strike. Employees who are on layoff status but have a reasonable expectation of re-employment in the near future have been deemed eligible to vote. Those who have been discharged for cause or who have quit between the date on which the election was set and the actual voting day are ineligible unless such employees have been discriminatorily discharged.[8]

Employees have the opportunity to vote in secret. They mark a simple ballot "yes" or "no" on the question of whether they wish to be represented by the specific union petitioning. A union must receive a majority of the valid ballots cast to be certified. If 50 percent plus one employee of the employees who voted in the election cast their ballots in favor of the union, the union will become the certified representative of the bargaining unit for the purposes of collective bargaining.

A simple illustration will underscore the importance of getting out the vote. If a bargaining unit of 500 service and maintenance employees at your institution is involved in an election, the union must receive a majority of the valid ballots cast. If only 400 of these employees actually vote, the union need only receive 201 votes. As you can plainly see, if 201 out of 400 voting employees cast their ballots for the union, the union will be certified to represent all 500 employees in the bargaining unit. The 100 employees who did not vote have no effect on the outcome of the election. Remember that many presidents of the United States have been elected by a majority of the votes cast but by a significant minority of the eligible electorate. *So go union elections.*

In *The 100 Best Companies to Work for in America,* the authors summarize policies of successful union-free companies:

1. Make people feel that they are part of a team or, in some cases, a family.
2. Encourage open communications, informing their people of new developments and encouraging them to offer suggestions and complaints.
3. Promote from within; let their own people bid for jobs before hiring outsiders.

4. Stress quality, enabling people to feel pride in the products or services they are providing.
5. Allow their employees to share in the profits, through profit-sharing or stock ownership or both.
6. Reduce the distinctions of rank between the top management and those in entry-level jobs; put everyone on a first-name basis; bar executive dining rooms and exclusive perks for high-level people.
7. Devote attention and resources to creating as pleasant a workplace environment as possible; hire good architects.
8. Encourage their employees to be active in community service by giving money to organizations in which employees participate.
9. Help employees save by matching the funds they save.
10. Try not to lay off people without first making an effort to place them in other jobs within the company or elsewhere.
11. Care enough about the health of their employees to provide physical fitness centers and regular exercise and medical programs.
12. Expand the skills of their people through training programs and reimbursement of tuition for outside courses.*

With such practices and philosophy, these institutions rarely become unionized.

KEY POINTS TO A UNION ORGANIZING DRIVE

1. More employees vote for or against their immediate supervisor than for or against top management, the board of trustees, or consultants.
2. Unions rarely organize employees; rather, it is administration's poor record in employee relations that drives employees into unions.
3. Institutions that provide all the benefits and conditions of the union shop will not become unionized.
4. There is a marked relationship between worker morale and the extent to which employees feel that their boss is interested in discussing work problems with their work group. If the boss is not interested, workers will discuss those problems with outside groups—in some cases, unions.
5. Employees who feel group loyalty and pride do not look outside to unions for need fulfillment.

---

*Reprinted from *The 100 Best Companies to Work for in America* by R. Levering, M. Moskowitz, and M. Katz, pp. 140–142, with permission of Addison-Wesley Publishing Company, Wesley, Mass., ©1984.

6. Improved managerial practices and the supervisor's attention to the best utilization of people and technology can increase job satisfaction and productivity. Satisfied and fulfilled employees do not look to unions.
7. Unions are looking for bona fide issues to use in the organizing drive. Although they often will latch on to petty gripes and perceived injustices, they also look for supervisors who are vulnerable. Such supervisors are usually not employee-centered, have not built up group loyalty, and are not interested in employee needs.
8. Labor unions capitalize on management mistakes.
9. You should not threaten employees or promise them any reward for staying out of the union. Do not interrogate them about their preferences during a union-organizing drive. These are unfair labor practices.
10. You can tell employees how the institution feels about unionization. You can share with them the employee disadvantages of belonging to a union.
11. You cannot call employees away from their work areas into your office to urge them to vote against the union.
12. You should tell employees that they do not have to sign union authorization cards or speak to union organizers if they do not so desire.
13. You should inform employees that even though they have signed a union authorization card they can change their mind and vote any way they wish at the time of an election.
14. You should encourage each member of your department who is in the bargaining unit (those employees eligible to vote) to cast a ballot in the election.
15. You should continue to enforce all rules and regulations in effect before the union's request for recognition.
16. You should keep top management apprised of day-to-day developments during the union-organizing campaign. You will be the person closest to the employees at that time. Your perception of trends is critical to administration planning.
17. Statistics indicate that the health care industry has been more effective in meeting the challenge of unions by adopting a more sophisticated and concerned management approach to employee needs.

NOTES

1. Lloyd Reynolds, *Labor Economics and Labor Relations,* 2nd ed. (Englewood Cliffs, NJ: Prentice-Hall, 1956), 60.

2. Charles L. Joiner, "Maintaining Nonunion Status," in *Handbook of Health Care Human Resources Management,* ed. Norman Metzger (Rockville, MD: Aspen Publishers, 1981), 627.

3. Ibid.

4. Warren H. Chaney and Thomas R. Beech, *The Union Epidemic* (Rockville, MD: Aspen Publishers, 1976), 45–46.

5. From an interview with Elliott Godoff conducted by Norman Metzger on 29 February 1972. The late Mr. Godoff was Executive Vice-President/Organization Director of District 1199 Drug and Hospital Employees' Union.

6. *A Guidebook for Union Organizers* (Washington, DC: AFL-CIO Industrial Union Department, 1965), 3.

7. Norman Metzger and Dennis Pointer, *Labor Management Relations in the Health Service Industry: Theory and Practice* (Washington, DC: Science and Health Publications, 1972), 143–44.

8. Dennis Pointer and Norman Metzger, *The National Labor Relations Act: A Guidebook for Health Care Facility Administrators* (New York, NY: Spectrum Publications, 1973), 72–73.

Chapter 12

Negotiating for Positive Outcomes

> *We characterize negotiation as a process of potential opportunistic interaction by which two or more parties, with some apparent conflict, seek to do better through jointly decided action than they could otherwise.*
>
> *David A. Lax and James K. Sebenius*
> The Manager As Negotiator
> *(New York: The Free Press, Div. of Macmillan Inc., 1986) p. 11.*

The art and science of negotiations underscore the need for persistence and determination: persistence in the face of often overwhelming resistance, and determination to offset an "adversary" who is unwilling or unable to compromise. Supervisors and managers often must negotiate staffing levels, salary increases for their subordinates, their own salaries, responsibilities, authority, promotions for their subordinates and for themselves, goals, schedules, and so on. Negotiators—those who succeed (and we will define "success" a little bit later)—are skilled practitioners of an art that is little understood. Personalities play a far more important role in most negotiations than the theoretical or academic formats, which has been suggested by the numerous writers on the subject. The art of negotiating has been called neglected and is far more complex than the mere resolution of the deal.

There are many forces, external and internal, that affect the bargain, and in the final analysis successful bargainers are familiar with all the forces brought to bear in the bargaining milieu. The personalities involved have a critical impact on the style and outcome of the negotiation. It is essential to understand not only your own personality but the personality of the other.

SOME DIFFICULT NEGOTIATING PARTNERS

Warschaw helps us identify certain styles:

1. *Jungle fighters.* Jungle fighters are the most dangerous negotiators of all. They are consummate "con artists." They are win-lose negotiators. They hate to be kept waiting for an appointment, they're the drivers honking in a traffic jam, the patients pacing in the doctor's waiting room. Psychologist Harry Levinson told the American Psychological Association at its 1977 conference that "such abrasive personalities are probably the most single frequent cause for the failure of bright men and women in executive ranks."
2. The next style is that of the *Dictators.* They are win-lose negotiators: they win, you lose. Warschaw says that they are gate-keepers of information: they are assertive, organized, poised, decisive, shrewd, analytical and efficient. But they are, as well, rigid, isolated, obsessive, opinionated, demanding, self-righteous, judgmental, and intimidating. You learn only what they want you to know. They have little tolerance for mistakes. Many of them are perfectionists, making impossible demands not only of others but of themselves. [I thought it interesting that she — Warschaw — said that they gravitate to those fields in which most people have little experience and knowledge. The field of gynecology is loaded with dictators, she says.]
3. The next style is that of the *Silhouette.* Silhouettes fear intimacy of any kind. They are lose-lose negotiators. They do anything and everything to ignore conflict and to avoid exposing their feelings. They have an effective response to pressure, more effective than anger: silence.
4. *Big-Daddies* and *Big-Mamas* are extremely manipulative. They will help you grow, but they must be in charge of that growth. They are successful because they offer the one human commodity that is essential for growth—tender loving care. [But Warschaw identifies the fact that they will do so only up to a point—the point at which their control over you is threatened. The big threat in dealing with Big-Daddies and Big-Mamas is that the strokes they offer are so comforting and the rewards are so good that you may never gain the independence you require to reach maturity.]
5. *Soothers.* This style loses more often than any other type of negotiator because
    - they start off every negotiation expecting to lose
    - they won't tell you what they want

- they seldom tell you the truth, if the truth is likely to upset you—instead they'll tell you what they think you want to hear
- they'll pretend that problems do not exist, or gloss over them—they seldom return phone calls
- they won't say "no" out of fear of losing your approval
- they blame themselves too quickly and make concessions too early*

The truly successful negotiators are win-win negotiators. They know that negotiating is not solely a question of how much they will win but how much the loss will affect the other person. They are master observers of the human condition. They know their purpose, needs, and goals as well as those of their opponents or partners. They won't humiliate you in public. They don't luxuriate in emotionalism; their regard for others is their greatest strength. They stay focused on the objective. They are risk-takers, but their risks are calculated. They don't try to out-muscle a combative force; more often they try to buffer and divert it. They don't feel that they need to be loved by everyone. They are objective, nonjudgmental, curious, clear, motivated, specific, sensitive, and open. These people usually start off with more self-esteem.

This marvelous panorama of styles must be augmented by an understanding that the individual you are dealing with may be simply a rogue. Lombardo and McCall catalog a rogue's gallery of bosses.

1. *Snakes-in-the-grass:* bosses who lack integrity and generally cannot be trusted.
2. *Killers:* little Napoleons or martinets who sit on people.
3. *Heel-grinders:* bosses who treat others like dirt.
4. *Egotists:* people who know everything, won't listen, and shirk responsibility.
5. *Incompetents:* bosses who just do not know what they are doing and won't admit it.
6. *Detail-drones:* bosses who go strictly by the book and delight in detail.
7. *Rodneys:* bosses who just "don't get no respect."
8. *Slobs:* bosses with personal habits, appearances, or prejudices that are intolerable to others.[1]

I start out with these two views of styles and rogues so that it is clear in your minds that there are at least two parties to the bargain. Knowing the

---

*Reprinted from *Winning by Negotiation* by T.A. Warschaw, pp. 18–20, with permission of McGraw-Hill Book Company, © 1980.

opponent or the boss that you will be dealing with is critical to effecting a successful win-win negotiation.

Raiffa offers a checklist for negotiators.

1. First know yourself.
2. Know your adversary.
3. Give thought to the negotiating conventions in each context.
4. Consider the logistics of the situation.
5. Remember that simulated role-playing can be of value in preparing your strategy.
6. Set and iterate your aspiration levels.[2]

REASONS FOR COMMON FAILURES IN NEGOTIATIONS

It is important to know whether the person across the table from you is a jungle fighter, a big-daddy or big-mama, or one of the rogues that we listed above; it is well to know how they have negotiated in the past. As far as knowing yourself, the critical element is searching for competing and substitute alternatives. The truly successful negotiator is not the one who goes in with an all-or-nothing attitude. The successful negotiator consistently thinks about alternatives and fall-back positions.

Be careful of a common failure in negotiations. Bazerman states that when both sides start with extreme demands, expecting to compromise somewhere in the middle, they get caught up in the struggle and feel that they have too much invested to back off; thinking that this is so, they take a hard line instead of adopting conciliatory or problem-solving approaches. Why does this happen? Bazerman says that there are at least four complementary reasons.

1. Once negotiators make an initial commitment to a position, they are more likely to know the information that supports their initial evaluation of the situation.
2. Negotiators' judgment is biased to interpret what they see and hear in a way that justifies their initial position.
3. Negotiators often increase their demands or hold out too long to save face with their constituency.
4. Finally, the competitive context of the negotiations adds to the likelihood of escalation.[3]

It is well to note that negotiations rarely are strictly competitive, but the players may behave as if they were; the players may consider themselves strictly opposed disputants rather than jointly cooperative problem-solvers. Raiffa points out that we really are not a zero-sum society: it is not true that what one gains another must necessarily lose. The trouble is that often we act as if this were the case.[4]

Fisher and Ury tell us that principled negotiation or negotiation on merits can be boiled down to four basic points.

1. *People:* separate the people from the problem.
2. *Interests:* focus on interests, not positions.
3. *Options:* generate a variety of possibilities before deciding what to do.
4. *Criteria:* insist that the results be based on some objective standards.[5]

Successful negotiations spring from a working relationship of trust. Ouchi defines trust as consisting of "the understanding that you and I share fundamentally compatible goals in the long run, that you and I desire a more effective relationship together, and that neither desires to harm the other."[6]

To be a successful negotiator, you must also be willing to see the situation as your opponent does. The key to successful negotiations is understanding the other party's positions, stresses, and needs. You must be willing to listen and alter your position. Charles Darwin said "I have steadily endeavored to keep my mind free so as to give up any hypotheses, however much beloved (and I cannot resist forming one on every subject), as soon as facts are shown to be opposed to it." On the other hand, José Ortega y Gasset has said "it does not worry him that his 'ideas' are not true, he uses them as trenches for the defense of his existence, as scarecrows to frighten away reality[7]." To be a win-win negotiator you cannot frighten away reality. You cannot stand with positions that are fallible in the face of facts.

It is essential that you understand (not always agree with) the other party's position. Therefore, you must attempt to see what motivates the other party. Fisher and Ury suggest that, if you want someone to listen and understand your reasoning, give your interests and reasoning first and your conclusions or proposals later.[8]

There are two typical styles that usually fail in negotiations. One is the *macho* or *cowboy-cowgirl* style, characterized by pitting your strength against the other party's strength. It is the dramatic, "high noon" confrontation. Here someone may have to give way, and it usually is a win-lose result with a great deal of bitterness as far as the loser is concerned. A variation on this, yet still very much a part of the macho approach, is the bottom-line approach. A bottom line is almost certain to be too rigid. It usually is set too high and more often than not it does not take into consideration possible options.

The second failing style, the *sycophant,* is very often found in modern institutions where we are forced to redefine reality. We rationalize positions and bury our creativity by submitting. Maccoby describes the typical sycophant: "He needs to be liked and accepted by strangers in order to gain a livelihood. The danger for him is not so much that it will harden his heart but that he will lose his integrity, sense of self-esteem and values in an attempt to adapt and ingratiate, to be what others want, to become more marketable."[9] The sycophant is similar to Warschaw's soother; they both expect to lose, they drown their integrity in submission, and they are frightened to state what they want. They fail the "I believe in my integrity" test. Join me in taking it. Answer to the following questions, "Usually," "Sometimes," or "Never":

1. I've gone home after work and muttered to myself "I should have told him this or that."
2. I sit in my office after a meeting with my boss and I think "If I only had. . . ."
3. I've had that sinking feeling in my stomach when I've thought I've sold myself out.
4. I have very little freedom to express myself at my job.
5. I am intimidated by my boss.
6. If I attempt to bargain with my boss over her or his decisions, I am considered disloyal.
7. I have been asked to do things that I know are improper.
8. I am caught up in office politics.
9. I feel that my boss listens to others and not to me.

Because the sycophant fails this test, he or she is a terrible negotiator—one who enters a room with expectations of losing.

PERSPECTIVES ON NEGOTIATORS

One 17th century writer defined the art of negotiations as follows:

> The compleat negotiator should have a quick mind but unlimited patience, know how to dissemble without being a liar, inspire trust without trusting others, be modest but assertive, charm others without succumbing to their charms, and possess plenty of

money and a beautiful wife while remaining indifferent to all temptation of riches and women.

This jocular albeit sexist definition is part of the legacy of the win-lose approach to negotiations. Further evidence is presented by Nierenberg, president of the Negotiating Institute of New York City, who describes the successful negotiator as follows.

> The successful negotiator must combine the alertness and speed of the expert swordsman with an artist's sensitivity. He must watch his adversary across the bargaining table with the keen eye of a fencer, ever ready to spot any loophole in the defense, any shift in strategy. He is prepared to thrust at the slightest opportunity. On the other hand he must also be the sensitive artist, perceptive of the slightest variation in the color of the opponent's mood or motivation. At the correct moment he must be able to select from the pallet of many colors exactly the right combination of shades, tints, that will lead to mastery. Success in negotiation, aside from adequate training, is essentially a matter of sensitivity and correct timing.[10]

A former director of the Federal Mediation and Conciliation Services, William E. Simkin, suggests ten qualifications of the "ideal" negotiator.

> The patience of Job, the sincerity and bulldog characteristics of the English, the wit of the Irish, the physical endurance of the marathon runner, the broken field and dodging abilities of a halfback, the guile of a Machiavelli, the personality probing skills of the psychiatrist, the confidence-retaining characteristics of a mute, the hide of a rhinoceros, and the wisdom of Solomon.[11]

Cohen writes:

> You can get what you want if you recognize that each person is unique and that needs can be reconciled. At the same time never forget that most needs can be fulfilled by the way you act and behave.[12]

A PRESCRIPTION FOR SUCCESSFUL NEGOTIATING

A. Samuel Cook, a labor attorney, offers this advice for successful negotiating.

1. Understand the satisfaction of needs; direct your attention to the interests and needs of the other party.
2. Be prepared. You cannot "wing it" and expect to win. Preparation requires first of all an intimate knowledge of oneself. Patience is essential. Voorhees tells us of an occasion where Walter Reuther, the famous union leader of United Auto Workers, was asked the same question 15 times. He never gave a sign of irritation and answered the question as carefully and as patiently on the fifteenth time as on the first. (Theodore Vorhees, "The Art of Negotiations," *The Practical Lawyer* 13 (April 1967) 64.)
3. Technical and economic research are essential. If you are bargaining over staffing levels, over your salary, or over the salaries of the people who are working for you, you should know as much as possible about the marketplace, the economic conditions at your institution, and what the parameters of the economic settlement encompass.
4. The versatile negotiator must learn the art of listening. This is the true key to a win-win negotiation.
5. The successful negotiator has the power of persuasion. This includes honest debate, exchange of facts, and arguments seriously considered by both sides with subsequent movement and compromise.[13]

Wessel outlines the salient points of a code of conduct for negotiators who believe in win-win.

1. Data will not be withheld because they may be "negative" or "unhelpful."
2. Concealment will not be practiced for concealment's sake.
3. Delay will not be employed as a tactic to avoid an undesired result.
4. Unfair "tricks" designed to mislead will not be employed to win a struggle.
5. Borderline ethical disingenuity will not be practiced.
6. Motivation of adversaries will not unnecessarily or lightly be impugned.
7. An opponent's personal habits and characteristics will not be questioned unless relevant.
8. Wherever possible, opportunity will be left for an opponent's orderly retreat and "exit with honor."
9. Extremism may be countered forcefully and with emotionalism where justified but will not be fought or matched with extremism.
10. Dogmatism will be avoided.
11. Complex concepts will be simplified as much as possible so as to achieve maximum communication and understanding.

12. Effort will be made to identify and isolate subjective considerations involved in reaching a technical conclusion.
13. Relevant data will be disclosed when ready for analysis and peer review, even to an extremist opposition and without legal obligation.
14. Socially desirable professional disclosure will not be postponed for tactical advantage.
15. Hypothesis, uncertainty, and inadequate knowledge will be stated affirmatively, not conceded only reluctantly or under pressure.
16. Unjustified assumption and off-the-cuff comment will be avoided.
17. Interest in an outcome, relationship to a proponent, and bias, prejudice, and proclivity of any kind will be disclosed voluntarily and as a matter of course.
18. Research and investigation will be conducted appropriate to the problem involved. Although the precise extent of that effort will vary with the nature of the issues, it will be consistent with the stated overall responsibility to the solution of the problem.
19. Integrity will always be given first priority.[14]

It is clear that the concept of win-lose that so preoccupies most individuals who are involved in negotiations of any sort is counterproductive. We are preoccupied with winning; in almost every aspect of life people want to be winners. The real measure of successful negotiations is when both parties come out thinking that they have won. Indeed, negotiations are really a cooperative endeavor. Your focus must be on the converging of interests, the satisfaction of the needs of both parties, and an approach that maintains the dignity of both parties. The goal, therefore, is to come up with nothing less than an arrangement that satisfies the needs of the parties. It is a simplistic view that all negotiations concern themselves with a give-and-take, trading, and, in the final analysis, splitting the difference.

Jandt states eloquently the viewpoint of win-lose negotiators.

> Positional bargainers articulate certain demands (their "positions") and they measure their success in terms of those demands to which their opposites accede. In positional bargaining, either I win or you win; either the majority of your "positions" prevail, or the majority of mine do.[15]

This is a destructive view. It clearly defines success in bargaining by making the position itself more important than the ultimate objective. Never get mired down in positions. Keep your eye on the point at which you and the other party will arrive at a mutually beneficial deal. There is an opportunity in sound negotiations to explore mutual problems; therefore, what some practitioners call "interest bargaining" is the recommended form. It takes into account the full range of the parties' interests and thus one negotiates problems rather than demands. As Jandt states:

> Practitioners of interest bargaining investigate the *real*—as opposed to the stated—desires of the opponents. (They) then seek ways to satisfy their opponents' desires—by, among other approaches, offering desiderata that they themselves control in exchange for desiderata that their opponents control. ("Desiderata" is defined as "Things lacking but needed or desired.")[16]

The key here is to make certain that you and the other party understand any hidden agenda.

The following are some rules of negotiating that may be helpful.

1. Write down your questions in advance, and make sure that nothing is left out.
2. Carefully review the phrasing of the questions—no one gains in the bargain by antagonizing the other individual or impugning their honesty. Politeness counts. Composure is mandatory.
3. Listen carefully to make sure that you understand the other party's views. Too many negotiating sessions are fruitless or counterproductive because one party or the other misses the real message. Listening is a lost art. A good listener does so:
   - without interruption
   - without jumping to conclusions
   - without evaluation
   - attentively
   - patiently
   - while looking at the speaker
   - with questions to clarify the speaker's meanings
   - without rushing the speaker or finishing his or her sentences
   - with body movements and comments that give the speaker a strong indication that the listener is following
   - with an attitude that conveys an appreciation that what the speaker has to say is important

Cancelliere suggests some positive steps that you can take to improve your ability to listen from the other person's point of view (so essential in fruitful negotiations).

1. Focus attention on the speaker and away from yourself.
2. Let go of your agenda. Let the speaker set the agenda, and follow where the speaker leads you.
3. Pursue understanding.
4. Control the need to assert yourself and impose your needs on the speaker.
5. Refrain from giving advice or making judgments.[17]

These work well when incorporated in negotiating efforts, but remember that your agenda is as important as the other party's.

SOME DO's AND DON'Ts

Bade and Stone offer the following list of Do's and Don'ts for negotiations.

1. Do not play it entirely by ear. Your strategy must be planned in advance. You should know what you are willing to accept. Even though you go in at a higher level, be honest with yourself about the bottom line you wish to accomplish.
2. Do not start with the hard issues. It is best to set a mood of compromise. Develop a mood that is conducive to give-and-take.
3. Use the appropriate language. Do not be subtle, pedantic, threatening, or hesitant. Be direct, clear, calm, patient, and tolerant.
4. Do not exaggerate or misrepresent the facts. A fact is a fact, and there is no substitute for honesty.
5. When responding to the other party's positions, give reasons.
6. Do not hide behind tricky, vague, or inconclusive language.
7. Keep control of the agenda that you wish to put forward.[18]

These authors also suggest that friendly, egalitarian attitude is the best approach to negotiations and that you not take a position that is construed as your final one, unless it has been thought out and truly is your final position.[19]

In one other negotiation style, the "end game ploy," a hail-fellow-well-met aura lulls you into a sense of receptivity directed toward closing the negotiations. Negotiations often are distasteful and tiring. An individual across the table from you may chip away at you near the end. Illiche, calling this style the "it's-a-shame-to" technique, illustrates it this way:

"Look. We resolved three or four most important issues. *It's a shame to* make that much progress without resolving the remaining issues. . . . *It's a shame to* give up without giving it a sincere try."[20] The point is to keep your eye on closing the deal. You should clearly know when enough is enough or when the negotiations need a time out.

Two particular salient points of the successful negotiator are identifying alternatives and having patience. There is no question that patience is a hallmark of the experienced negotiator. Chester Karrass, director of the Center for Effective Negotiating in Los Angeles, writes:

> Patience gives an opponent and his organization time to get used to the idea that what they wish for must be reconciled with what they can get. . . . It gives (opposers) time to find out how best to benefit each other. Before a negotiation begins it is not possible for either to know the best way to resolve problems, issues, and risks. New alternatives are discovered as information is brought to light.[21]

Beware of being in a hurry to close the deal, and beware of your opponent's rush to closure. The erosion of patience plays an important role in the end game ploy. Arbitrary deadlines are usually counterproductive. Final offers are usually followed by other offers. Both the arbitrary deadline and the final offer are often a sign of impatience.

The exploration of alternative positions before the bargaining begins is a critical and worthwhile investment. A key element in preparing your negotiating positions is an exploration of the possibility of the non-agreement. You must come to grips with a realistic evaluation of whether some agreement is better than no agreement; you must understand what the ramifications of "no agreement" are. In exploring alternatives—no matter how unpleasant that exercise might be—you must understand that agreement must not only satisfy your self-interests but the self-interests of the other as well. A one-sided solution can have a worse effect than no solution. Broaden your options. Look for mutual solutions, and remember that the party is not over when you have made the deal. Remember that stressing shared interests will facilitate agreement. Also, lower your expectations. One of the cornerstones for successful bargaining is a need for pragmatism and minimal subjectivity. You need to set high targets, but there is an inherent risk in aspiring to more to get more: the non-agreement. Effective bargaining requires a flexibility of approach.

Here are a few more do's and don'ts that may be helpful.

1. Do not think of negotiations as a Roman gladiator's battle or as a test of strength.
2. Preconceived notions of the other party's responses, which bring you into the bargaining with a chip on your shoulder, are to be discouraged.
3. Prepare! Prepare! Prepare! Make the hard choices of positions and a realistic analysis of interests before you start.
4. Success in negotiating involves an informed awareness and understanding of the compulsions that are operating in the other party. Keep your eye on the "why" of the other party's position.
5. Assumptions as to your opponent's understanding of what he or she can gain in a settlement are not to be made lightly.
6. Do not make the fatal error of underestimating your opponent.
7. Personal integrity and courage are the pervasive traits of successful bargainers.
8. Talk less. Listen more.

LISTENING SKILLS IN NEGOTIATIONS: ANOTHER REVIEW OF COMMUNICATION SKILLS[22]

Active listening and deliberative listening both require energy plus a desire to understand, yet these two types of listening have some important differences as well. Kelly explains that the desired result of the two types is similar: the accurate understanding of verbal communication. This understanding, however, is achieved in different ways.

> The deliberative listener "first" has to desire to critically analyze what the speaker has said, and "secondarily" tries to understand the speaker. . . . The active listener has the desire to understand the speaker "first" and, as a result, tries to take appropriate action. This does not mean to suggest that the active listeners are uncritical or always in agreement with what is communicated, but rather that their primary interest is to become fully and accurately aware of what is going on.[23]

Active listening plays an important role in supervisor-employee relationships, but it is also important in relationships between neighbors, roommates, friends, parents and children, and teachers and students. Unfortunately, active listening is not highly valued in our society. It is brushed aside by many of us who were taught to listen only in the deliberative style. It should be remembered, however, that we do not listen only with our ears. We also listen with our eyes and our sense of touch; we listen by becoming aware of the feelings and emotions that arise within us because of our contact with others. We listen with our mind, our heart, and our imagination.

Good active listening requires that we listen for all possible meanings, those behind the words as well as the obvious meanings. We find such meanings in facial expressions, gestures, and numerous body movements. This requires the listener to make eye contact with the talker. Beyond the body movements we must appraise and be aware of the talker's use of vocabulary and the tone and the volume of the message. This totality, which goes beyond the surface reception of the message, will enable us to understand better the full meaning of the communication.

This is especially applicable to the negotiating process. To be effective, the negotiator must actively listen for feedback. The negotiator must be able to listen to all meanings of what has been said and, in some cases, of what has been left unsaid. The negotiator should remember that even silence can be communication. As was stated earlier in this book, we cannot *not* communicate.

Before the skills of active listening can be learned, certain preconditions must be met. We have discussed in an earlier chapter the needs for the listener to be receptive. In addition, the listener must be nonjudgmental. If one expects to communicate effectively, then a sensitivity to the feelings of the other individual in the communication process is necessary. While the listening process is going on, interruptions should be kept to a minimum.

Rogers notes "the major barrier to mutual interpersonal communication is our very natural tendency to judge, to evaluate, to approve or disapprove, the statement of the other person.[24]" He goes on to say "real communication occurs when the evaluated tendency is avoided, when we listen with understanding. What does this mean? It means to see the expressed idea or attitude from the other person's point of view, to sense how it feels to him, to achieve his frame of reference in regard to the thing he is talking about."

Once the prerequisites of active listening are met, the listener is psychologically ready to listen. This psychological preparation is not enough, however, to achieve fully the results of good listening. The achievement of empathy is important, but the listener must also communicate that empathy through "attending" and "responding." Egan has noted "if I am to let you know that I understand you, I must first pay attention to you and listen to what you have to say about yourself."

Table 12-1 lists some of the attending (nonverbal) and responding (verbal) behaviors by which an active listener expresses empathy. The nonverbal ones that indicate that the listener is attending are primarily

Table 12-1 Attending and Responding Behaviors

Attending (nonverbal)	*Responding (verbal)*
• Facing the other person squarely	• Evaluative responses
• Adopting an open posture	• Interpretive responses
• Leaning toward the other person	• Supportive responses
• Maintaining good eye contact	• Probing responses
• Being relatively relaxed	• Understanding responses
• Reflecting attention through facial expressions	
• Attending with vocal cues	

physical. Egan states that your body can either emphasize the message you are trying to communicate with words or erase the message you are sending with words and even substitute an opposite message. Mehrabian noted the following division of the communicative process. He discovered that, of the total message, 7 percent is verbal, 38 percent is vocal, and 55 percent is facial.[25] Mehrabian's findings emphasize the importance of the 93 percent of the message that is nonverbal. He also notes that such nonverbal attending behaviors are indications of caring manifested in immediacy of liking.

Becoming aware of the nonverbal content of a message is important to negotiators as they attempt to listen. First, they can become sensitive to the value of their own verbal cues in communicating to the person sending the message that they are listening. Negotiators can say through their attention "We are here, we are interested in you, we want to listen." Attending thus confirms for the talker that listening is occurring. Second, negotiators as listeners can become sensitive to the total message of the talker through attention to the latter's nonverbal as well as verbal cues. Negotiators' recognition of both the verbal and nonverbal parts of messages will aid them in developing understanding and empathy.

Although paying attention is important, it does not always lead to accurate, empathetic understanding between talker and listener. It is also important to let other people know how you interpret their messages. Stewart and D'Angelo call this process "perception checking." They state "When you are perception checking, you verbalize your interpretation or inferences about what was said or left unsaid, and you ask the other person to verify or correct your interpretation."[26] A poster found in many university speech departments reads "I know that you believe you understand what you think I said, but, I am not sure you realize that what you heard is not what I meant." Perception checking allows us at least to attempt to develop common meaning.

Another difficulty in understanding the verbal communications that go on in negotiations springs from the several messages that are present in any communication.

1. what you mean to say
2. what you actually say
3. what the other party hears
4. what the other party thinks he or she hears
5. what the other party says
6. what you think the other party said

In this complex panorama of multimessages our message is often not heard. We often choose the wrong words. We often are "misunderstood." Therefore, there is a need for paraphrasing or checking the message. The next time you are in a negotiation session or in a discussion, debate, or argument, invoke "Metzger's Rule of Reason in Communication": *Before you can respond to me you must tell me what you believe I said. Before I can respond to you I must tell you what I believe you said.* It is interesting how filters enter into our ability to listen. Biases, predispositions, and self-fulfilling prophecies all play a role in presenting static in conversations. This "Rule" can help eliminate that static.

Peck has written on the psychodynamics of the negotiating process. He strongly suggests that an intuitive understanding of the process of negotiations is probably one of the most valuable traits of the successful negotiator. The significance of understanding personality types involved in a particular negotiation cannot be overestimated. As important is the appreciation of the need to "be your true self" in negotiating situations. If you attempt to be something other than what your sense of integrity dictates, you are unlikely to succeed. The reason is clear: you have to rehearse the new role and are likely to make mistakes; indeed, the falseness of your adopted position will be clear to the other in the negotiations. Peck brings to our attention typical personality traits that you must recognize and appreciate if you are to succeed in negotiations.

1. *Transference.* This is when you attribute to the other in the negotiations value judgments and motivations based not on what you have observed or heard but on what you are reminded of from other experiences with other people, whose characteristics are attributed to the other. This can be either a positive view of the other or a negative view. If it is a positive view, you tend to be convinced in advance of the other's position and often susceptible to unnecessary concessions or compromises. If it is a negative view you tend to be defensive or

overly aggressive. Transference can result in a feeling that the other is incomplete, unreal, or mechanical. It is, therefore, essential to guard against transference by engaging in introspective evaluation and careful analysis of the person across the table.

2. *Nonverbal communications.* The nonverbal communications of the other may be the most important indicator of the chances of gaining agreement. An observant negotiator will attempt to understand the signals coming from the person across the table, such as the level of the voice, nervous laughter, giggle, hand gestures, clenched fists, and jabbing motions of the fingers. What was the cause of the signal? Should you discontinue the negotiations or hasten a conclusion? The person who is confident of her or his position in the negotiations will be willing to sit at the table or desk, whereas the person who is dissatisfied with the current posture of negotiations will be inclined to manifest his or her desire for a change by movement in his or her chair or even by moving about in the room. Eye contact is most important in understanding the body language of negotiations. Looking sidewise and not making eye contact may indicate a lack of confidence in either the accuracy of one's statement or the power of one's position. Lack of confidence may also be displayed by partially covering one's mouth with one's hand while speaking. The positioning of arms and legs often indicates tension, concern, frustration, or openness. I have learned over the years that facing an individual in a chair that is unencumbered by a desk is a sign of openness. I keep my rolltop desk against the wall, and put nothing between me and the individual to whom I am talking. If an individual insists on standing up, you stand up as well. The successful negotiator watches the physical movements of the other for indications that more often than not reflect the other's position and willingness to reach agreement. These signals are often more revealing than the spoken words. Although they are not infallible, they cannot be ignored. You must, if you are to be an experienced negotiator, learn which of the nonverbal communications you can trust.
3. *Uncertainty and silence.* The art of negotiating is not for those who have a low threshold for frustration and limited patience. A successful negotiator lives with uncertainty and often sets up conditions of uncertainty so that the other, in the hopes of eliminating such uncertainty, will come to agreement. The use of silence is a profound mechanism in negotiations. Most people cannot tolerate long periods of silence while in the company of others. If you can remain silent you force the other to speak, to give information, and, more

often than not, to look for ways to bring you back into the discussion—possibly by altering a position.

4. *Sex.* It may be true that most people prefer to negotiate with members of their own sex, but this is certainly neither always possible nor defensible. Women believe that men are more likely to lie in negotiations than women, perhaps because of the traditional romantic male pursuit of a woman. Carefully evaluate the role of sex in a negotiating process. If the other is a man, does the fact that you are a woman weaken your position? Are sexual stereotypes present in the exchange? Do you bring into the room sexual stereotypes?[27]

KEY POINTS ON NEGOTIATING FOR POSITIVE OUTCOME

1. The successful negotiator understands the personalities across the table from him or her. It is desirable to know, in advance, the expectations, priorities, and limits established by the other.
2. Bargaining should be a rational process, although bluff, luck, power, and the articulate nature of the proponents do play roles.
3. Bargaining is not a contest nor a forum for angry exchanges. It should not produce a win-lose result.
4. You should not lightly assume that the other knows what she or he has to gain from a settlement; it is a vehicle for educating the parties.
5. Persistence and determination are often necessary to bring about compromise.
6. The successful negotiator focuses on the objective and takes calculated risks.
7. A critical element in successful negotiations is finding competing and substitute alternatives. Therefore, you must be willing to listen and alter your position.
8. Final positions should not be lightly presented; do not take a position termed a "final" one unless it is just that.
9. Beware the erosion of patience after long negotiations. The end game in negotiations is as critical as the opening game.
10. Cook tells us "If a negotiator knows where he stands and bargains from a position of integrity and courage, he might not always conquer a formidable foe but he can and will have the satisfaction that he acted upon the highest conviction and gave the best that is within him."[28]

NOTES

1. Michael M. Lombardo and Morgan W. McCall, Jr., "The Intolerable Boss," *Psychology Today* (January 1984): 45-48.

2. Howard Raiffa, *The Art and Science of Negotiation* (Cambridge, MA: Belknap Press, 1982), 126-7.

3. Max H. Bazerman, "Why Negotiations Go Wrong," *Psychology Today* (June 1986): 56.

4. Raiffa, *The Art and Science of Negotiation,* 14.

5. Roger Fisher and William Ury, "Getting to Yes—Negotiating an Agreement Without Giving In," *Harvard Negotiation Project* (Boston: Houghton-Mifflin, 1981), 21.

6. William Ouchi, "Going from A to Z: Thirteen Steps to a Theory Z Organization," *Management Review* (May 1981): 5.

7. José Ortega y Gasset, *Revolt of the Masses* (New York: Norton, 1957), 157.

8. Fisher and Ury, "Getting to Yes," 133.

9. Michael Maccoby, *The Leader, A New Face for American Management* (New York: Ballantine, 1981), 48.

10. Gerard I. Nierenberg, *The Art of Negotiating* (New York: Simon & Schuster, 1981), 185-86.

11. William E. Simkin, *Mediation and the Dynamics of Collective Bargaining* (Washington, DC: Bureau of National Affairs, 1986), 53.

12. Herb Cohen, *You Can Negotiate Anything* (New York: Bantam, 1980), 62.

13. A. Samuel Cook, "The Neglected Art of Negotiation," *The Daily Record,* Baltimore (date unknown).

14. Milton R. Wessel, *The Rule of Reason: A New Approach to Corporate Litigation* (Reading, MA: Addison-Wesley, 1976), 164-65.

15. Fred E. Jandt, "The Art of Negotiation," *The Royal Bank Letter* 67, no. 4 (July/August 1986): 2.

16. Ibid., 4.

17. Frank Cancelliere, *Listening . . . Key to Productivity* (Rockville Center, NY: Listening Dynamics, 1985), I-3.

18. W. J. Bade, Jr. and M. Stone, *Management Strategy in Collective Bargaining Negotiations* (New London, CT: National Firemen's Institute, 1951), 80-81.

19. Ibid., 81.

20. John Illiche, *Power Negotiating* (Reading, MA: Addison-Wesley, 1980), 103.

21. Chester Karrass, *Give and Take* (New York: Thomas Y. Cromwell, 1974), 160.

22. Portions of this section are excerpted from Harry E. Munn, Jr. and Norman Metzger, *Effective Communication in Health Care: A Supervisor's Handbook* (Rockville, MD: Aspen Publishers, 1981), 60-63, 66.

23. Charles M. Kelly, "Actual Listening Behavior of Industrial Supervisors as Related to Listening Ability, General Mental Ability, Selected Personality Factors and Supervisory Effectiveness," in *Small Group Communication: A Reader,* eds. Robert S. Carthcart and Larry A. Samovar (Dubuque, IA: William C. Brown, 1970), 252-53.

24. Carl R. Rogers and Richard E. Parson, "Problems in Active Listening," in *Communication Probes,* eds. B.D. Peterson, G.M. Goldhaver, and R.W. Pace (Chicago: Scientific Research Associates, 1974), 30-34.

25. Albert Mehrabian, *Silent Messages* (Belmont, CA: Wadworth Publishing Co., 1971), 43.

26. John Stewart and Gary D'Angelo, *Together: Communicating Interpersonally* (Reading, MA: Addison-Wesley, 1975), 19.

27. Cornelius J. Peck, *Cases and Materials on Negotiations,* 2nd ed. (Washington, DC: Bureau of National Affairs, 1980), 226-36.

28. Cook, "The Neglected Art of Negotiation."

Part III

A New Management Credo

Chapter 13

The Road to Excellence

> *Our young people are born into a society that is huge, impersonal and intricately organized. Far from calling them to leadership, it appears totally indifferent to them. It does not seem to need them at all and gives them instead a sense of powerlessness.*
>
> *Fred M. Hechinger*
>
> *"Help Wanted: Leaders"* The New York Times, *Tuesday, August 18, 1987 p. C6. Citing John W. Gardner.*

Caring about people is the backbone of organizational strength and success. A new management credo includes the broadening concern with aspects of people's lives, both individually and collectively, which, unfortunately, received little credit in the past. The thousands of health care employees, who have been little and invisible people, are calling out for attention. They want their contributions appreciated, and they want an end to their alienated feeling and their sense that they have no stake in the outcome. The modern supervisor and manager must lead the drive to change the organizational climate to a more positive one. He or she looks for common ground, is not easily angered, feels positive about himself or herself, encourages boat-rockers, and is a truth teller.

In many of our organizations there is a strong immediate pressure on the individual to conform. The typical health care hierarchical structure has as its role model a doctor, a financial expert, or a strategic planner, all of whom are often so preoccupied with their own expertise that all other concerns—including interpersonal relationships—are at best secondary. We often find the troubling adversarial relationship between groups in the institution; goal definition and agreement receive little or no attention. Too often decision-making is protected by the chosen few, and control is unshared.

Hayes, in discussing the utility of industrial democracy, states:

> This movement towards greater participation of employees in the decisions that affect their everyday work lives—not the politically-oriented power thrust of some movements towards "industrial democracy"—seems to reflect the desire of free men to have

> greater control of their own lives. To the extent that this occurs, and to the extent that free men commit themselves to the goals of the organization because of their participation in its decisions, we are likely to have organizations of spirited, vivacious people who are working together to accomplish their common goals—not bossed, not "hired," but free committed men.[1]

Such outcomes require a new management style within a new management organization. Kanter tells us:

> "In short, while workplace reform has the potential to fulfill many of the expectations of the new workforce, it also points to more fundamental problems in the design of organizations. The ideal-typical twentieth century bureaucracy could be showing cracks and strains, tensions and contradictions which point to the need for a new concept of the corporation."[2]

These cracks and strains call out for new organizational restructuring. What is necessary is to change the culture of the organization. Many researchers and observers believe that we must transform individuals, who have been assigned limited tasks and have worked without the drive for interdependence and the awareness of how jobs interrelate within the entire organization, into groups of employees who perforce have a broader understanding of commitment to the total enterprise.[3] It is clear that employees of the new breed expect greater meaning in their work, a feeling of making a difference. The fear of insignificance is pervasive in our large institutions. Kanter warns us:

> This new workplace involves opportunities for greater employee initiative, for entrepreneurial effort, and for greater participation in problem-solving. However, this new workplace cannot exist easily in the conventional command-and-control hierarchy of status and authority relations that have been the dominant organizational form in the twentieth century.[4]

THE HOARDING OF POWER

There is a need to reshape organizations that are built around an environment with policies that control and implement freedom for all but a few. Drucker states:

> Far too few of today's managers realize that management is defined by responsibility and not by power. Far too few fight the debilitating disease of bureaucracy: the belief that big budgets and a huge staff are accomplishments rather than incompetence.[5]

The successful supervisor or manager is so defined not by the power that he or she harnesses but rather by the accomplishments of the work force that he or she manages. It is time to empower others. The work arena has too long defined success by a selfish accumulation of power.

Sharing power does not mean abdicating responsibility. On the contrary, the most responsible act a manager can take is to broaden the base of decision-making and problem-solving. If we encourage democratic collaboration it is likely that our employees, who are involved in that process, will help us to sharpen and refine ideas. If we listen to what others have to say and offer, it may change our own positions. Contrary to a common myth, tasks performed cooperatively rather than competitively are accomplished more efficiently, and the participants have a higher degree of motivation and morale. When an employee believes it was his or her idea or suggestion that we are implementing, he or she is more likely to make it work. It should be clear, therefore, that the hallmark of the restructured organization is a pervasive willingness to share power.

It is equally clear that the successful health care organization of the future will be less bureaucratic and have fewer managerial levels. Less is better when it comes to the hierarchical structure. In building such a thin managerial structure, attention must be paid to encouraging subordinates to be free to tell the truth, to make suggestions, and to participate in problem-solving and decision-making. Research continues to indicate a strong desire on the part of employees to be involved in their jobs. A new management credo insists on the sharing of managerial prerogatives between line-supervisors and workers on a systematic institutional basis. There is a need to revamp the workplace.

Brown and Weiner put this task in perspective.

> Traditionally, organizational structure has been defined as a pyramid with a few people at the top and many at the bottom. The truth of the recent past, however, is that U.S. corporations more closely resemble footballs: few at the top, few at the bottom, and many crowded around the middle. We are now moving into an era in which the Mae West, or hourglass shape will be the predominant configuration. The reasons are economic and tech-

> nological. A new reality has hit American business. There has been a growing realization that the bloated management ranks of corporate America—a product of affluent times, or educated workers, world dominance in many markets, predictability of cost and profits—are now an extra weight borne by a weary swimmer.[6]

Such an analysis is as applicable to the health care industry as it is to corporate America.

A METANOIC ORGANIZATION

Kiefer and Senge describe an organization with a creative orientation, in which the individuals are creating together. That organization has the following characteristics.*

1. *Clarity of mission, vision, and values.* Each person is clear about what the organization exists to do. The organization is vision-driven and value-based, with structure norms and culture explicitly derived from these.
2. *Personal ownership of mission, vision, and values.* People identify personally with what the organization stands for. Each person feels responsible for the organization's accomplishments. They will do whatever it takes for themselves and the organization to realize the vision.
3. *Diverse individuals with congruous visions.* Diversity of vision is encouraged, valued, and exploited in the organization.
4. *Attunement interpersonally.* There is a deep rapport and empathy that allows each person to care for another, based in a capacity to "stand in one another's shoes."
5. *Attunement with natural order.* There is a deep sense of service to life in general and to customers and colleagues in particular.
6. *Certainty of vision, trust in the process.* The realization of the essence of the organization's vision is felt to be inevitable; that what we choose together will come to pass, even if not exactly as originally envisioned.
7. *Aspiration.* There is a tone throughout the organization of always reaching for the highest.

---

*Excerpted from *A Behavioral Description of a Metanoic Organization* by C. Kiefer and P. Senge pp. 2-5, with permission of Innovation Associates, © 1986.

8. *Outstanding performance in all dimensions relevant to purpose.* The organization is successful in achieving its purpose. Over time the purpose of the organization becomes progressively clearer by virtue of the results it accomplishes.
9. *Assessment of performance.* The ultimate criteria against which performance is measured are mission and vision.
10. *Clear standards.* Standards for performance are clear, universally understood within the organization, agreed upon, and managed against. Rewards, incentives, and punishments are consistent with the organization's purpose, values, and philosophy.
11. *People judge their behavior, not themselves.* People feel unconditional acceptance. Therefore, they do not judge themselves as good or bad, but they do judge their behavior aggressively, particularly as it relates to their ability to individually and collectively achieve desired results.
12. *Focus on results, not roles.* People are more concerned about end results than their role. They are players rather than people occupying a position.
13. *Open, honest communication.* All communication between individuals within the organization and between the organization and its members is open, honest, informal whenever possible, goal oriented (continually oriented to "What do you want?"), and supportive ("How can I help?").
14. *People continually seek the truth.* The organization is curious, inquisitive, and wants to know all the facts, good and bad.
15. *Learning mode.* There is a tolerance for ambiguity, paradox, and not-knowing. The organization consciously supports learning as a primary activity along with doing.

The Metanoic Organization has the following design characteristics.

1. *Local decision-making.* No decision is ever made in the organization at a level higher than is absolutely necessary.
2. *Autonomous business units.* These units are as small as possible while remaining consistent with organizational purpose to provide for a higher degree of informality and shared personal responsibility for results. (This, indeed, is transferable to health care organizations: substitute "operational units" for "business units.")
3. *Minimum layers of management hierarchy.* The organization has only as much formal hierarchy as is absolutely needed.
4. *Nonhierarchical reward and recognition systems.* The organization eliminates all unnecessary and dysfunctional hierarchy. Financial

rewards are geared to an individual's contribution to the enterprise's success, not to his or her place in the management hierarchy.
5. *Freedom of access to information.* There is wide and ready access to all necessary information. People are not special, nor do they possess special power, by virtue of having access to information not available to others.
6. *Open performance review processes.* Performance review is the responsibility of all members of the organization. Peer review processes and individual self-assessment are common.

Kiefer and Senge offer us the ideal model for the road to excellence. The leadership pattern in such Metanoic Organizations sees leaders as coaches, mentors, and designers as well as decision-makers. Most important, people in such organizations are free: they are doing what they want. Such an organization need not be utopian but certainly practical.

A NEW MANAGEMENT CREDO: CHALLENGE TO HEALTH CARE SUPERVISORS

The singular challenge is presented to you to create some of the basic conditions of human community, which are absent from many of our health care institutions. That is, you must provide work experiences that make people feel that they make a difference. This requires an inordinate amount of trust and confidence in your own ability, judgment, and willingness to change. Let us, by a review of all the preceding chapters in this book, embark on a new management style directed toward achieving excellence.

1. Your effectiveness is built on your own strength, the strengths of your superiors and colleagues, and, not the least, the strengths of your subordinates.
2. There is a self-fulfilling prophecy in management: if you expect superior performance you are more likely to get it.
3. An effective supervisor must understand and appreciate employee motivations and needs.
4. Behavioral scientists indicate a clear road to employee commitment: the lesson of the Hawthorne study is the big difference that the little difference of paying attention to employees makes to them.
5. Need fulfillment or frustration produces either constructive or

defensive behavior; concentrate on identifying the needs of your employees and methods to fulfill them.

6. The critical relationship between you and the people who work for you includes mutual understanding and agreement on goals and rewards.
7. It is up to you to restructure the work situation. Such restructuring must include job enrichment and redesign and broadening of responsibilities.
8. The successful supervisor is the people-centered supervisor: good people relations produce good patient care.
9. Possibility is the watchword for excellent supervision. Grasping possibilities should be a constant goal of managers.
10. Good leadership includes the willingness to be a risk-taker.
11. You must build an atmosphere where your people are willing to take risks; they should know that you will tolerate mistakes and that they can grow with their experiences.
12. As we have been told, a manager who knows that his or her subordinates are his or her equals becomes the equal of his or her superiors.
13. Successful managers have a "high touch" style of management: they share credit and give rewards.
14. Don't lose interest in the indoctrination process: it has big payoffs. One of the important responsibilities you have is to absorb new employees into the work team. Remember that the first few days have a strong effect on the employee's future. It is your responsibility to reinforce the employee's confidence in his or her ability to cope with the new work assignment.
15. Immediate positive recognition is a necessary stimulus for continued efficiency. Once-a-year performance evaluation is not the answer; ongoing communication of appreciation or redirection is much more important.
16. Work performance is improved appreciably when the employee knows that it is possible to influence the expected results.
17. Strive for self-commitment among your employees: self-motivation and self-discipline are the strongest forces for a plan to obtain excellence.
18. We have been told that "feedback is the breakfast of champions," that "achieving good performance is a journey, not a destination," and that "people who produce good results feel good about themselves."
19. To be successful an organization requires managers who can recognize the need for change, who can initiate change, and who can adapt to change; you do this through communication.

20. The key to the process of effecting change is establishing a plan toward ameliorating the effect of the change on the person involved.
21. Active listening—sitting up and listening—plays an important role in supervisor-employee relationships. You must *want* to listen.
22. We have been told that the four basic questions to which most employees desperately seek answers are "Where am I going?" "How am I going to get there?" "Who will I be when I arrive?" and "Can I feel good about myself in the process?"
23. One cannot mandate cooperation by punishing, by threatening, or by legislating.
24. The goal of positive discipline is to salvage the employee and to correct the behavioral pattern that is either antisocial or anti-institution.
25. Self-discipline develops where employees trust the supervisor and the management, where employees feel that their job is important and appreciated, and where employees feel that they belong.
26. We have been told that the most meaningful measure of any system for resolving employee complaints is employees' perceptions of its overall fairness.
27. The handling of employee grievances affords the supervisor with the greatest opportunity to win employee respect and gain employee confidence; handling employee complaints is an opportunity rather than a chore. You can minimize the grievances by being alert for the common causes of irritation within your department, by keeping promises, by letting your employees know how they are getting along, by encouraging constructive suggestions, by assigning and scheduling work impartially, and by acting promptly on reasonable requests from your employees.
28. More employees vote for or against their immediate supervisor than for or against top management, the board of trustees, or consultants in a union-certification election.
29. Unions rarely organize employees; rather, it is the administration's poor record in employee relations that drives employees into unions.
30. The way to maintain nonunion status is clear: make people feel that they are part of a team, encourage open communications, promote from within, allow employees to share in rewards for productivity, and expand the skills of your people.
31. Employees who are taught the right way to do a job, the efficient way to do a job, will be more productive and more knowledgeable and will become more committed.
32. We have been told that authority is granted by constituents to their

leaders only so long as these leaders satisfy the needs and standards of the governed.

33. The new work force comprises employees who expect a greater voice in decisions at work and who want opportunities beyond those contained in their present jobs.
34. Our employees expect greater meaning from their work. They want to be able to innovate, and they want to be able to contribute.
35. You must develop an atmosphere of trust that permits employees to participate in problem-solving and decision-making as partners and not as junior partners.
36. An alienated worker does not believe that his or her work can give fulfillment and meaning.
37. Fulfilling and meaningful work comes from a relationship of trust, appreciation, and caring.
38. Workers respond best and most creatively not when they are tightly controlled by management but rather when they are given broader responsibilities and helped to take satisfaction in their work.
39. You must be sensitive to contemporary work values: the new breed of employee expects more equal treatment, expects to be listened to regardless of his or her job category, and is less likely to accept differences in privilege and status.
40. Whether the work ethic is dead or alive, it is within your grasp to improve it.
41. When employees are permitted to be collaborators rather than tools of management, they will be less alienated.
42. The old organization chart needs to be scrapped; we must have an emphasis on organization and informality and fluid, flexible lines of communication in reporting relationships.
43. You must develop plans to assist workers to develop the ability to manage themselves.
44. The sharing of managerial prerogatives with your workers will bring us the excellence we so desperately need in the health care industry.
45. It is time to empower employees by having them participate in the organization's decisions and goal-setting.

CONCLUSION

What we have been discussing is a plan for excellence, a new management credo for an organization that has as its core rationale a creative orientation. This organization encourages diversity of vision and permits people to take risks, to participate, to collaborate, and to share in rewards.

Such an organization has an open system rather than a rigid hierarchical and bureaucratic one. In such organizations, you, the manager and supervisor, assume the role of coach, mentor, and visionary. You go down a new path. It is time to shed the inane propensity to move along the comfortable road of redundancy and obscurity.

NOTES

1. James L. Hayes, *Memos for Management Leadership* (New York: AMACOM Division of American Management Associations, 1983), 14.
2. Rosabeth Moss Kanter, "The New Workforce Meets the Changing Workplace: Strains, Dilemmas and Contradictions in Attempts to Implement Participative and Entrepreneurial Management," *Human Resources Management* 25, no. 4 (Winter 1986): 516.
3. R. J. Bullock and E. Lawler, "Gainsharing: A Few Questions and Fewer Answers," *Human Resource Management* 23 (1984): 123.
4. Kanter, "The New Workforce," 534–35.
5. Peter F. Drucker, "A New Discipline," *Success* 28 (January/February 1981): 18.
6. Arnold Brown and Edith Weiner, *Supermanaging* (New York: New American Library, 1984), 107.

Index

E

F

G

Q

R

S

T

About the Author

Norman Metzger occupies an endowed chair, the Edmond A. Guggenheim Professorship, in the Department of Health Care Management at the Mount Sinai School of Medicine and is vice-president for labor relations at The Mount Sinai Medical Center in New York City. He is also an adjunct professor in the Graduate Program in Health Care Administration at the Bernard M. Baruch College of the City University of New York.

Professor Metzger is the 1987 recipient of the Exceptional Contribution Award of the American Society for Healthcare Human Resources Administration. He was president of the League of Voluntary Hospitals and Homes of New York from 1968 to 1972 and from 1980 to 1982. He is currently chairman of the League's Labor Relations/Negotiating Committee. He was president of the American Society for Healthcare Human Resources Administration for the term 1985–86.

Professor Metzger has written more than 100 articles on the subjects of motivation, labor relations, evaluation of employee performance, recruitment, orientation, job evaluation, communication, discipline, and, most recently, as a result of extensive research, the issues of changing leadership styles and worker participation. His latest research is in the area of changing worker attitudes and the new breed of supervisor. He is a six-time recipient of the annual award for literature given by the American Society for Healthcare Human Resources Administration in recognition of his outstanding contribution to hospital personnel administration literature. He is the author, co-author, or editor of 12 books.

About the Author